PENGUIN BOOKS

CARPENTERS AND KINGS

Siddhartha Sarma is an author and journalist based in New Delhi. His first novel, *The Grasshopper's Run*, won the Crossword Book Award (2010) and the Sahitya Akademi Award for children's literature (2011).

Carpenters and Kings

Western Christianity and the Idea of India

SIDDHARTHA SARMA

PENGUIN BOOKS

An imprint of Penguin Random House

PENGUIN BOOKS

USA | Canada | UK | Ireland | Australia
New Zealand | India | South Africa | China

Penguin Books is part of the Penguin Random House group of companies
whose addresses can be found at global.penguinrandomhouse.com

Published by Penguin Random House India Pvt. Ltd
4th Floor, Capital Tower 1, MG Road,
Gurugram 122 002, Haryana, India

Penguin
Random House
India

First published in Hamish Hamilton by Penguin Random House India 2019
Published in paperback in Penguin Books 2021

Copyright © Siddhartha Sarma 2019

Illustrations copyright © Sankha Banerjee 2019

ISBN 9780143453512

Typeset in Adobe Caslon Pro by Manipal Technologies Limited, Manipal
Printed at Replika Press Pvt. Ltd, India

www.penguin.co.in

'A lawyer asked Jesus what he should do to inherit eternal life, to which Jesus asked, what does the Law say? The lawyer replied: love God, and thy neighbour as thyself. Jesus said he had answered correctly. The lawyer then asked: who is my neighbour?

Jesus said: A man went down from Jerusalem to Jericho, and fell among thieves, who stripped him of his raiment, wounded him and departed, leaving him half-dead. A priest came that way, saw him, and passed by. Similarly a Levite saw him and passed on. But a certain Samaritan saw him and had compassion on him. He bound the man's wounds and brought him to an inn and took care of him. The following day, the Samaritan gave money to the landlord and told him to care for the injured man, telling the landlord he would repay him for additional expenses. Which of these three was the neighbour of the man who fell among thieves?

The lawyer said: He that showed mercy on the man.

And Jesus said: Go, and do likewise.'

—Luke 10:25–37

'And this is the true religious devotion, this the sum of religious instruction: that it shall increase the mercy and charity, the truth and purity, the kindness and honesty of the world.'

—From the inscription on the Ashokan Pillar at Feroz Shah Kotla, Delhi (tr. James Prinsep)

Contents

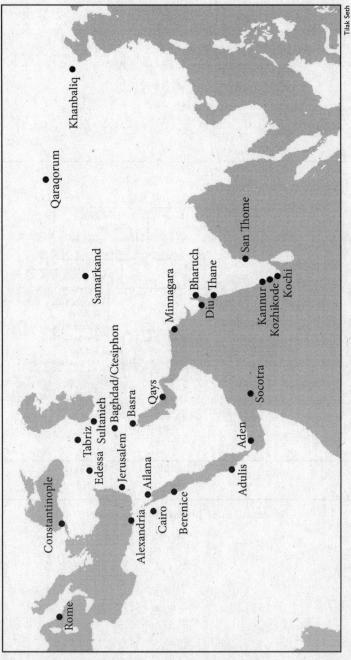

Anachronistic map of major cities and ports

Tilak Seth

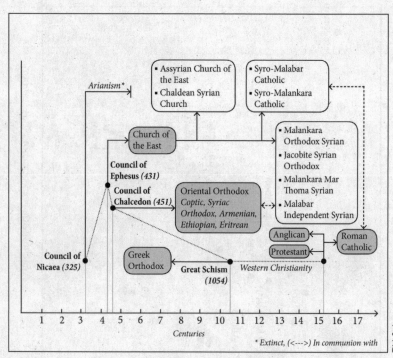

Formation of Christian denominations

Note on geography and nomenclature

This book explores an approximately 2000-year history involving three continents. Over this time, the names of old urban centres and regions have changed considerably. For the sake of uniformity, cities whose modern names are similar to or derived from medieval or ancient names will be called their modern names—such as the Malabar port of Kollam, which was at various times known as Quilon, Columbum, Coulão and others, or Bharuch, which was called Barygaza by the Greeks, Bargosa by the Romans and Broach by medieval and colonial-era Europeans.

In the case of cities which have completely different names today than what they had in the Middle Ages—such as Istanbul, called Constantinople for most of its history, or Beijing, called Khanbaliq during the Yuan Empire—the older names have been retained to evoke a sense of the period.

Considering the very long and relatively complex history of Christianity in the Malabar Coast region, the oldest grouping of Christians in India has been termed Syrian Christians. This broad term today includes denominations in communion with the Catholic Church, or which are part of Eastern Orthodoxy and the Church of the East. Although Nestorianism was an important element of Syrian Christianity in India till the advent of the Portuguese, the term has been used only to refer to Eastern Christians in Central Asia or China, in order to draw a distinction between their specific histories and that of Syrian Christians in India.

The Church of Rome has been referred to as the Latin Church in the section dealing with the Medieval Period, to distinguish it from the Roman Catholic, Anglican and Protestant denominations which emerged from the Latin Church after the Reformation in Europe.

The names of Mongol rulers and generals, several of whom have entered popular imagination, are spelt differently by writers depending on context or preference. In this book, their names have been transliterated to English from Mongol sources, while their honorifics have been placed in the right order. For instance, Genghis Khan, as his name is popularly spelt, has been called Great Khan Chinggis here.

Introduction

The history of Christianity in India is a nearly two-millennia-long story whose complexity rivals the history of the subcontinent itself. Christians comprise a significant minority population, which has played a key role in the post-Independence period in the country, as have Christian institutions and clergy. In terms of historiography, however, the treatment of Christianity in India has remained problematic. As the political climate of India changes, as the Hindu Right extends its political dominance into the intellectual sphere, and as revisionism becomes a key tool for reimagining Indian history through a very narrow nativist and bigoted lens, it has become increasingly necessary to examine the history of Christianity in India and to set the record straight.

The problem is twofold. For the Right, it is necessary to delegitimize the presence of Islam and Christianity by creating a narrative that claims that the history of these two Abrahamic faiths in the subcontinent was a disruption in an otherwise harmonious society. Therefore the claim that Islam spread primarily by the sword, ignoring the evidence of conversions, such as in eastern Bengal, by charismatic Sufi preachers, or the long history of the faith on the Malabar Coast predating Turkic invasions from the north-west. These aspects of the history of Islam in India are related to complex social changes in geographically disparate regions. However, the Right's narrative views the history of the religion purely in terms of invasion, large-scale violence and conversion by the sword, in an attempt at convincing other communities that the Muslims of the subcontinent, particularly India, are inheritors of a continuous legacy of disruption and turmoil.

Similarly, Christianity is considered an inevitable adjunct to the colonial experience; modern Christians of India are considered descendants of Hindus who chose the religion of colonial administrators, thus simultaneously betraying the faith and culture of their ancestors and the native political structure which resisted colonialism. This narrative often ignores the presence of Syrian Christians in Malabar, a history which is as old as Christianity in Syria, Persia and the eastern Mediterranean. Nor was it only a geographically limited presence, for as this book shows, Christian communities existed and thrived on the Indian coast from Gujarat to Sri Lanka and the Coromandel Coast from a very early period of the Common Era, and had well-established ecclesiastical structures which were seamlessly integrated into Indian societies.

The second problem has been the post-colonial narrative, which has classified Indian Christians into two categories. While acknowledging the Syrians, this narrative has not dealt adequately with how Syrian Christians became an integral part of Indian society, how the West was aware of Christianity in India long before the colonial period, or how Syrians reacted to Portuguese imperialism and attempts by the Catholic Church to enforce communion with the Church of the East in India. One reason for this narrative is the inadequate presence of the history of south India in the overall historiography of the subcontinent, where more emphasis is placed on events and personalities from the Indo-Gangetic region.

The second category of Indian Christians is understood to have derived from proselytism by Portuguese and British colonial-era missionaries, thus labelling Western Christianity, including Catholic and Protestant denominations as well as the Anglican Communion, a by-product of the colonial period. In this failure or unwillingness to engage with the complexities of the history of Christianity in India, at least, post-colonial historiography appears to have inadvertently agreed with the Hindu Right. As this book demonstrates, this view too is historically incorrect, because Western Christianity in India predates the colonial period by more than two centuries.

Christianity arrived in the subcontinent in the Apostolic Age, sometime in the first two centuries CE, and took root among the Jewish communities of the western coastal region, communities whose presence in India went back to the Achaemenid Persian Empire and the Hellenistic world which supplanted it in the Persian Gulf and Arabian Sea littorals.

As Christian ecclesiastical order and official doctrine was being codified in the Roman Empire in the fourth century CE, the faith was spreading in the subcontinent, and by the sixth century, Christian communities and their ecclesiastical structures in India were known to travellers from what was Roman-ruled Egypt. Greek-speaking traders were a vital part of India's maritime commerce with Egypt and Persia, and through this commerce the ties between Christians in India, Persia and the Roman world were strengthened.

With the coming of Islam in the seventh century, while the Byzantine Empire's direct contact with India was lost after Egypt was conquered by the Arabs, Eastern Christianity, centred in Persia and Syria, forged stronger ties with India and spread to the Far East, including China and Tibet. This period also saw the introduction of Buddhist stories into the Middle East, stories which would ultimately reach Europe and acquire renown among Latin and Greek Christians.

The key inflection point in this sequence of events was the emergence of the Mongols on the global stage. The establishment of the Mongol Ilkhanate in Persia created, for the first time, conditions suitable for Western Christianity to establish its presence in the Middle East. In the period following the early Crusades and the establishment of the Ilkhanate, Christian missionaries from the mendicant orders, such as Dominicans and Franciscans, would set out from Persia to India and China, officially establishing the Latin Church in India in the late thirteenth century. This missionary movement was approved and encouraged by popes during what would come to be called the Avignon Papacy.

The missionaries of this period, working singly or in small groups, were a remarkable part of the growing European consciousness of the world. Partly with the understanding of popes who were personally interested in the East, and partly on their own initiative, Dominicans and Franciscans based in or travelling through India wrote extensive accounts of the topography, wildlife, agriculture and, most importantly, people of the subcontinent. These writings constitute an invaluable resource in understanding both how Indian society was in the

Middle Ages, and how Europeans were intimately aware of India as well as China in the time before the Age of Exploration and the beginning of European colonialism. There were also early humanist scholars in Europe who saw the strategic implications surrounding India and maritime trade between the subcontinent and Egypt, and wrote about them in treatises which form part of medieval crusading strategy.

The picture that is painted here, of an Indian society welcoming in its attitude towards missionaries and the idea of conversion, and of a Church of Rome willing to seek an ecumenical relationship with Syrian Christians, shows how faith, when working without the impediment of imperialist structures, could have been a tool to foster a truly multicultural society. It was a period that could have led to the creation of a world much different from what it eventually became.

A series of disruptive events would end this direct and informed European contact with India and China in the fourteenth century. Civil war in China, plague and the depredations of Timur together changed the shape of political structures in Eurasia. The Yuan dynasty of China was supplanted by the native Ming dynasty, which effectively ended the diplomatic relations that had been forged between the Yuans and western European kingdoms as well as the Church of Rome. The Mongol Ilkhanate collapsed because of the plague in Persia, which made the Western Christian presence in the Middle East untenable. Timur is chiefly remembered in India today for the sack of Delhi towards the end of the fourteenth century, but his campaigns were also instrumental in the decline of Eastern Christianity in the Middle East and Central Asia, and the end of European contact with the subcontinent.

At the end of the fifteenth century, when this contact was re-established by the Portuguese during the Age of Exploration, the paradigm had changed. What had become the Roman Catholic Church, in alliance with the Portuguese crown, pursued an imperial policy that was diametrically different from the philosophy of medieval missionaries, and which caused disruption in India both among Syrian Christians and people of other faiths. The Portuguese Empire in India was forged on the idea of perpetual war against Islam and other faiths, while the Catholic Church, grappling with the Protestant Reformation in Europe, was interested in uprooting heresy and enforcing the faith through increasingly violent means. The traumatic history of the Goa Inquisition is a cautionary tale of how imperialism and religion can be a potent toxic mixture. The policies that led to the Goa Inquisition resulted from the convergence of several events, including the loss of Constantinople to the Ottoman Turks and the problematic legacy of the Reconquista in the Iberian Peninsula. The Portuguese colonial legacy in India is an example of how Indian history is intimately connected with events and people around the world and illustrates, once again, how Indian history need not be studied in isolation from the history of Europe, Africa or the Far East.

The Protestant Reformation too had its effect in India, with the arrival of Dutch and Danish merchants. The objection of these merchants to Protestant missionaries from their home countries shows how these trading companies did not want business and proselytism to mix. But this period was also the beginning of a missionary model which saw Protestant preachers engaging with Indian languages, culture and literature, and researching them, a model which would be continued by later Anglican and Protestant missionaries during the British Raj.

The victory of the British over the French and their rapid expansion in India in the late eighteenth and early nineteenth centuries created its own form of disruption, which would have a long-term impact on the Indian society that was emerging in response to modernity. The Hindu Right in India today is concerned with 'bringing back' Indians who had converted to Abrahamic religions in the Middle Ages and the colonial period. This was not a concern for Hindu society in the Middle Ages, when European missionaries recorded how converts were accepted by their former communities without rancour. In the early period of the Raj, the principal opposition to conversions, as the book shows, was not by orthodox Hindus, who maintained that there was no scriptural sanction for accepting back a person who had given up his caste. The early attempts at bringing back Hindu converts into the caste fold were by liberal Hindus, as illustrated by the case of a young Brahmin boy in Bombay who wanted to convert to Christianity.

The Rebellion of 1857, and the underlying caste and religious concerns of Hindus and Muslims, was another inflection point in modern Indian history. British administrators from then onwards would be circumspect in encouraging conversions or proselytism by missionaries. Europe itself was moving towards a secular model of government, and the church and the state would be, in most European countries, separated.

The history of Christianity in India, as with the larger history of the subcontinent, therefore needs to be studied in the context of local and global events. In the process, one can perhaps arrive at a greater understanding of how Europeans have considered the idea of India in the past 2000 years.

Equally importantly, it could help Indians understand some of the complexities of their own history. The country is at present passing through a period when an attempt is being made to create an idea of India which has never existed. This ersatz India is based on the denial of legitimacy to faiths such as Christianity and Islam. As this book shows, this is not a new idea, and has been tried before in other parts of the world. But wherever the core beliefs of the faith, such as Christianity, or the core principles of a society, such as the natural multiculturalism of Indians, are at odds with such revisionism, these attempts have either failed or caused catastrophic and irreversible discord within the society or faith. The Hindu Right can only pursue its policy of bigotry and revisionism at the peril of India.

Antiquity

The Second Carpenter

'Send me where you want, but send me somewhere else. Not to India.'[1]

Thus begins *The Acts of Thomas*, an account of the coming of the apostle Thomas to the subcontinent. Now part of the large body of literature termed New Testament apocrypha, *The Acts*, written in the third person, does not, unlike the four canonical gospels, talk about the life, ministry, crucifixion and resurrection of Jesus Christ. Instead, it begins with a gathering of the apostles in Jerusalem, to decide who would spread the message of the Son of God in which part of the world. The writers seem to have assumed that the readers, or listeners, are already familiar with the life of Christ. Although it says 'we the apostles', it does not specify who the narrators are.

All eleven of the surviving apostles are present, and named, at the beginning of the First Act: the brothers John and James the son of Zebedee, Peter* and his brother Andrew, James the

---

* The Greek and Syriac versions of the text mention that he was called both Peter and Simon.

son of Alphaeus, Simon from Canaan, Philip, Bartholomew, Matthew, Judas the brother of James, and Thomas himself. The Risen Christ has met them and instructed them to travel among the nations with his teachings. It is a gathering of friends, witnesses to the miracle of the resurrection and conscious of their role as the closest followers of Christ. It is a momentous discussion, for the task given to them is to save the world. Christian tradition would come to call this the Dispersion of the Apostles.

The apostles then divide the regions of the world among themselves, and Thomas is tasked with going to India. Insofar as even a draw of lots for the apostles is determined by the will of God, Thomas makes for an interesting choice to travel to India. What would the fate of the Church have been if Peter, instead, had been chosen by divine will? Peter, the rock of the Church, so aware of how far short he fell of the ideals of Christ that he insisted, according to Christian tradition, that he be crucified upside down, in a symbolic inversion of the way Jesus was crucified. How might he have preached in India? It can only be speculated, because the task goes to Thomas, while Peter would travel through the great cities of Antioch and Corinth to Rome.

Diffidence and doubt seem to be recurring themes in the personality of Thomas, according to *The Acts*. In the canonical Gospel of John, when Jesus tells the apostles that he is leaving to prepare eternity for those who follow him, Thomas is made to say: 'We do not know where you are going, so how will we know the way?'

Again, after the resurrected Christ appears to the apostles, Thomas declares he will not believe in the resurrection unless he sees Christ with his own eyes and touches the nail wounds on his limbs and the spear wound on his side. Thomas finally believes in the resurrection after he does precisely that, to which Christ says, 'Because you have seen, you have believed; blessed are those who have not seen but still believed.'[2] Scepticism was not new for the apostle.

Thomas, who from these episodes came to be called 'Doubting Thomas' in later Western Christian tradition, behaves in a similar manner at the beginning of *The Acts*, and refuses to go to India. 'I am a Hebrew. How can I go among the Indians and preach the truth?' he tells his fellow apostles at the gathering.[3]

Later, Jesus himself appears to Thomas, and tells him to take up the task and spread the message in the subcontinent. But Thomas is adamant. 'Send me anywhere else,' he says, 'and I will go. But not to India.'[4]

The solution to this impasse comes about in the form of Abbanes, a merchant sent to Jerusalem by King Gundaphorus of India, and tasked with getting him a carpenter.[5] Christ finds Abbanes in the market and tells the merchant that he has a slave, a carpenter, and is willing to sell the man. He then leads the merchant to the reluctant apostle, and Abbanes tells Thomas that he has been sold. Thomas accepts the will of God and finds himself embarking for India, after all. What transpires is among the most magical of New Testament apocryphal stories.

The first halt for Thomas and Abbanes is at the city of Andrapolis, of which no other details are given except that it is 'a royal city'. Here Thomas is asked by the king to pray for his daughter, it being her wedding night. However, Christ appears before the newly-weds in the form of Thomas and tells them not to develop physical relations, but keep themselves pure for the Lord.

The king on hearing this is enraged and seeks Thomas who, by this time, has finished preaching in the city and departed with Abbanes.

The merchant and the carpenter eventually reach the unnamed city of Gundaphorus, where Thomas tells the king that he is a master carpenter and can build both furniture and buildings, in wood and stone. The king asks him to build a palace. And Thomas tells him: 'That is why I am here.'

Thomas then spends all the money the king gives him, but not in constructing the palace. Instead, he gives it away to the poor and the sick, preaches to them and, on occasion, heals them. Time passes, and the king wants to see how much of the work has been done. Thomas tells him that his palace is indeed ready, but is in Heaven, and shall be his reward in the afterlife.

Gundaphorus is, understandably, livid and imprisons Thomas. Meanwhile, the king's brother dies, and is resurrected by divine will, with a message for Gundaphorus: 'Your palace is indeed ready for you in Heaven, if you recognize the messenger who has come to you on Earth.' Gundaphorus and his court become disciples of Thomas.

The apostle then sets out on his journey into the Indian heartland. Along the way, Thomas meets a gigantic serpent, and discovers it is no ordinary reptile, but the one which had caused Eve to taste the fruit of the Tree of Knowledge, and made Cain slay Abel. Thomas compels it to suck back the poison from a young man the snake has just killed, and the giant serpent meets its end from its own toxin.

He then meets another fantastic creature, a talking donkey which says it is descended from Balaam's famous pack animal, which in the Old Testament story had seen an angel whom Balaam had not. The donkey, on being punished by Balaam for refusing to move, had spoken human words admonishing the man. Its descendant is similarly gifted and pious. It not only preaches to Thomas and recognizes his divine mission, but lets him ride on its back to the next city.

Here Thomas, like Christ during his ministry, performs an exorcism and saves a woman who has been possessed by a demon, an incubus. At this point in the story, Thomas receives an invitation from a king named Misdaeus, who declares himself 'one of the richest in India'. His wealth and power, however, have not saved his wife and daughter from being beset by demons and Misdaeus wants Thomas to exorcise them. Thomas travels on a chariot drawn by wild donkeys and arrives at the city.

Thomas confronts the demons, and finds that one of them is actually the incubus he had driven out from the woman previously. The creature is considerably annoyed to find his old nemesis has cornered him again and tells Thomas: 'Like you, who have come to preach the Good News, I have come to destroy. Just as you will be punished by your Master if you do not obey his will, I will be punished by mine.' Thomas is firm, however, and the demons vanish.

The apostle then preaches to the grateful Misdaeus's family and to others in the land, and acquires a considerable following which includes the king. However, among his preachings is the dominant theme of abstinence, and Misdaeus finds that his wife no longer wants to have physical relations with him. This leads to a falling-out between the king and the apostle, and eventually Misdaeus orders the execution of Thomas. The apostle accepts his fate and is pierced with spears, and his body is kept in a tomb.

Sometime later, one of Misdaeus's children is possessed by a demon. The king remembers the holy man who had once saved his wife and daughter. Misdaeus wants to use Thomas' relics as a cure, but on opening the apostle's tomb, finds his body has disappeared.

This is no miracle, however. As *The Acts* explains, the body has been taken by one of Thomas' disciples to upper Mesopotamia. Meanwhile, the king rubs some of the dust from the tomb on his son's body, and the child is healed. Thus the king repents, becomes a believer again and spreads the word of Christ.

The Acts survives in several complete manuscripts and some fragments in both Greek and Syriac, the Aramaic dialect which flourished at that time in northern Mesopotamia. The origins of *The Acts*, like other writings of the Apostolic Age of Christianity, are difficult to pin down. The text can be reliably dated to the early third century CE, from the mass of writings, references and nebulous legends that constitute the earliest period of Christianity.

The Acts is noted for the hymns it contains, including the beautiful 'Hymn of the Pearl' and 'Come, Holy Spirit', which continues to be sung by Christians today, albeit in altered forms. Its composers appear to have believed in Docetism, an early Christian belief that the human form of Christ was an illusion. Docetism also includes the belief that physical relations are inherently sinful, reflected in what Jesus preaches to the newly-weds, the story of the incubus demon, Thomas preaching celibacy to Misdaeus's family and defeating the serpent which had caused the fall of Eve and Adam.

Like other New Testament apocrypha, *The Acts of Thomas* was considered Scripture by early Christians of both Asia and Europe. But over several ecumenical councils, the official view of the Church was that it could not be considered part of the

Bible. During the Protestant Reformation, at the Council of Trent in Italy in the sixteenth century, the Catholic Church formally declared *The Acts* a heretical work, although it continues to remain significant for understanding the history of Christianity, particularly in the subcontinent.[6]

The Acts is likely to have been composed in the city of Edessa, now Sanliurfa, a provincial capital on Turkey's border with Syria, where the relics of Thomas were supposed to have been brought from India and venerated. The people who composed it were a mix of Jewish expatriates and Gentile local citizens.

The text is not a source of historical or geographical information, nor was it ever meant to be. As with other apocrypha, it was meant for use among the scattered Christian communities of the Middle East, Egypt and Greece. But amid the cast of kings and fantastical creatures, amid the miracles and exorcisms, it is possible to get an idea about early Christians and how they saw India.

Trade routes between the subcontinent and the Middle East by sea and land had been established in prehistory. Archaeological finds in Sumeria and Egypt show that the people of these Bronze Age civilizations had a commercial network extending to the Indus Valley. By the time of the Second Urbanization period in the Gangetic plain, in the sixth century BCE, these trade networks had become more sophisticated and saw the movement of ideas in addition to cargo. Centres of maritime trade had developed along the Indian coast from Sindh and Gujarat to the Malabar and Coromandel regions.

The expansion of the Achaemenid Persian Empire in the sixth century BCE created a new world order. The first real world empire brought diverse people, who had only distantly heard of one another, into a single political grouping. Trade along carefully administered—and meticulously taxed—routes increased and diversified. By c.521 BCE, Jewish exiles from Babylon had returned home and built the Second Temple in Jerusalem. A few years later, Achaemenid Emperor Darius the Great conquered the Indus Valley with the northern part becoming the new province of Gandhara and the southern part, Hindu (deriving from 'Sindhu', the name of the river in Sanskrit). Jews and Indians found themselves part of a well-organized polity whose constituents were conscripted into armies for other conquests. In 480 BCE, an Indian contingent of bowmen, clad in cotton clothes and armed with reed bows and iron-tipped arrows, was present with Nubians, Scythians, Egyptians, Persians, Judaeans and Phoenicians at Thermopylae during the invasion of Greece.[7]

The first Jewish communities in India are likely to have established themselves in coastal cities in the north-west around this period. Eventually, Jewish diasporic groups would settle along the Konkan, Malabar and Coromandel coasts. These, the oldest of India's Jewish communities, are known as the Cochin Jews. But there have been others down the centuries, particularly after the formation of the Jewish diaspora following the destruction of the Second Temple in Jerusalem by the Roman Empire in 70 CE. Later Jewish communities include the Bene Israelis who are mainly concentrated in the Konkan, in Mumbai, and inland cities like Pune. The Middle Ages saw the arrival of Paradesi Jews, said to be fleeing persecution in Europe. The Baghdadi Jews from Mesopotamia arrived in the eighteenth century and became a prominent part of Mumbai's mercantile community.

By the fourth century BCE, mainly because of Achaemenid expansion, the known world had become a little smaller and the people, including Jews and Indians, had become a little more familiar with each other. In the Gangetic plains, indigenous empire builders were at work, and the Nanda dynasty, with its capital at Pataliputra (modern Patna in the state of Bihar) had expanded to the west.

The weakened Achaemenids were replaced by Alexander, whose conquests included Judaea and the two old Persian provinces in India. The passing of the conqueror fractured his empire, as the Diadochi, his generals, fought among themselves in ever-changing alliances. Seleucus Nicator inherited the largest portion of Alexander's conquests, from Judaea to India. To oversee this vast land, Seleucus, like generals before him, built cities straddling the trade routes to the East, and one of these was Edessa. Over time, it became a vital city in northern Mesopotamia, populated by expatriate Greeks, Jews and the diverse peoples of the Middle East.

In the years after Alexander, Hellenism, that mix of Greek culture, language and the arts, flourished in Asia and Northern Africa, reaching as far as southern India and China. Hellenism and political power, however, did not often walk together. In a war which lasted two years, Seleucus lost the Indian provinces to a new emperor whom the Greeks would call Sandrocottus and the Indians, Chandragupta Maurya.

Seleucus' descendants, ruling from the great eastern Mediterranean port city of Antioch, were not up to the task of retaining Alexander's eastern conquests. Over time, the Seleucid Empire crumbled. The Central Asian and Persian provinces were lost to new dynasties or peoples.[8] Edessa became a frontier city for the Seleucids. In northern Mesopotamia, the years of peaceful trade with Indian cities over land and sea, under the *Pax Achaemenia*, became a distant memory. In time the Seleucids, reduced to Judaea and Syria, were subsumed by the Roman Republic, which was to become the Roman Empire by the beginning of the Common Era.

But even without imperial peace, trade and travel continued, and the people of Edessa certainly had their views on India, some of which can be found in *The Acts*. The subcontinent still retained a great deal of mystique. Of all the places in the world, the Serpent of Eden, grown to monstrous size, could only have hidden in the vastness of India to prey with impunity on wayfarers. Talking creatures and demons pleading occupational hazards were to be found by travellers. The Ancient Greeks, who had fantastical tales about these lands, had not been the only people to locate supernatural entities in India. There was no dearth of either gods or monsters there.

A theme in *The Acts* worth examining is the portrayal of the people of India. It is interesting that, during the entirety of Thomas' stay in the land, his principal difficulties come not at the hands of the people or the mob, but from the fickleness of kings. There is no entrenched priestly hierarchy to plot against the apostle. No character in *The Acts* points out the Jewishness of Thomas, nor is he persecuted outright for reasons of belief, ethnicity, dietary habits or country of origin. Indeed, the first person he meets on his journey is a Jewish dancing girl, and the subjects of both Gundaphorus and Misdaeus appear to be receptive to his preaching. There is no significant *doctrinal* objection to Christianity among the natives, merely the petulance of royalty, and the people of Edessa were as familiar with this as Egyptians or Indians. This, the hospitable nature of ordinary Indians, was to be discovered by Europeans when the Latin Church would first arrive in the Middle Ages. There were many kingdoms in India, the message went, and countless more people, but there was always space for a new god or a messenger from the divine.

Whether this subtext reflects the welcome that early Christians found among the polytheists of India or not, *The Acts* does reinforce what must have been apparent to its intended audience in the Middle East: persecution does not occur from or among the powerless; rather, it is a by product of the trappings of power and the inadequacies of those who wield it.

The Jews of Edessa and the early Christians appear to have had some idea of the polytheism that characterizes Hindu beliefs. There is of course the reference to 'all types of images' created by the people of India, but this would not have been unusual in a world which, even outside the subcontinent, was still predominantly polytheistic. It would be a subject of greater scrutiny in the Middle Ages, when the memory of pagan Europe had faded away.

Of the rich cast of characters in *The Acts*, the two kings, Gundaphorus and Misdaeus, could be worth a look for those seeking to place the text in the tapestry of subcontinental history. There was indeed a Gundaphorus, or Gondophares, an Indo-Parthian king who ruled from what is now eastern Iran to north-western India. Four kings of that name in that dynasty have been individually identified, and at least one was on the throne late in the first century CE, around the time of the first Christians.

The name 'Gundaphorus' would eventually become, in medieval European imagination, 'Gaspar', and would be identified in some traditions as one of the three Magi who visited the infant Jesus with gifts. At various times, Europeans located the Magi at different cities of eastern Persia. But this would present a bit of a problem: Why would a Magus, of all the kings of the East, not recognize an apostle of Jesus afterwards, or be unfamiliar, even unreceptive to his teachings?

As far as Misdaeus is concerned, a likely historical candidate is Vasudeva I, a Kushan ruler of Bactria and western Punjab in the third century CE, which coincides with the period of composition of *The Acts*.

By the end of the Apostolic Age, Christianity had spread among Jewish communities and Gentiles in Greece, Rome, Egypt, Persia and north-western India, but perhaps no farther than the coastal areas of the subcontinent. As the ecclesiastical structures to minister to these communities grew, it would have been difficult for smaller communities of Christians in the interiors of India to be closely connected to centres like Edessa. In coastal India, the first Christians were almost certainly converts from Judaism. There might not even have been a conscious break from the religion of their ancestors. As in Mesopotamia, in India too the first Christians are very likely to have been part of a gradual reformist movement within Jewish communities, or part of baptizing cults such as the one to which John the Baptist had belonged.

In the third century CE, Edessa finally returned to the West, but not to the Greeks. The Hellenistic Age, or at least its political manifestation, had ended. Now the Roman Empire was at war with the Parthians, who sought to inherit the Achaemenid mantle of masters of the world. By then, the Christianity practised by the people of Edessa, northern Mesopotamia and Syria—and through them the early Christians of India— had started taking on a different doctrinal form compared to what was emerging in Roman-ruled Egypt, Greece and Italy.

The basic ideas—the life, ministry, death and resurrection of Christ, the ideas derived from Jewish prophetic traditions, the messianism—were the same. But, as scholars began writing and debating on different issues of faith, divergent views on fundamental questions had begun to be aired. An emerging and very contentious point would be the question about the nature of Christ.

India too had changed from what it had been during the time of Sandrocottus. At the end of the third century CE, a new empire united most of north India. The Guptas oversaw a vast dominion built on a thriving commercial network that was connected to the Roman Empire in the west and to the Chinese in the east. Indian royalty may not have sent envoys to Jerusalem just to fetch a carpenter for a palace, but international trade was thriving.

In the Roman Empire, it was a time of councils.

Schism

The veneration of the relics of the apostle Thomas had been established at Edessa by the third century, and early Christians had connected Thomas' ministry in India with the eastern Syrian city by then. A hundred years later, Eusebius of Caesarea, one of the founders of biblical studies, began investigating the numerous New Testament texts and apocrypha which had proliferated by his time. His objective was to check the reliability of the Gospels and to ferret out discrepancies, thus establishing what he hoped would be a reliable bibliography of early Christian writings.

In his magisterial *Historia Ecclesiastica*, Eusebius says it was believed by his time that the apostle Thomas had preached in the East, 'including in Parthia'. Eusebius appears to have agreed that Thomas preached in Gondophares' kingdom at the very least, and might have included, in his definition of Parthia, areas east of the Indus. The choice of the word 'Parthia' is significant. If Eusebius had definite evidence that Thomas had been in India, he would have used the term. 'India' was a region loosely defined by chroniclers of that period: in several records of councils of the Persian Church, it refers to the eastern African coast as well. This conflation stayed on in the Medieval period, when parts of eastern Africa were still referred to as 'India' or 'India Tertia' (Third India) and only ended towards the middle of the fourteenth century, when the term was applied specifically to the subcontinent.[1]

The idea of 'Parthia' in the West too was fluid, although this was due to the borders of Parthian rulers shifting with chaotic rapidity, sometimes extending to what is eastern Balochistan in Pakistan today, at other times crossing the Indus. By the beginning of the Common Era, Hellenistic remnants in Bactria (now northern Afghanistan) had metamorphosed into Indo-Greek kingdoms, of which the most famous ruler was Menander I (d.130 BCE), who ruled from Sakala, the city of Sialkot in Pakistan today. Indo-Greek kingdoms extended east of the Indus into the subcontinent, and several rulers including Menander became Buddhist. In Vidisha in the central Indian state of Madhya Pradesh is the Heliodorus pillar, named after the man who commissioned it, an ambassador from the Indo-Greek king Antialcidas to the court of King Bhagabhadra of the Shunga dynasty in 113 BCE. The inscription is dedicated to Vasudeva, identified as an early Vaishnav god, of whom Heliodorus calls himself a devotee.[2]

The Indo-Greeks were succeeded by the Indo-Parthians around the Apostolic period. Therefore, Eusebius was referring to an amorphous geography when he used the term 'Parthia', and was including regions around the Indus as well, territories which at other times were included in the geography of India. Since Jewish communities would have been established on the coastal trade routes from Persia to western India, it appears that for Eusebius, the ministry of Thomas was located in the lower Indus region.

Eusebius also accepts the veneration of the apostle's relics in Edessa, although he does not mention the site where Thomas was martyred in the subcontinent. This passing of the 'Eusebius Test' indicates the official acceptance in the West of the Thomas mission in India.[3]

To this appearance of India in the early Roman Christian imagination must be added the views of the theologian and historian Jerome who among other writings compiled, in the late fourth and early fifth centuries, accounts of prominent Christian preachers and thinkers preceding him. One of these was Pantaenus, a Christian philosopher who taught in Alexandria in the late second century. Pantaenus was widely respected for his knowledge of ecclesiastical and secular literature, and was a man of impeccable probity. So great was his reputation that Christian preachers in India requested Demetrius, the Bishop of Alexandria, to send Pantaenus to the region. Pantaenus made an astounding discovery in India: the apostle Bartholomew had preached among the people there and read from the Gospel of Matthew, a copy of which he had left behind among the Indians. Pantaenus brought this text, written in Hebrew, from India to Alexandria and continued with his scholarly pursuits.[4]

Jerome, who like Pantaenus would later be canonized, did not mention the ministry of Thomas at all, nor did he appear to be aware of this tradition among the Indians. Instead, he wrote that according to Pantaenus, a quite different apostle had preached among the Indians. The solution to this confusion may lie, once again, in geography. Other sources had mentioned that Bartholomew preached in western Anatolia and the Black Sea region. In the early Christian period, the Crimean Peninsula and parts east were within the Bosporan Kingdom, and one of the provinces of this kingdom was called Sindia, after the Sindi people who lived in the Taman Peninsula between the Sea of Azov and the Black Sea. Pantaenus, it appears, had travelled only to the Black Sea but Jerome, coming 200 years after him, placed the Alexandrian in India.[5]

The early Christian imagining of India and its people also directly referred to pre-Christian motifs, stories and symbols connected with that land. In the collection of legends called the *Alexander Romance*, of which the earliest surviving version in Greek is from the third century CE, there is an account of a correspondence between the Macedonian conqueror and Dindimus, 'king of Brahmins', where the word 'king' might have referred to what the Hellenistic world considered noted Brahmins of the subcontinent. In their exchange, Alexander first enquires about the life and customs of Brahmins, to which Dindimus enumerates the virtues his people hold in esteem: vegetarianism, a frugal life, an avoidance of excesses and a love of nature. Alexander retorts by calling this 'a miserable life' which could be neither envied nor imitated. The conqueror says his philosophy and those of his fellow soldiers is to work hard but also enjoy well-earned pleasures.

The *Alexander Romance*, including the section on Dindimus, was the subject of considerable discussion among the early Church fathers. It is inferred today that the response of Dindimus reflects the position of the Cynic school of philosophy of the pre-Christian period. Like the historical Cynics, the fictional Dindimus supports asceticism, self-mortification, freedom from physical desires and a rejection of art and learning, particularly about the material world. This doctrine was not only close to the Buddhist position, but also to Christian ideals of self-sacrifice, rejection of wealth and dependence on the love of a god. Dindimus' position was based to a large extent on how Hellenistic Greeks considered Indian Brahmins to be, ideas which had remained in the early Christian period and had entered the *Alexander Romance*.

In this congruence of ideals and virtues, Christian thinkers like Jerome, Origen and Tertullian found much to admire about Brahmins and the Indian idea of asceticism, even if they were not familiar with India as a geography or society.[6] If they had been more familiar with Buddhist philosophy, this admiration would have extended to Buddhism as well.

Meanwhile, from the accounts of Eusebius and Jerome, sifting through the geographical misunderstandings, one gets an idea of how Christian scholars in the Roman Empire recorded the history of the faith in India. Certainly the Persian Church, being directly connected with the Indians and much closer to them, had a clearer idea. By the third century CE, Christian communities had expanded in the cities of Mesopotamia and along coastal Persia to India, and representatives of the missions regularly travelled between Persia and the subcontinent.

In the West, however, Christians had been facing persecution across the Roman Empire. The early Church hierarchies in imperial cities like Alexandria, Antioch and Rome tried to minister to their flock under scrutiny and the constant threat of violence by the authorities. The political structure which, according to Christian belief, had been responsible for the crucifixion of the Messiah was still very much present and hostile to the faithful.

It had begun after the Great Fire which destroyed large parts of Rome in 64 CE during the reign of Emperor Nero, who blamed the calamity on the Christians of the city, then considered a splinter group of Jews.[7] Christians were despised by the citizens of Rome already by then, because of claims about the Resurrection—an idea which the pagan Romans found unnatural and deeply offensive—and large numbers of people who were accused of being Christians or had confessed were arrested and convicted, not for the fire itself but for 'hatred against mankind'. They were executed by different means, from being torn to pieces by dogs to being crucified, while others were burnt alive in the evenings. But although Christians were unpopular, the gruesome manner of their deaths in Nero's gardens, which had become a public spectacle, made Romans uncomfortable because it appeared that persecution of these people was being done not so much for the public good as for Nero's sadistic pleasure.

For two centuries after Nero, no Roman emperor matched his brutal treatment of Christians, although citizens continued to persecute local communities of the faithful around the Mediterranean, and the imperial administration either collaborated with the persecutors or encouraged such treatment. In 177, during the reign of Marcus Aurelius, the pagan citizens of Lugdunum (now Lyons in France) began shunning Christians in public places. The authorities stepped in, and the Christians of Lugdunum were arrested, tried on a wide range of charges from incest to cannibalism, and either sentenced to long periods of imprisonment or fed to the animals in the arena.[8] By the end of the third century, persecution against Christians had become institutionalized, although their communities had grown and had some sympathizers among pagan Romans and even within the elite.

By the early fourth century, the empire had been divided, for administrative convenience among other reasons, into an eastern and a western part, and a system of co-emperors had been instituted. At the close of the first decade, the empire was plunged into civil war among four rival factions. One of them was led by Constantine, son of the late co-emperor Constantius. In October 312, his forces met the army of co-emperor Maxentius at the Milvian Bridge on the Tiber, near Rome. Either in a dream on the eve of the battle, or in a vision in the sky on the way to the battlefield, Constantine appears to have seen a Christian symbol (in some accounts a cross) and the message, in Greek: *En touto nika.* 'With this sign, conquer.' His troops arrived at the Tiber carrying shields and flags emblazoned with the Chi-Rho, a Christogram containing the first two Greek letters of the name of Christ: X and P.

Constantine's army defeated Maxentius at the Milvian Bridge. Among the dead was Maxentius himself, drowned in the river during battle. Constantine was master of the Western Roman Empire, and eventually reunited both sections of the empire, becoming the first sole emperor in four decades.

Shortly after his victory at the Milvian Bridge, Constantine issued the Edict of Milan, under which persecution of Christians was finally stopped, and they were recognized as one of the many religions permitted to be practised across the empire. Constantine would convert to Christianity, but only on his deathbed in 337.

Administering his vast empire, Constantine was also aware that there were different forms and rites practised by Christians and their literature was diverse. What the faith needed, he felt, was a touch of Roman structure and order.

In 325, he invited Christian bishops of the empire and beyond to the city of Nicaea, now Iznik near the Sea of Marmara in western Turkey. The idea was to arrive at an imperially approved idea of Christianity and decide on questions such as the nature of Christ, his position relative to God the Father, the official date for Easter and codification of rites. The number of invitees reflected the diversity that Christian congregations had acquired by then. Over 1800 bishops had been called from Alexandria, Rome, Jerusalem, Antioch, Edessa and other centres of the faith. Only a fraction of these eventually attended. Eusebius of Caesarea was present as expected, and so was a bishop named Ioannes, representing Persia and India. But so was Arius.

Scholars of the Church had been debating on certain very divisive ideas for some time, and these were placed under examination at what would come to be called the First Council of Nicaea. The most controversial of these ideas was what Arius, a Berber bishop in Alexandria, had propounded. The core belief of Arianism was that Christ had been born of God the Father at some point, and although still divine, this meant he was subservient to God himself. This went against the orthodox belief called Trinitarianism that God the Father, Christ and the Holy Spirit were equal in every way.

At Nicaea, watched by Constantine—who made an ostentatious entrance at the council to let the bishops know the might of the empire—Arius defended his theory. It did have its proponents among the bishops of North Africa and elsewhere, but the Trinitarians carried the day. Constantine himself did not have a vote—he was no bishop—but approved the final verdict. Christ the Son was co-eternal with God the Father, and an equal. Arianism became a heretical sect and was suppressed within the Roman Empire, although it proved remarkably resilient. After Constantine, when the empire split once again into two and the Western Roman Empire was overrun by

Germanic tribes, these people, including the Goths, Visigoths and Vandals, had already converted to Arian Christianity. By the seventh century, however, with the fall of the kingdoms founded by these tribes around the Mediterranean, Arianism was extinct.

Constantine's gathering of bishops also drafted a summary of officially recognized Christian beliefs. The Nicene Creed declared the belief that God created the world and everything in it; that Christ was co-eternal and of the same substance as God the Father, as was the Holy Spirit, and that Christ was incarnated as a man, suffered on the cross and ascended to heaven and, finally, that he would return in the End of Days. As a footnote, the Nicene Creed roundly condemned Arian beliefs about the subservient nature of Christ compared to the Father.

Arius and some of his supporters were removed from their positions and exiled, although he was allowed to return to Alexandria after making some changes to his doctrine as a concession to the emperor. A little more than a decade after Nicaea, the octogenarian passed away. It is very likely that he was poisoned, although some of his bitterest Trinitarian critics would continue to entertain themselves with fantastical stories of how he met his end from divine wrath. A particularly trenchant opponent, the fifth-century historian Socrates of Constantinople would write of how Arius died after evacuating his intestines after being afflicted with dysentery brought about by sudden remorse. Divine justice, said the Trinitarians, had come at last for such an incorrigible heretic.[9]

Having settled divisions within the bishops, Constantine then began construction of a new Rome at the site of an ancient Phoenician-turned-Greek village called Byzantion on the Bosporus Strait. Constantinople became his new capital and, after the empire split again, the capital of the eastern half, which would become the Byzantine Empire.

Shortly after the Council of Nicaea, wrote Eusebius, a delegation of Indians arrived with gifts of precious stones and exotic animals for Constantine, and acknowledged his imperial authority over them. Eusebius does not give further details about these Indians or this peculiar embassy. Roman imperial ambitions to the east had been thoroughly checked by the Persians, so this unexplained appearance of Indians and their acceptance of a remote western empire is an extremely unlikely event. In this case, Eusebius's sources seem to have made that familiar conflation of eastern Africa with India. Ethiopian and Nubian proximity to the Romans in Egypt had increased in the time of Constantine.

But Arianism and other heterodox beliefs lingered. In 380, Emperor Theodosius I, the last to rule a united Roman Empire, declared that Nicene Christianity was the only legitimate form of the faith, and would be the official religion of the empire. The state's support for pagan religions, including funding of temples and other shrines, also ended.

After Theodosius, the western empire began disintegrating under pressure from Germanic tribes. The eastern fragment endured, ruling over Syria, Palestine, Egypt and North Africa. Persia, the eternal rival of the Romans, now had a new empire, of the Sassanids. Eastern Syria became a contested region between the two powers. The Christians of Persia, by the beginning of the fifth century, had at least forty bishoprics or sees, under the authority of a *catholikos* at the Sassanid capital of Ctesiphon. These included bishoprics in India.

The Sassanid Empire's official faith was Zoroastrianism, whose clergy had a hierarchical structure and whose fortunes were intimately connected with the fate of the empire. Jews and Christians had been permitted in the empire—as long as they acknowledged the primacy of Zoroastrianism—but after Christianity became recognized in the Roman Empire, Christians in Persia became targets of persecution and were viewed as possible fifth columnists. Persian Christians could only try in vain to convince Sassanid officials and Zoroastrian priests that they were not agents of Constantinople. Sassanid emperors would repeatedly levy large taxes on the Persian Church, and senior clergymen were frequently imprisoned, exiled or executed.

Arianism, which caused the first major doctrinal crisis in Christianity, had been about the position of Christ in relation to the Father. The second crisis was about the nature of Christ himself. By the beginning of the fifth century, the episcopal sees of five major cities in the Roman Empire—Jerusalem, Rome, Constantinople, Alexandria and Antioch—had achieved prominence over all the others in the Christian world. Because of their significance, the teachings and doctrinal positions of archbishops of these sees were considered significant.

At Antioch, a dogma had gradually evolved over the question of the nature of Christ and about how much of this nature was divine. There was the view that Christ, being divine, was eternal and could not be considered to have been born in the way humans are. The opposing view was that Mary had given birth to a divine Christ, and therefore she should be called *Theotokos* or 'God-bearer'. The Antiochene position was that in Christ, human and divine natures were separate and distinct. Nestorius, a clergyman born in the Roman province of Syria, had studied at Antioch before becoming archbishop of Constantinople. He gave further shape to the dogma and tried to solve the debate by declaring that in Christ, the divine and the human had coexisted as separate entities.

But since the human part was tainted by Original Sin, Nestorius argued, Mary should be more correctly called *Christotokos* or 'Bearer of the Messiah'. If Nestorius thought that would solve the debate amicably, he was mistaken. Both sides of the doctrinal debate were outraged. Those who insisted Christ's nature was human and divine in complete union denounced Nestorianism as a heresy as egregious as Arianism had been. From Alexandria to Rome, the debate split the ecclesiastical hierarchy. Alexandrian Patriarch Cyril became the bitterest foe of Nestorius, and other church leaders were forced to take sides.

As the debate became increasingly acrimonious, Eastern Roman Emperor Theodosius II recalled the policies of Constantine and announced another council, which met at Ephesus on the Anatolian coast in 431. The suggestion came from Nestorius himself, who wanted the opportunity to best Cyril and prove the Alexandrian was a heretic. Cyril wanted to do just this to Nestorius.

The sessions at the Council of Ephesus lasted for more than a month and grew progressively more acrimonious. Finally, the assembly pronounced that Nestorianism was wrong. The nature of Christ was both human and divine, and the two could not be separated. Mary would be called the 'God-bearer'. Nestorius was branded a heretic. Meanwhile, his supporters, many of them from Antioch, who had also been condemned of heresy, issued their own proclamation condemning Cyril.

The emperor's reaction was to order both Nestorius and Cyril into exile. Gradually, the anti-Nestorian camp prevailed and his supporters were removed from their positions. In 435,

Nestorius was exiled by the emperor yet again from Antioch to an isolated monastery in Egypt, where he eventually died.

The Council of Ephesus was a traumatic moment in the history of Christianity. While Nestorius' opponents in Alexandria and Rome prevailed, his supporters from Antioch and Syria never forgave their counterparts in the West. Nestorianism was gradually uprooted from the Roman Empire, but followers of the doctrine migrated eastwards, establishing themselves in Mesopotamia and Persia and arriving in India.

The legacy of Ephesus lingered, and resentment grew among the centres of Christian thought. In 449, another council was convened at Ephesus, with the patriarch of the Church of Alexandria being appointed the president by the then emperor. The Pope of Rome did not attend, but sent representatives. By the time of this council, the churches of the East, led by the Alexandrian clergy, were in a dispute with those in Rome about the nature of Christ. In a victory for the Alexandrian faction, the Second Council of Ephesus declared that in Christ, human and divine natures existed together as one nature without separation.

The Pope of Rome then sought another council, and in 451, Emperor Marcian granted it. The bishops and senior clergy of the Christian world this time assembled at Chalcedon, on the eastern shore of the Bosporus. The Church of Rome and its allies won the debate, and declared that Christ's human and divine natures existed together, but as separate forms.

The Alexandrians and other factions of the eastern Mediterranean did not accept this, and accused the prelates of Rome and their allies of being imperial agents. In Alexandria, the factions excommunicated and issued decrees against each other. Meanwhile, the churches in Sassanid Persia, which had accepted Nestorian preachers and ideas, gradually distanced themselves from churches within the Roman Empire. By 544, the rift had become permanent. The Nestorian Schism, as it came to be called, saw the Christians of Persia and eastern Syria separate from their counterparts in the Roman Empire and become the Church of the East. Thus, Western and Eastern Christianity began diverging from each other.

In Alexandria, the rift caused by the Council of Chalcedon would lead to another schism resulting in Oriental Orthodox Christianity, from which the Coptic Orthodox Church centred in Alexandria, the Armenian Apostolic Church, the Ethiopian and Eritrean churches are descended.[10]

While the Church of the East became progressively more Nestorian, the old rivalry between the Sassanid Persian Empire and the Byzantine Empire was worsening. In 540, Sassanid Emperor Khosrow I invaded Byzantine territory and sacked a number of cities, including Antioch. Two years later, a great plague, thought to be bubonic, scythed through the cities of the Byzantine Empire. The plague is supposed to have originated in China and to have arrived on merchant ships through India to the Red Sea and Egypt, where it was first recorded in the empire. Later writers would call it the Plague of Justinian, after the ambitious Byzantine emperor of that time. Justinian himself was infected by the disease, but he survived. Large numbers of his people did not. The plague then spread through the Sassanid Empire and crippled both great powers.

In 553, Justinian declared the official religion of the empire would be the form of Christianity that had been distilled through the series of councils in the previous 200 years. While he confirmed imperial support for this official version of the faith, the prelates of the empire confirmed that the Church would not contravene the directions of the emperor. The Church and the state had expressed themselves to be in agreement, and to be of one purpose. It was an arrangement that echoed the system already in place in Persia, where the Zoroastrian hierarchy and imperial administration were co-dependent.

The immediate victims of this alliance between the Church and the state were heretics, including Arian remnants and Nestorian malcontents, many of whom were in Alexandria. Those who were not Nestorians but still opposed the Council of Chalcedon were also under a cloud. Jews, who had progressively been suffering ever since Christianity began to be promoted by the emperors, now faced increased persecution, leading to a large-scale exodus eastwards, with many migrating to the Arabian Peninsula. The old pagan polytheistic faiths were suppressed, and their shrines attacked or demolished.

The Church of the East and its Nestorians were safe from Justinian's purges, but Christians in general faced restrictions in Persia. The Zoroastrian clergy ensured Nestorian missionaries did not have complete freedom to venture into Central Asia on proselytizing missions. Zoroastrianism was so completely identified with the Persian imperial state that it could not spread beyond the borders of the empire—the steppe tribes of Central Asia were too suspicious of Zoroastrian missionaries' intentions to accord them welcome. In Western Europe, the Church of Rome did not have this problem by the sixth century. The Western Roman Empire had ceased to exist, and among the tribal chieftains of what used to be Roman Gaul, Britain and Germania missionaries brought the growing religion to the pagans. But in Persia, the Nestorians had to be content with their flock in the Sassanid Empire and their ministries in India. This arrangement would not change till the third decade of the seventh century, when the world would be remade.

The Many Errors of Mani

Exercises in alternative history hinge on key inflection points, on events and people of suitable complexity. One such person is Mani. What if the religion he founded, at one time among the most influential in the world, had endured? In our own unaltered timeline, in the period when Manichaeism was at its zenith, how much of it arrived in India, and what impact did it have on the Christian communities in the subcontinent? How did Mani see India? Did Manichaeism itself survive in some form in that land?

For a long time, the study of Manichaeism was based on analysing its reflections in accounts of Christians and people of other faiths. From the middle of the twentieth century onwards, primary sources directly dealing with the faith have been re-examined, and some portion of the mists around Mani has been cleared. And yet not always, for where Manichaeism's detractors were trenchant in their criticism of the preacher and his beliefs, hagiographies by apologists created a fantastic set of myths around him. In the modern era, the virulence of commentaries against Mani in Late Antiquity has been replaced by a tendency to consider his legacy more influential than it actually was.

We do know that Mani was born c.216 CE in a settlement by a river north-east of Babylon. We also know that his father was named Patteg. Everything else about his early life veers into the unverifiable or the clearly embellished. Mani's followers in Iran would say Patteg was descended from an old Parthian family. His mother, who was given different names depending on the text, was said to be from a Parthian family related to the ruling Arsacid dynasty of Persia, in keeping with the desire of disciples to give noble lineages to their masters.

Elsewhere, followers with an eye on potential Christian converts said Mani's mother's name was Maryam and that his father was an emigrant from southern Mesopotamia, much like Joseph and Mary's journey to Bethlehem and baby Jesus being taken to Egypt or other lands afterwards. Besides being considered a descendant of royalty such as Christ and the Buddha, Mani was said to have been an only son in some of the accounts, or, in others, to have had a brother.[1]

Patteg, by these traditional accounts, appears to have been a follower of a traditional Mesopotamian religion that, unlike Zoroastrianism, worshipped idols. While wandering around the Persian capital of Ctesiphon shortly after Mani's birth, Patteg heard a voice giving him three stern instructions: eat no meat, drink no wine and abstain from sexual relations.

Mani's father, and later his mother, appear to have joined a cult that believed all matter was inherently evil, and therefore physical relations were a sin. Their rituals were centred on the idea of physical and dietary purity. All forms of life were divided into male and female, and 'male' vegetables had to be washed and blessed before they could be eaten.

Sifting through the diverse and conflicting accounts of Mani's early life, one catches a glimpse of Mesopotamian society in that period: a world where the newly arrived Christian doctrines contended with the old Zoroastrian and Jewish beliefs. The founder of Patteg's cult, a Babylonian Jew named Elchasai, was rebelling against fire sacrifices in the religion of his ancestors, and turned to water for salvation, possibly influenced by baptizing cults of Palestine, such as the one to which John the Baptist belonged. The very act of baptism, Elchasai's cult believed, would purify a person, body and soul.

In other matters, the cult apparently borrowed from early Christian belief, including the idea that Christ was the last of the prophets. But while the Christianity that went to the West under Paul of Tarsus had become a new faith, followers of Elchasai were actually Christians following Jewish religious practices.[2] By the time Mani's parents joined it, the cult had become quite popular in southern Mesopotamia and the Trans-Jordan area.

Mani was brought up as a believer in this cult, a product of the tremendous cross-cultural and inter-religious churn in the Middle East during the early Christian period. Later hagiographies claimed he started getting revelations and insights when he was twelve years old, which continued till he was twenty-four. Then, he received a visit from a divine and radiant entity which was his 'twin'. This was named 'tawma', which is derived from the same Aramaic word from which the name of the apostle Thomas, who has also been called 'the Twin' in biblical apocrypha, has been derived. Mani's followers were clearly aware of all the accounts about Thomas, who was held in such a prominent position by Christians in Syria around that period. The appearance of the radiant figure is also similar to Zoroastrian accounts of the first revelation of a shining presence called 'Vohu Manah', which taught Zarathustra about Ahura Mazda and the eternal struggle between truth and falsehood. As Mani would have known, there are hallowed patterns to the prophetic tradition.[3]

The grown-up Mani, armed with his divine revelations, now began disputing the fundamentals of their faith with his fellow Elchasaites. This too was in the tradition of Christ.

Some of Mani's objections appear to have been rational. On the matter of baptizing male vegetables before eating them, Mani was wholly justified in questioning the point of it. There was no visible way in which these vegetables were being cleansed of whatever flaw they possessed, he said, so why could believers simply not abstain from them if dietary purity was so essential?

And what worked for vegetables, by extension, could very well work for humans. Mani told the Elchasaites that bathing and ablutions conferred no purity on a person. Jesus, he said, had not talked about baptism in his teachings, and the body, an inherently impure vessel, could not be cleansed by water. The solution, said Mani, was to 'separate light from darkness, death from life'.

Mani's ideas, expectedly, were not received well by the Elchasaites. A few were inclined to believe the young man was privy to some divine revelation. Others accused him of shocking heresies, including the unpardonable one of announcing that it was perfectly all right to eat Greek bread, which, being foreign and impure, ought to have been anathema. The Elchasaites said only Jewish bread was to be eaten, and besides, it was the food of the poor.

Cornered by such serious allegations about unbaptized vegetables and Greek bread, Mani was hauled up before a council of elders. Mani defended his beliefs by referring to the example of Christ, who associated with the apparently impure. Sometime afterwards, Mani made his break with the Elchasaites.

Arising from the ferment in that part of the world, Mani's ideas were unique compared to his contemporary cults in two ways: first, they were not exclusivist, and much like Pauline Christianity, meant for the entire world; second, Mani explicitly declared that he was the seal of the prophets. Manichaean literature places him at the centre and culmination of a lineage that draws from Zarathustra, the Buddha and Jesus, essentially making him the inheritor of all three belief systems.

This innovation of Mani made the religion extraordinarily malleable, depending on geography and culture. As it spread outside Mesopotamia, Manichaeism took on the contours of already established faiths, from Christianity and Judaism in the West to Buddhism and Taoism in the East. Salvation for everyone, Manichaean or not, depended on acts of mercy and kindness shown to believers.

The term 'Manichaean' has survived in contemporary usage to denote a simplistic division of the world, or a part of it, into contending parts. By inference, a 'Manichean' position refuses to acknowledge the greyness within and around ideas. Mani's doctrines were, of course, somewhat more complex than that. Originally, he said, good and evil existed in two separate realities, until evil became aware of good. This led to three phases of creation, the third and ultimate one resulting in the creation of Adam and Eve from emanations of light from demons.

The complex cosmogony apart, the duality of good and evil, and their existence as effectively equal entities has been problematic for believers of later Abrahamic religions. For all the Manichaean talk of syncretism, Mani was deriving most of his doctrines from the Judaic faith of his father, including the flawed nature of the first man and woman. Christians and Muslims of a later age, horrified by the idea that Creation was not an entirely divine plan, or that evil had emerged in rebellion to God, condemned the Manichaean 'heresy' in strong terms, despite this Abrahamic connection. But the duality of light and dark, and even the names of some of the chief dramatis personae on both sides of this celestial conflict, were ideas taken from Zoroastrianism.

Making a break with strict legalistic Judaism, Mani embarked on a journey that mirrored the one already made by Paul of Tarsus, and the one made by Christ in Judaea. But whereas Paul went from Jerusalem to Rome, spreading his message among Jews and Gentiles in the vast Roman world of the first century, Mani, a little more than 100 years later, went East, finding Jews and, inevitably, Christians, from Mesopotamia to India.

Manichaeism was still surviving in the Middle East when ninth-century Arab Muslim chroniclers wrote about its history, and according to them Mani travelled along an old trade route which carried tin eastward to a port in the Persian Gulf, from where it was taken to an Indian port, which the Arabs identified as Deb (Debal), which by their time was capital of Sind and under Arab rule.[4]

This route appears to have mirrored the one taken by Thomas on his long journey from Jerusalem. Mani and those who wrote about this period of his life were familiar with the legends surrounding the apostle and his deeds in India. Along and much beyond the Strait of Hormuz were Christian communities who were intimately aware of how the reluctant Thomas eventually converted Indians, kings and commoners alike, battled the Serpent of Eden and trounced sundry demons. Mani's hagiographers, coming upon this rich layer of belief, strove to create an equally magnificent Indian career for the later prophet.

By Mani's time, the subcontinent was predominantly Buddhist although Brahminical Hinduism was beginning a resurgence. By most accounts, he spent two years among the Indians, too short a period for either the prophet to fully engage with Buddhist doctrine, or for the Buddhists to integrate Manichaean ideas with their own. Mani would certainly have had an easier time explaining his ideas to the Christian and Jewish communities of the subcontinent, and it is not unlikely that he found some followers, at the very least.

His hagiographers would certainly not be satisfied with such small successes. To Mani they attributed fantastic prodigies. Entire regions and vast swaths of countryside and kingdoms readily embraced Manichaeism, they said. Hundreds and thousands of Indians converted to Manichaeism in swarms, across cities and villages. In two years, so successful was Mani that on returning to Persia c.243, he sent his father, Patteg, and his brother, Hanni, to India to minister to the multitudes of converts he said he had there.

His India stint seems to have added considerable lustre to Mani's following in the land of his birth. Shortly after his return, he told the Sassanid Emperor Shapur I of how he 'stirred the whole land of the Indians', of how his teachings were embraced by the natives, and of the persecution that he (in another parallel with Thomas) suffered, but only under the kings. It is another matter that while Thomas was martyred in India, Mani appeared to have endured his persecution and emerged none the worse for wear. The prophet then got a guarantee of safe passage through the Sassanid Empire for his followers. Later Manichaeans would say this conferred on them the position of a state religion, but this was far from the truth: the wily Zoroastrian mowbeds (priests) would never have let that happen.

Mani then began a period of frenetic travel through Persia, repeatedly coming up against his old foes, the Elchasaites, who were still sore about the matter of the vegetables and bread. Settled across the river from Ctesiphon, he composed for the emperor the *Shabuhragan*, a summary of the principles of his religion. He then sent his missionaries in all the directions. To Palmyra and Egypt he sent old Patteg, while a trusted follower, Ammo, went east through Nishapur and Merv into the Central Asian strongholds of the Kushans, a steppe confederacy which had in the preceding centuries spread through Bactria and India. Like the Indo-Greeks just before them, the Kushans became Buddhists. By the time of Mani, they had retreated from India, but were still neighbours to the north-east of the Sassanid Empire.

And then Mani himself set forth for the cauldron of faiths. His journeys among the Christians of India had made him see where the nerve centre of Syrian Christianity lay, and for six years from 264, he travelled around Mosul, north-western Mesopotamia and Syria, establishing strong communities of dedicated followers. By 270, Manichaeism was an established presence in Persia, while outside it, a network of missionaries extended both east and west.

Some of these missionaries entered the Roman Empire, where they won some converts. Not too many to make much of a difference, but apparently quite enough to be noticed by the authorities as another trouble-making sect from the east with some indefensible ideas. By the end of the third century, Emperor Diocletian, who was already persecuting the Christians with a vengeance, ordered the arrest of all Manichaean missionaries across the realm and had them burnt at the stake. Their followers and writings too met with the same fate. For most of the following century, while Christianity became legal, Manichaeans continued to be hunted down ruthlessly by the Roman authorities. Emperor Theodosius I, who made Nicene Christianity the state religion, also announced that all Manichaean monks found anywhere in the empire were to be summarily put to death. Mani's faith never took hold in the West.[5] In the Middle Ages, the Cathars, a Christian sect, emerged in the Languedoc region of France, and some of their ecclesiastical structures—and the idea that the flesh is inherently sinful—have echoes of Manichaeism. The Cathars were said to have been influenced by people returning from the Crusades, and ultimately by the Paulicians, a heretical dualistic Christian sect which emerged in Armenia in the mid-seventh century. It is possible that Manichaean ideas had influenced the Paulicians.

In the rest of the world, in Mani's own lifetime, his church was divided into the Elect, who had taken the vows of the faith, and the Hearers, who were lay believers. Some of the structure consciously mimicked early Christianity: Mani too had twelve apostles, including Patteg and Ammo. Below them were seventy-two bishops, who in turn commanded 360 presbyters.

It was, by all measures, a formidable achievement: a doctrine and a church within a prophet's own lifetime. Later

Manichaeans would considerably expand on the founder's cosmogony and doctrines, although hagiographies would attribute a lot of them to Mani himself. His chief contribution, it appears, was in the establishment of the Manichaean church structure.

Later Manichaeans could not help being aware that the prophets Mani had modelled himself most closely on had a very different trajectory. Christ had suffered before his resurrection, but had not gone around seeking legitimacy from an emperor. His teachings had been interpreted and carried into the Roman heartland by Paul, and Christians still endured unspeakable atrocities in the West in Mani's time. The Buddhists, meanwhile, were limited to the East, while the Zoroastrians, despite the efforts of several imperial dynasties, had not been able to break out of Persia. Manichaeism, in contrast, was at least tolerated in the land of its origin. In the East, by targeting Christian and Jewish communities, Mani's missionaries appear to have had some success with them, if not always with the larger Buddhist people. The faith was even making inroads in Egypt and Europe.

Mani himself was aware of the special position his missions and apostles had given him. Enumerating the ten reasons why his faith was superior to every other which came before, the first reason, he says, is that his faith had spread to every land, while others had been mainly limited to their area of geographical origin. In eulogizing the universal nature of his religion, Mani presaged the claims of Christianity and eventually, Islam. Mani had declared his faith a world religion while the contours of the world—and the idea of religion itself—were still being formulated.

Conscious of his unique position, the 'seal of the prophets' then decided to force the verdict of history. Shapur I was succeeded by Hormizd, and Mani turned up in the imperial court to immerse himself in schemes to get his faith declared the official religion. But Hormizd passed away quickly and in 273, his brother Bahram I became king of kings. Mani was still without what he sought, but the Zoroastrian clergy were getting alarmed. Here at their doorstep was a man promoting a faith which, he said, was a culmination of the three greatest religions of their time, an inheritor of Jesus, Buddha and, to their acute discomfort, Zarathustra. It would not do at all.

A very senior Zoroastrian priest, Karder, led the fightback. The Zoroastrian clergy purged the outlying regions of priests with Manichaean sympathies, while Bahram's soldiers 'pacified' far-flung hamlets and settlements where the new faith had taken root. Mani had played for the highest stakes of all and his reach had finally exceeded his grasp.

Railing at the iniquities of the world, prophesying the fall of tyrants, Mani left Ctesiphon and, journeying through the region of his birth, set out for the East, intending to preach among the Kushan in Khorasan, where his apostle Ammo had established a considerable following. But the runaway prophet was stopped at the Persian border and brought back to the king of kings.

Questioned about his conversion of Zoroastrian clergymen and defiance of imperial orders, Mani made his last, fatal error. He told Bahram that the shahanshah's father, Shapur, had respected him a lot. Mani even produced a letter to show this. Bahram, incensed at this affront, immediately ordered the priest's arrest. Fettered with more than 50 kg of chains, Mani spent some weeks in prison, weakening rapidly, and died aged about sixty.

Depending on the hagiography—which give different dates for the event—Mani's corpse was either dismembered, flayed, stuffed with straw and displayed for public edification, decapitated and the head was stuck on a spike at the entrance to the city, or even cut in two and nailed separately.[6] All these gruesome endings were, for the writers of the widely divergent accounts, ways to show their listeners that Mani had met an end appropriate for a prophet. As a biography by Uighur Manichaeans in the tenth century would note, thus passed 'the Buddha Mani'.[7]

The faith and church he had founded, however, endured. Mani's beliefs had been derived from other faiths, and he appears to have spent more time dealing with the political aspects of religion and the administrative questions concerning an ecclesiastical structure, than in working on developing or refining the beliefs he preached. As a political operator, too, Mani was quite outmatched by the Zoroastrian clergy and paid for it. But to the consternation of the mowbeds, Manichaean prelates across the Sassanid Empire continued to prophesy an imminent End of Days, and a confrontation between an equally matched good and evil across the Sassanid Empire. Among the Kushans, too, Manichaeism found strong roots, and ultimately reached China.

The main weakness of Manichaeism in relation to its competitors was the difficulty that lay believers experienced in practising some of its tenets. The human body being demonstrably impure, celibacy was considered ideal and not just for the prelates. Mani's faith also never had the security of a stable political patron. In failing to triumph over Zoroastrianism in Persia, Mani and his followers lost their strongest bid to have a formidable state mechanism to sustain them or promote missionary activities. Unlike Christianity, which had champions such as the Byzantines and the Ethiopians, or Islam, which had the Arabs at the beginning, or Buddhism, which had the Mauryan Empire, the Manichaean church was always contending with established faiths in whichever land it reached. Such is the fate of a pioneering world religion.

Over time, under the onslaught of Islam and Christianity in the West and Central Asia, Manichaeism withered away. In the fourteenth century, the first Ming emperor, Zhu Yuanzhang, whose loathing of Manichaeans exceeded even that of Bahram, banned the faith almost immediately on taking the throne, and Manichaeism was effectively wiped out from the world.

It did leave legacies in surprising places. In the fourth and early fifth centuries, Augustine of Hippo, the great Berber Christian theologian, developed the doctrine of Original Sin which was to play such a fundamental role in later Christian beliefs and imagery, particularly within the Church of Rome. Augustine was at first a Manichaean, a Hearer for nearly a decade, before being convinced there wasn't much substance to what Mani had preached and converting to Christianity. And yet, Original Sin and its inheritance by humankind as well as the idea that the flesh is sinful have echoes of Manichaean dogma, which in turn was derived from ideas about sin and the human body among early Christian communities in Mesopotamia, including the Docetists who composed *The Acts of Thomas*.

But in all this, the question remains: What about the Indians? Certainly there were Manichaeans in the subcontinent, converts from the Jews and Christians already living there. Manichaean missionaries were too active in the known world not to have had some degree of success among these communities. As the faith disappeared from the rest of the world, Indian Manichaeans would either have converted back to the larger Christian and Jewish faiths or would have been subsumed into indigenous belief systems such as Buddhism. In India, Buddhist chroniclers appear not to have noticed Mani's arrival and claimed triumphs, and there is little to show exactly what impact this extraordinary faith had on Buddhism. Uighur and Kushan Manichaeans might have readily accepted Mani as a Buddha figure, but of his influence in India, either among Buddhists or Hindus, there is no trace. No isolated band of clearly identifiable Manichaeans turn up at a later stage in history; no treasure trove of Manichaean texts, unlike the finds in Egypt and China, shed light on how the man's doctrines were recorded in India. If they were internalized in Hindu scripture, the process was too subtle to provide definite evidence.

This absence of evidence about Manichaeism in India is an irony. In basing the beginning of his prophetic career almost entirely on his exploits in India, Mani was inadvertently paying homage to the strength and endurance of Syrian Christianity and those of the believers living in the subcontinent. Just as Paul of Tarsus, in journeying to Rome and preaching among Jews and Gentiles fulfilled the instructions of Jesus, Mani, the latter-day Christ and self-proclaimed seal of the prophets, in travelling among the Indians was living in the ultimate analysis a very Christian messianic life. It is another matter that his very earthly goals were not based on fundamental Christian values. The apostle Thomas knew he was a carpenter tasked with creating an eternal palace in the kingdom of heaven. Mani patterned himself as a prophet seeking very earthly powers. In the eternal contest between earthly kings and ecclesiastical empire builders on the one hand and divinely inspired, humble carpenters on the other, Mani chose the more attractive but ultimately doomed path.

Fruits of the Wisdom Tree

The apostle Thomas might have been the first Christian martyr in India, but few stories of martyrdom from the East can rival, both in the details of the legend and its subsequent influence on Christians, the tale of Barlaam and Josaphat.

It has been found in written primary sources in at least seven Eurasian languages: Greek, Latin, Arabic, Hebrew, Syriac, Pahlavi and Georgian with some variations, and currently exists in translation in languages across the world. Josaphat in the legend is a prince, son of King Abenner of India. The king, however, persecutes Christians, and is furious on being told by a soothsayer that Josaphat is destined to be a Christian. Abenner then builds a beautiful palace in a remote part of his kingdom, and there the young prince is brought up surrounded by luxury and shielded from the perils of the world. Josaphat grows up, and one day leaves the palace to take a look around. He comes upon a leper and then a blind man, and is told that these and other disabilities and illnesses are part of the human condition. Josaphat then meets an old man, and his attendants tell him about mortality. The prince is pained to see the suffering in the world and asks himself if there is a solution, either in this world or the next.

At this point in the story, the wise old hermit Barlaam arrives at the palace in disguise, preaches to Josaphat through several pithy parables and converts him to Christianity. Josaphat becomes a hermit too, although he continues to live in the palace.

King Abenner, on discovering his elaborate attempt at shielding his son from Christianity has failed, tries to coerce Josaphat into renouncing the faith. Then the king arranges for a Christian man to impersonate Barlaam and lose a public debate, but Josaphat convinces the impersonator to be true to his faith and the man wins. The king also gets a woman to seduce Josaphat, but the young prince is resolute and finally has his way. Josaphat leaves the palace and becomes a hermit and preacher himself.[1]

The legend and, in particular, the parables contained in the frame narrative of the prince and the hermit, became extraordinarily popular in the Christian world. The Greek Church readily recognized Barlaam and Josaphat as saints, commemorating their joint feast day on 26 August. The Roman Church listed their feast day on 27 November. The Greeks, it appears, got to Barlaam and Josaphat first, recognizing them officially sometime after the turn of the tenth century. The earliest mention in the Roman Church's list was in a catalogue from 1370. In 1583, the Roman Martyrology, the definitive list of martyrs, saints and beatified persons in the Church, was published. Barlaam and Josaphat were in it, and continued to be till the modern period.

In the case of the Romans, it is possible the Church included the legendary Indians only after their story had already become very popular and influential in the West. And there was much for the lay believer and preachers to like in the legend. Christian piety triumphing over an obdurate but powerful king; a shielded prince who discovers, much like a child contemplating the world, the true nature of the human condition and who rejects the wealth and privilege he was born to; the possibility of an afterlife redeeming the sorrows and the peril of mortality in this one; rectitude and humility, all couched in homely parables which must have been a delight for itinerant preachers to expound on.

That both eminent personages of the Church and ordinary Christians believed completely in the existence of Barlaam and Josaphat, and that the two were unarguably the best known and most admired Indians in medieval Europe is indisputable. And where sainthood went, relics were bound to follow. In November 1571, the Doge of Venice, Alvise Mocenigo I, a formidable antiquarian himself, presented what was said to be a fragment of the spine and a bone splinter of Josaphat to King Sebastian I of Portugal. The Portuguese had been in India for eighty years by then, and admirers of the two Indian martyrs were supposed to have located the relics and sent them back to the mother country. The provenance of these relics was based on Mocenigo's reputation as a pious man who knew a thing or two about valuable antiques. The relics immediately became priceless possessions for Portuguese royalty. Nine years later, a pretender to the Portuguese throne would cart them away after Spain invaded Portugal. In 1633, the members of the Cistercian Order were able to get the relics of Josaphat and a number of other saints, and brought them to Antwerp. In 1672, a large procession of the citizens of that Belgian city brought the relics to the cloister of Sint Salvator, where they were installed with considerable rejoicing.[2] Sint Salvator was closed during the French Revolution, after the French occupied Antwerp in December 1796. The last abbot of the venerable cloister and all his monks were marched out by the revolutionary army, and its possessions, including its books, sold. The relics passed out of history.

The influence of the legend of the two Indian saints appears in unexpected places in medieval European culture. In 1260, Jacopo Fagio, the archbishop of Genoa, compiled the *Legenda Aurea*, a collection of hagiographies of the more popular saints, and the two Indians featured prominently in it. The Latin work was read, and quoted, throughout Europe, till William Caxton printed it in English, as *Golden Legend*, in 1438, making it one of the first books to be printed in that language. By the 1450s, printers were bringing out copies of *Golden Legend* in as many European languages as they could, and by 1500, it had gone into more editions than the Bible itself. Barlaam and Josaphat, not to mention their other fellow saints, were medieval bestsellers.

In the late fourteenth century, Geoffrey Chaucer turned to the parable of the Robbers' Nemesis from the Barlaam legend in writing his *Pardoner's Tale*. The Persians turned this story into verse, from which there were two Arabic translations, but with a slight tweak. While in the original Jataka tale it was Buddha who predicts the grim fate awaiting the robbers, the Arabs gave the role to Christ in both their versions. A hundred years after the saints became printed bestsellers, William Shakespeare too would turn to them for inspiration. He based the story of the three caskets, one each of gold, silver and lead, which played such a vital role in the wooing of Portia by Bassanio in *The Merchant of Venice*, on a parable narrated by Barlaam. Shakespeare is most likely to have come across the story in the

Gesta Romanorum, the fourteenth century anthology of fables which was such a rich source of stories for Chaucer, Boccaccio and him.[3]

At the beginning of the colonial period, there was hardly a European of passing scholarship who would not associate India with Barlaam and Josaphat, and there was considerable curiosity about what the Indians themselves had to say of their most famous saints.

Writing about the presence of his fellow countrymen in India, Portuguese historian and ex-soldier Diogo do Couto mentions a curious discovery at the beginning of the seventeenth century. Among the Indians he heard about a certain teacher named Buddha, whom he called 'Budao'. Couto observes that this Budao, who was said to be of great antiquity, was the son of a powerful king, and had renounced a royal life to become a monk. In this and other details of the Budao legend, Couto finds similarities with the life of St Josaphat. Was it possible, he asks his sources in India, that the Budao legend might have been based on the life of the Christian saint?

Couto did not have the resources to investigate this, and he was not the first European to raise this matter. In 1446, an unidentified editor of a reprint of Marco Polo's account *Il Milione* added a comment in a section where Polo describes (in passing, as was characteristic of the Venetian merchant's approach to the culture, society and religion of the places he visited) rituals in temples across the Yuan Empire dedicated to a teacher called 'Chagamoni Burkhan'. The editor remarked on the parallels between stories about the life of this teacher and the legend of Josaphat.[4] The remark seems to have gone unnoticed in Europe.

It was left to scholars in the nineteenth century to make the connection which would be apparent to a reader in India or South East Asia. They discovered that Couto had accidentally been on the right track, but from the wrong end, as it were. For the legend of Josaphat was derived from tales of the Buddha. By the beginning of the twentieth century, after decades of analysis, scholars had retraced the journey of the legend, and answered the question: How did the Buddha manage to become, in a manner of speaking, a saint in Western Christianity?

The parallels that Couto saw in the lives of Josaphat and Buddha were obvious. The prince who was to become Buddha is brought up in luxury. On coming across human misery and mortality, he becomes dejected. Then he meets a hermit, an ascetic who has renounced ambition and passion. The prince declares he has found the solution to human misery, and wants to become an ascetic. His father tries to dissuade him, including by getting him married, but eventually, the prince does become an ascetic. In the original Buddha biography, in the Pali Canon, he fathers a boy from his marriage with Princess Yashodhara. The boy was named 'Rahula' because the father found the baby to be a 'fetter' that would bind him to the material world and thus prevent the prince from seeking enlightenment. After the Buddha began preaching to the world, Rahula and Yashodhara would join his congregation and become followers.[5]

Prince Josaphat does not get married at all, which makes it much easier for him to follow the hermit. The other main difference between the two stories is whereas Prince Josaphat finds his answers in the possibility of a Christian afterlife, Prince Siddhartha finds his in asceticism and renunciation. The Buddha's followers then become a distinct group among the many sects in the Gangetic plains of that period. And then there are the numerous parables contained in the Barlaam legend, all of which have been shown to have roots in Buddhist Jataka tales, some with very little modification or embellishment except the absence of some elements of Buddhist philosophy.

Even the supporting characters from the Buddhist original have survived. In Europe, the name of the prince's father would become the suitably biblical Abenner from the original Suddodhana. 'Abenner' comes from the Greek version, while in Georgian it is 'Iabenes' and in Arabic, 'Janaiser'.[6] Josaphat's tutor is named Zardan in an Arabic version, said to be derived from the name of Prince Siddhartha's charioteer, Chandaka.

By the sixth century CE, two competing philosophies had been locked in a long and bitter tussle in the subcontinent: Buddhism and Brahminical Hinduism. Under the patronage of various imperial and kingly dynasties, the two idea systems had experienced periods of dominance over each other. The principal problem that teachers on both sides faced was: How best to present their ideas to the masses? For stern lessons in moral rectitude, virtue and renunciation, or complex secular and political theories are not easily accepted by the people. Renunciation, it could be said, comes easier to a prince who has already lived the good life than to a peasant who has never tasted the joys which the prince has grown dissatisfied with. As the best teachers have known down the ages, these ideas need to be coated in simple, homely parables or fables if the characters are animals.

Buddhism came up with the *Jataka Tales*, in which the Buddha is shown to have lived in different eras as different kinds of humans or animals. The actions of the Buddha figure were to be lessons on the virtues of ascetic life, of self-negation and moderation as a means to escape earthly misery.

The Brahminical response included, among other works, the *Panchatantra*, which through a large cast of animal characters across the entire moral spectrum, mainly gives sound advice on how best to negotiate the secular life. The characters in these stories are frequently morally ambivalent, cunning, ruthless or just pragmatic. The stories are narrated by a hermit teaching the sons of a king how to administer their realm and manoeuvre through complex political problems.

The *Panchatantra* is an attempt by Brahminical Hinduism to counter the Buddhist narrative about renunciation and to explain that a secular, practical life can be lived, and lived successfully. Princes can still do their duties virtuously without becoming hermits, even though the definition of virtue itself is open to interpretation.

Buddha biographies, *Jataka Tales* and the *Panchatantra* became popular by turn in Indian royal courts. The fact that both sets of stories featured kings and princes was of tremendous help. By the sixth century, a lot of these stories, particularly the Buddhist ones, appear to have been retold without the addition of specifically Buddhist doctrines, such as rebirth, the Eightfold Path and Nirvana. These altered stories eventually found their way out of the subcontinent. And so did their rival, the *Panchatantra*.

Percolating through East Iran, which by then was an established melting pot of religious and philosophical ideas, these stories reached the court of the Sassanids, where they appear to have been received well. Khosrow I, Sassanid shahanshah for nearly fifty years till 579, bitter foe of the Byzantines, destroyer of Antioch, ambitious palace builder and patron of art and culture, ordered the translation of these tales into the Pahlavi script used by the Persians. In translation,

'Bodhisattva', as the Buddha is called in some of the stories, became 'Budasaf'. In a later Arabic translation, the 'b' became 'y', apparently by mistake, because the two letters differ by a single diacritical mark in the Arabic script. Yudasaf was how the character would come to be known among the caliphs of Baghdad in the Middle Ages.

Meanwhile, a Syriac translation from Persian turned 'Balauvar', the old hermit's name, into 'Barlaam'. Some years after the Pahlavi version was released in the Sassanid court, a Greek translation was authored by a monk at the turn of the seventh century near Jerusalem. The legend then entered European languages through Latin. Whereas Josaphat is clearly based on the young prince who would become Buddha, Barlaam is also a Buddha figure, just as the original composers of the Jatakas had intended. But amid these changes and alterations in translation, parts of the original keep shining through. In one of the Arabic versions, Josaphat gives up wealth, power and his family, walking out of his magnificent palace in the middle of the night, and meditates under the Bo tree. After preaching for years, Josaphat, whom the Arabic text specifically refers to as 'al-Budd', dies in the arms of his favourite disciple.

The life of Buddha, gleaned from this and other stories, was referred to as *Kitab al-Budd* by the Arabs of the Islamic Golden Age and the encyclopedic tenth-century Arabic catalogue of books *al-Fihrist*, compiled by Ibn Ishaq al-Nadim includes the *Kitab* among its notable works, in the section on books dealing with the doctrines of Hindus and Buddhists.[7]

The *Panchatantra*, meanwhile, was also translated into Pahlavi at the same time as the Barlaam legend was, in the middle of the sixth century. A Sassanid physician named

Borzuya is said to have travelled to India to look for medicinal herbs and chanced upon the text, or a version of it. He added stories from other Indian texts, such as the *Mahabharata*, and named it *Karirak ud Damanak*, from Karataka and Damanaka, the two conniving jackals from the second frame story of the *Panchatantra* who convince their lion king Pingalaka to kill his friend, the bull Sanjeevaka. Borzuya, whose translation no longer survives, appears to have added elements from Sassanid court life and legal systems in his version.[8] In the eighth century, it was translated into Arabic as *Kalila wa-Dimna*, with the jackals still retaining their claim on the title. By the eleventh century, the story had been translated into Greek and Syriac, and in the thirteenth century, it turned up in Spain, with the Old Castilian title of *Calila e Dimna*. Through a Hebrew version, the *Panchatantra* was translated into Latin. The two jackals finally lost their hold on the title, and the book became known as *Directorium Humanae Vitae*, or 'Directory of Human Life'. This, too, was one of the earliest books printed, with Johannes Gutenberg himself bringing out the German version, *Das Buch der Beispiele*, in 1483. By the seventeenth century, the *Panchatantra* was known in Europe as the *Fables of Bidpai*, with Bidpai being the Indian sage to whom the work was attributed. The author of the original Indian story was said to have been a Brahmin named Vishnusharman.

Elements from the life of Buddha also appear in another Christian legend, that of the saint Alexis, or at least his early life including the part where he abandons his wife and child and becomes a hermit. This may have been derived ultimately from the life of Buddha as mentioned in *al-Fihrist* and translated into Greek at some point. Alexis was venerated in Eastern Christian tradition, because he was believed to have lived near Edessa as a mendicant. His veneration then progressed westwards through the Church of Constantinople to Rome by the tenth century.

The establishment of the chain of transmission of the Barlaam and Josaphat legend left many Christians in the early twentieth century in a difficult position, namely, as to how to reconcile themselves to the veneration of the Buddha as a Christian saint, and a particularly popular one. Doctrinally, this is not as problematic as it may sound. For one, when the Greek and Roman churches chose to legalize the veneration of the two Indian martyrs, the process was not exactly the same as the beatification and canonization of latter-day historical figures, like Mother Teresa. The two churches simply acknowledged the piety of Barlaam and Josaphat as apparent in the story. Medieval Christians were recognizing, prima facie, the Christian virtues of the old hermit and the young prince rather than specifics of geography or historicity. In Barlaam's piety and Josaphat's striving for answers to human questions there were endearingly universal lessons, even though there might be an eventual divergence between the Buddhist solution to these problems and the Christian one. Even Arab Muslims of the ninth and tenth centuries found much to appreciate in the life of Buddha, although most Arabic versions tended to excise the part about Buddhist veneration of relics, finding it an un-Islamic practice.

One would like to think that neither Christ nor Buddha would have chastised medieval Christians for holding Barlaam and Josaphat in such high regard. The two teachers would, perhaps, have gently reminded their listeners to also practise in their own lives the virtues enumerated in the legend.

The similarities between the life of Christ and Buddha, particularly their thoughts and methods of preaching have been pointed out by scholars. The imparting of lessons by means of parables easily understandable for laymen; the stress on the spirit as opposed to the letter of moral codes; the personal nature of ideas of purity; the striving for some form of salvation are all common to both. Moreover, as early Christian and Buddhist histories record, the formation of an ecclesiastical or monastic order in both cases was to perpetuate, at least at the beginning, the ideals of the two teachers after their passing. There are also similarities in these monastic structures and traditions in both faiths, as medieval travellers to India and South East Asia were to discover.

All of which has led to considerable speculation on the extent to which early Christians were influenced by Buddhism. In the 400 years between Alexander's arrival in India and the departure of early Christians from Jerusalem, Buddhist teachings had travelled steadily westward. Some of this was the result of Mauryan Emperor Ashoka's diplomatic outreach to Hellenistic kings in Syria, Egypt and even Greece. A lot of it, as with other religions and ideas, was the result of individuals venturing out into the world by land or sea.

Around 21 CE, an embassy of Indians arrived in the city of Antioch. The name of the king who sent them was either Porus or Pandion, according to the Greek geographer and historian Strabo. The ambassadors had travelled by the Red Sea, and most of them had died, with only three surviving the long journey. The letter from the Indian ruler said he was overlord of 600 kings, and sought friendship with Augustus Caesar, who had ended the Roman Republic and become the emperor of Rome not much earlier. The Indian king assured Augustus of safe passage through his realm whenever he wanted, and an alliance in any campaign the Romans had in mind. The ambassadors had brought gifts, including some exotic animals, but were also accompanied by an ascetic named Zarmanochegas, who was naked. He travelled to Athens, where he met Greek philosophers awaiting the arrival of Augustus. The Indian informed his listeners that he had lived a very successful life, and did not want to face misfortune in the future, so he wanted to end his life. A fire was built and the Indian jumped into it. A tomb was built in his name, which mentioned that he was a native of Bargosa, the Roman name for the port city of Bharuch in Gujarat today.[9]

The Judeo-Roman writer Flavius Josephus recorded how classical Greek philosophers had considered Judaic theology to have been influenced by Eastern philosophies. The name of the mendicant from Bargosa has led to speculation that he was from the 'Sramana' or ascetic tradition in India, but this tradition covers several sects and movements, including the Buddhists, Jains and Ajivikas. Of these, the Jains still have a sect of naked ascetics. There are no other clues in the accounts of this singular episode. The man's native city had some of the strongest connections with Roman Egypt and with the Hellenized Near East during Antiquity. Zarmanochegas could certainly not have been the only Indian ascetic to arrive in the West.

As for the powerful Indian emperor who sought an alliance with Caesar Augustus, at the beginning of the Common Era there was the Satavahana dynasty ruling over a substantial part of the Deccan and the Konkan Coast extending to southern Gujarat and its ports. Strabo's 'Pandion' or 'Porus' could have been one of the Satavahanas, who were patrons of both Buddhism and Brahminical Hinduism. On the other hand, there was also the long-lived Pandyan kingdom which extended at various times from the Malabar to the Coromandel Coast, and whose name corresponds to Strabo's 'Pandion', although they had no influence in Bargosa. Certainly the Greeks of Egypt were familiar with the Indian coast by then and would not have mis-recorded Zarmanochegas's port of origin.

Material culture travelled even farther. In the 1950s, a small bronze statuette of the Buddha was found during an archaeological excavation on the lake island of Helgo near Stockholm. The statuette was in the north Indian Gupta style and has been dated to the fifth or sixth centuries CE. Helgo was a key trading post from that period till the early Viking Era, so the statuette appears to have made its way to Sweden sometime during this period through the Byzantine Empire. This of course does not necessarily indicate Buddhist ideas had percolated with it into pre-Viking Scandinavia. The figure could have been just a curious piece of exotica for the merchants of Helgo, just as the later Vikings were eclectic in their collection of pillage. It is even possible that pagan Norsemen would have understood that the statuette was some kind of an object of veneration and not merely the commemoration of a noted person.[10] What the Helgo Buddha mainly demonstrates is how interconnected the world had been at that period. And if figurines could travel so far so relatively quickly, the marketplace for ideas too stretched from one urban centre of civilization to the other.

Concrete evidence about the precise influence of Buddhism on Christianity is scant. However, scholars who have marvelled at the circuitous westward route taken by the Barlaam and Josaphat legend do observe this: if Buddhist stories like these had indeed turned up in Syria by the sixth century—or perhaps even the fifth—and then became an integral part of Christian belief, it was entirely likely that as early as the first century,

Buddhist beliefs had syncretized with Judaic cults in Babylon and the resultant set of beliefs, ideas and doctrines could have influenced Christianity just as it was emerging.

As for why the *Panchatantra* did not quite match the popularity of *Barlaam and Josaphat* in medieval Europe, it has been suggested that it was not easy to give an appropriately Christian doctrinal slant to the former. Josaphat's disaffection with the attractions of the world and his search for answers to human misery and death bring him to the idea of salvation. That in the original Buddhist version this salvation was not the Christian afterlife was not known to medieval Christians. But the idea of sacrifice was common to both faiths and Josaphat's story resonated strongly among Christians. Barlaam and Josaphat, essentially decent and gentle persons seeking answers that have vexed humanity throughout history, could have just as easily been European instead of Indian.

It is also possible that, among the *Panchatantra*'s unapologetically Machiavellian characters, the medieval mind simply did not find much in the way of Christian virtues as easily as it was possible with Barlaam and Josaphat. The meek may not always inherit the earth, but sometimes by curious byways they do become bestsellers.

An Amateur at Sea

By the early sixth century, the Western Roman Empire had ceased to exist. The cities of Gaul, Iberia, the Italian peninsula and Britain were islands in a fractured Europe, left behind by the receding tide of Roman might and inherited by people such as the Franks and Anglo-Saxons. The Middle Ages had begun in Western Europe. But the Roman Empire still endured in the East. From Constantine's city on the Bosporus, the Byzantine emperors ruled a still vast domain from Syria to southern Egypt and North Africa. The great port city of Alexandria on the Nile estuary stood at the centre of the most complex and valuable trade network the world had ever seen. The farmers of the Nile Valley still produced more than they needed and Byzantine ships carried Egyptian grain and cotton to the cities of the empire dotting the Mediterranean coast.

But there was another trade route which was equally valuable for the Byzantines. On the extreme east of the Nile Delta lay the city of Pelusium, from where caravans would travel south to the Red Sea ports of Clysma, now subsumed by the Suez Canal, and Ailana, now the port of Aqaba in Jordan. The route connected all shipping that came up the Red Sea with ports on the Mediterranean.

For the Byzantines, the Red Sea was the route to the East, but much more was at stake than just shipping. By the beginning of the sixth century, the Byzantines had inherited the Roman Empire's confrontation with Persia. Ever since the Romans had taken Jerusalem, Syria and Egypt, their empire's Asian ambitions had collided with successive Persian imperial houses who in turn dreamt of a return to Achaemenid glory and mastery over Europe.

The Parthian Empire, from the middle of the first century BCE to the middle of the third century CE, fought several campaigns against the Romans along the border that ran through eastern Syria. At the Battle of Carrhae in 53 BCE, the Parthians annihilated the army of Marcus Licinius Crassus, who, when he was killed in the field, was the richest man in the world and the third member of Julius Caesar's First Triumvirate.

Under emperors such as Trajan in the second century CE, the Romans expanded their territory in the region. From the fourth century CE, the war had been inherited on the Persian side by the Sassanid Empire. The Byzantines and Sassanids maintained complex alliances with neighbouring kingdoms and power centres in a continued struggle that, at least for contemporaries, was apparently without end.[1]

One of the Byzantine allies was Ethiopia, with its capital in the city of Aksum. Christianity had arrived in Ethiopia in the first century CE and believers had found the land a welcome contrast to the Roman Empire's relentless persecution of their co-religionists. In the fourth century CE, Christianity became the state religion of the Aksumite Empire. When the Byzantines probed and planned against the Sassanids, the Aksumites were a natural ally. The Christian powers focused their attention on the land just across the Red Sea: Arabia. The peninsula was to become a proxy battleground for a world war.

For the Byzantines of the early sixth century, the land route to India, lost long ago by the hapless Seleucids, was in the hands of an enemy determined to keep it. Only the sea route remained: down the Red Sea, around the tip of the Arabian Peninsula and onwards to the Erythraean Sea, as the Arabian Sea was called. Sailors returned to Ailana and Clysma, and merchants turned up at Alexandria with petrifying tales of massive storms and reefs and adverse winds. But there were fortunes to be made as well from this trade.

The ports of India were very familiar to Byzantine sailors. Of the goods that could be traded at these cities, Alexandria's merchants had an exhaustive list as attested by the *Periplus of the Erythraean Sea*. A first-century CE list written in Greek, of the major ports and cities from Egypt to Ethiopia and India, it is a document revealing the true sophistication of trade in the Arabian Sea in Antiquity.

The *Periplus* paints a rich and vivid picture of a vibrant sea lane. Hugging the coast of Arabia or Africa, ships would embark from Clysma via the great port of Berenice in what is now the southern coast of Egypt. From Berenice the route lay south to the ports of Aksum, of which the principal one was Adulis, now an abandoned site on the Eritrean coast. Southwards from there lay the uncharted waters of the south-east African coast. The people who lived some distance south of Adulis were not sophisticated enough for the Greek sailors of Alexandria, but were familiar with Hellenistic culture and could speak Greek, while one of the chieftains was even said to be acquainted with Greek literature. Other ships would turn east seeking favourable winds and travel along the Arabian coast. Western Yemen was frankincense country. The next great port on the journey was Ommana, a voyage of six days up the eastern Persian Gulf. This region and the eastern coast of Arabia were within the Persian sphere of influence. To Ommana came Indian ships with teak, sandalwood, ebony, blackwood and other kinds of timber which were in demand among the Persians and Greeks. Between Ommana and Arabia plied smaller boats called 'madarata'. Ommana and other Persian towns also exported pearls to India and Arabia, but the Greeks considered these inferior to Indian pearls. Other Persian exports were purple dyes, clothes, wine, a considerable amount of dates, some gold, and slaves. Ommana would remain an important halt in the timber trade from India even in the Middle Ages.

From here, preferably in July, with strong winds pushing the sails onwards, merchant ships would travel along Persia, past the extensive marshes of coastal Scythia to Minnagara, its greatest city.

The Sinthus (Indus), greatest of all the rivers flowing into the Erythraean Sea, had seven mouths, which were shallow and marshy and difficult to navigate, except the one in the middle. On the banks of this mouth was the prominent market town the Greeks called Barbarikon and the Romans Barbaricum, corresponding to modern Karachi in Pakistan. On the river in front of it was a deltaic island, while behind the town lay Minnagara on the river.

At the time of composition of the *Periplus*, Minnagara was ruled by Parthian princes famous among Greeks and Romans for civil war because 'they were constantly driving each other out'.[2] But the merchants would unload their wares and sail farther east, beyond the mouth of the Sinthus, from where India began.

Beyond the Sinthus was the Small Gulf of Eirinon, now known as the Rann of Kutch, while the Great Gulf of Eirinon was the name for the Gulf of Kutch. The Small Gulf was not navigable, and sailors had to be careful near it because of its shallow water and shifting sandbanks, where ships often ran aground, and a stubborn captain, attempting to force his way south, could get shipwrecked. The voyage was particularly dangerous in July, but the winds were also the most favourable for a southward journey.

Rounding the coast of Syrastene (Saurashtra) and via the Gulf of Khambat, ships would head for the great port of Barygaza (Bharuch). The country thereabouts was fertile and noted for its wheat, rice, cotton and sesame oil. From inland cities like Ozene (Ujjain) were brought agate and carnelian, muslin and other, 'ordinary' cloth, spikenard—which was prized by the Byzantines for its use as perfume—and bdellium, the fragrant resin that Alexandrian merchants brought back from India and said was just as good, perhaps even better, than myrrh.

In return, the cosmopolitan traders of Barygaza wanted from the Greco-Roman merchants a long list of items with wine, preferably Italian, top of the list, although they did not mind Laodicean (now in south-western Turkey) or Arabian wine if Italian was not available. Other imports were copper, tin, lead, coral, topaz, glass and antimony. The Indians also wanted, in large quantities, gold and silver coins and the *Periplus* advises Greek merchants that they could make a tidy profit on these two precious metals by trading with the Indians. Another item on the import list was ointments from Alexandria, but only the relatively inexpensive ones, and not in large quantities.

The tastes of the governors of Bharuch ran along conventional lines: well-crafted silver vessels of the sort in fashion with Alexandrian nobility, singing boys, beautiful women for the harem, fine clothing and, of course, fine wines.

A Greek merchant wandering among the shops of Bharuch would have found, pressed into his hand by his Indian counterparts, gold and silver drachmae issued by Indo-Greek kings, inheritors of the legacy of Alexander, Apollodotus or Menander, with inscriptions in Indic and Greek scripts. And on returning to Egypt, the merchant would show his stay-at-home friends these tokens from a world away. The Mediterranean at the beginning of the Common Era might have been a Roman pond, but the Erythraean Sea was still a Greek oyster.

South of Bharuch was a region infested with pirates, and sailors were advised to be cautious on their journey farther down the coast. Crossing the Nammadus (Narmada), merchantmen would then enter Dachinabades (Dakshina Pradesh), the southern lands. Here, says the *Periplus*, was the important port of Calliena (now the Mumbai suburb of Kalyan), a city which would play a starring role in medieval accounts by European travellers, and a very valuable trading post for the Byzantines. Calliena was at that point governed by Sandares, the Greek name for Sundara Satakarni, a prince of the Satavahana dynasty who would be king for a year till 84 CE. Some distance north of Calliena was Suppara, now the city of Surat in Gujarat. Suppara, an ancient city which has been identified with locations in Hindu scripture, was also a vital port, and would continue to be important in the Middle Ages.

Crossing a multitude of ports on what is now the Konkan Coast, the ships would arrive in Damirica (Tamil lands) and anchor at cities well known among merchants of Alexandria, Ommana and Berenice: Naura, Nelcynda of the Pandian kings, Canna (Kannur) and Muziris on the Malabar Coast. Local merchants would exchange pepper, ivory and precious stones for gold, silver, topaz, coral and fine wines.

The *Periplus* shows the Greeks and Romans of the Byzantine Empire had an intimate knowledge of Indian ports and the economy of those parts to which they travelled. Interspersed in the enumeration of the coastal cities of India is an understanding of the trade routes and requirements of the people in the interiors, and the cosmopolitan life of those cities which were most closely connected with Persia and Egypt. But it is mainly a trader's guide, not a scholar's, and tells very little about the rest of the land or its people. We do not know about the complex routes which connected Ozene with the great cities of the heartland, or the Gangetic plains. Indeed, it appeared to have been exceedingly rare for visitors to venture inland from the ports, nor were they supposed to. Curiosity about peoples and cultures has never been a mercantile personality trait. But the *Periplus* also shows the routes by which ideas, religions and communities travelled to India, routes which were to remain virtually unchanged in the closing years of Antiquity and the beginning of the Middle Ages.

In 525, a monk named Dionysius Exiguus was at work changing the way the world would calculate time itself. In Rome, on the request of Pope John I, Dionysius was creating a calendar to calculate Easter and the years since the life of Christ. This would be the Anno Domini reckoning, now the Common Era.

Far to the south-east, across the forbidding plateau of Ethiopia, another man was on a very different journey. But in his eyes, the mission of Cosmas the Alexandrian was no less important. For his life's task was to calculate the extent of the earth and the very vaults of the heavens.

Of the numerous characters, colourful and prosaic, great and meek, who populate the Early Middle Ages in the Byzantine world, the figure of Cosmas must be among the most striking. He was almost certainly of Greek heritage, born and raised in Alexandria. Most of his biography can be gleaned from passages and references in *The Christian Topography*, the culmination of his travels and thoughts, written in Greek.

His education, he tells us, was limited to practical subjects which helped prepare him for the life he was meant for, that of a merchant. Knowledge of philosophy, Scripture or rhetoric, 'the learning of the schools', was denied to him. Nor did he learn how to 'compose a discourse in a fluent and embellished style', so he hoped to sway his readers by the content of his works alone. He was trained to be a man of the world, but so keen was his curiosity and so piercing his intellect that in his later life as a monk he became, he tells us, a man of learning no less capable than the finest scholarly minds of Alexandria, with scriptural knowledge that rivalled theirs.[3]

Cosmas's business made him travel considerably in the Mediterranean, the Red Sea and the Persian Gulf. He even ventured out, he says, into the open Erythraean Sea far off the Arabian coast, a region of thick fog, massive waves and unknown perils. In these voyages, Cosmas travelled extensively in Ethiopia and India, and he leaves behind a detailed account of what he found in these lands. Cosmas was more than a traveller and amateur scriptural scholar, for he was also seeking knowledge about Christian communities in these parts. But his main task, his life's work as he saw it, was not just as chronicler of far-flung Christian peoples.

The fate of the world might have hung in the balance between the Byzantines and Sassanids. The war between the East and the West might have entered a cataclysmic phase, extending to Arabia. But Cosmas saw himself as standard-bearer in a different conflict. This was his war against ancient astronomy and geography.

No monk railing against pagan beliefs could have rivalled the intense contempt Cosmas held for ancient Greco-Roman scholars, chief among them Claudius Ptolemy, a fellow Alexandrian of the second century CE and among the greatest polymaths of Antiquity, whose works from astronomy to music and optics were to be extraordinarily influential even in the Late Middle Ages in Europe. Christian scholars of the Early Middle Ages, contemporaries of Cosmas, were largely in agreement with the theories of Ptolemy and Pliny the Elder. The latter in his *Naturalis Historia* (Natural History) in the late first century CE had summed up scholarly consensus in his time by confirming that the earth was circular or perhaps irregularly spherical. Barely 100 years before Cosmas, the Roman Macrobius in his commentary on Cicero's *Republic* wrote that the earth was certainly spherical and the sun's diameter was estimated at twice that of the earth.[4]

Using verses from Scripture and, as he called it, common sense, Cosmas attempted to debunk the idea of a spherical earth. Based on the Tabernacle of Moses mentioned in the Old Testament—said to be patterned on the earth and heaven—Cosmas wrote that the earth was a rectangular plane, twice as long as it is broad and surrounded by an unnavigable ocean.

Beyond this lay another earth, from where the Ark brought Noah and his family after the Flood.

The heavens, meanwhile, formed a box around this base, with the top being shaped like an oblong vault. Cosmas very helpfully made an illustration of the world, and the resulting box resembled, as the nineteenth-century British officer and translator Henry Yule wrote, 'One of the huge receptacles in which female travellers of our day carry their dresses'.

The earth, declared Cosmas, was at the very bottom of the universe, as intended by divine will, although pagan scholars, he scoffed, professed the utterly absurd belief that the earth was in the middle of the universe. But surely this meant there was something under the earth, and since the Book of Genesis did not mention it, this was not true.

Cosmas then took the aid of what he considered common sense in his attack on pagan geography, saying that if the world were indeed round, people in the Antipodes would be walking around on their heads and rain would fall up. Pagan scholars, therefore, were in conflict not only with Scripture but also with common sense.

It was not easy to debunk the Ptolemaic model of the shape of the earth, however, and Cosmas's model had to show considerable dexterity in explaining the matter of the sun. That is, if this were a flat earth, with nothing underneath, where did the sun go at night? This Cosmas explained in the form of a huge mountain in the north which stretched from west to east. The sun sank behind the mountain in the west, travelled behind it and emerged in the east. The stars themselves, he said, were propelled around in heaven by the angels.

Cosmas accommodated the geography of India in his scriptural interpretation of the world. The Pheison, one of

Cosmas imagined the earth to be flat and bound by the firmament like a box

the four great rivers which were believed to emerge from the Garden of Eden, he conflated with the Indus and the Ganga, a considerable feat of geographical misunderstanding which indicates that he was not familiar with the Gangetic plain and assumed that the two Indian names referred to the same great river whose mouths he crossed at the port of Barbarikon.

Cosmas also spoke with the 'brachmani' (Brahmins) of India, but strictly about geography, and noted their belief that a straight line from eastern China to Persia would geographically bisect the earth. He also calculated that the distance by road from China through Bactria to Persia was considerably shorter than the sea route. Medieval Indians, like the Chinese and other people, appear to have largely believed in a flat earth.

The Christian Topography is primarily a vessel for Cosmas to forward his scripturally sound but scientifically incorrect theories on the heavens and earth, but it also contains descriptions of the sights he found in his travels. And here we find the most remarkable conundrum of the Alexandrian merchant. He was, on the one hand, a willing believer in scriptural geography and astronomy even when they went against observed facts, such as the curvature of the earth. On the other hand, as a traveller, Cosmas was remarkably accurate and drew a distinction between the sights he had seen with his own eyes and those places and people about whom he had only heard from other sources and had not been able to independently verify.

Cosmas mentioned his travels in the Aksumite Empire in Ethiopia, where he appeared to have been the first writer to have documented the source of the Blue Nile. He also mentioned the great trading port of Adulis on the Ethiopian coast. Long before Cosmas, the *Periplus* had mentioned the importance of

Adulis and its wares, including gold, ivory and frankincense, and the port had grown in power and wealth in the intervening centuries.

When Cosmas was visiting the Aksumites, the Sassanid-Byzantine war had spilled over into the Red Sea after years of rivalry, both military and mercantile. The Himyarite kingdom of southern Arabia was an important power in the peninsula. Its rulers were widely believed to have descended from the Queen of Sheba, and were Jewish. The Himyarites, conscious of the great powers in the neighbourhood, kept a delicate balancing act between the Byzantine and Aksumite Christians to the west and the Sassanids to the north-east.

After years of tension, in 523, the Himyarite king Dhu Nuwas attacked and killed Christians including Aksumites in the town of Najran, now on the Saudi-Yemen border. As later Arab historians would record, Dhu Nuwas then formally entered the existing world war by declaring that his act was revenge for the atrocities Jews were suffering in Christian lands. He then sent letters to the Sassanids telling them to act against Christians in their lands as well. The Aksumites were outraged. Two years later, Cosmas, visiting the court of the Aksumite emperor, records the Ethiopians preparing for an expedition against the Himyarites, after a request from Byzantine Emperor Justin I. In 527, the Aksumite expedition would destroy the Himyarite kingdom.[5] Yet another old political power would crumble in that long-running conflict.

Meanwhile, in 525, Cosmas was making observations on the fauna of Ethiopia, prominent among them being the rhinoceros. He noted the animal's curious hostility to the elephant, and said Ethiopians used its horns to plough the earth. Cosmas also claimed that the rhinoceros makes its horns erect when it charges, which was a common myth among Greco-Romans of his time.

Cosmas had a lot more to say about animals he found in India, including the bull-stag and the wild ox. Several of the stories found in *The Christian Topography* would become standard tales in the medieval European imagination of India. About the wild ox, Cosmas narrated the belief that if its tail was caught in a tree or a trap, the beast would not try to break free, because it feared losing a single strand of hair from its tail. The locals would then turn up and cut its tail off, which army commanders would use to decorate their horses and banners. Cosmas, of course, saw in the legend a cautionary tale about losing everything from avarice.

The merchant also wrote about the musk deer or 'kasturi'. The scent glands from the males were prized throughout the known world for making perfumes and were an important export from India. Cosmas also mentioned the hog deer which he remarked he had 'both seen and eaten'.

Cosmas devoted a section to the unicorn, contributing a substantial part to the legends about the animal. By his time, the unicorn had been firmly established as a creature to be found somewhere in the East, perhaps in India. The man who travelled to the farthest lands across the sea and yet believed in an utterly flat earth admitted that although he was writing about the unicorn, he had never actually seen one himself. In the palace of the Aksumite king, Cosmas found four carved figures of unicorns, and he included his drawing of one in the book. This unicorn of Cosmas resembles a horse and is close to how the animal has been usually represented.

The unicorn was important for Cosmas and he wrote about the legend that on being cornered by hunters, the animal would leap off a precipice, land on its horn and escape. Cosmas quoted from Scripture about the strength and glory of the animal. His travels, it is clear, were about discovering divine glory among fauna too.

Among the descriptions of crocodiles in the Indus and the geography of coastal India, Cosmas finally found, like the good merchant he was, the exotic goods he had spent so much time looking for: Christian people in the far corners of the earth.

The subcontinent by the first half of the sixth century was different from the period when the *Periplus* was written. The flourishing Indo-Greek kingdoms of north-western India were gone by the end of the first century. There would be no more Greek diplomats like Heliodorus at the courts of Indian kings. There was not much likelihood of Cosmas and his fellow merchants happening upon Indo-Greek coinage in coastal cities. But trade still flourished, including in spices such as pepper, that eternal grail for western merchants which Cosmas too mentioned.

The old ports were also as vibrant as ever, and there was still a vast market for western goods. Sailing south from Bharuch, Cosmas arrived at the town of Kalyan where he found a resident Christian community with a bishop ordained and sent from Persia. The old connection with Edessa, then, was thriving and Syrian Christians had a well-entrenched ecclesiastical order in the coastal cities of northern Konkan. In 'the country of Male', that is the Malabar Coast, Cosmas found both pepper and a church of respectable size.

These were not isolated settlements. On his voyages, the Alexandrian found Christians settled in stable, thriving communities in an arc extending eastward from Egypt. On the island of Dioscorides, now Socotra, he discovered that the residents were not just Christian; they spoke Greek, being descendants of colonists sent by the Greco-Egyptian Ptolemid dynasty. The clergy on the island were ordained in Persia before being sent there. The Christians of Socotra were seafarers too, and Cosmas met some of them in Ethiopia.

From these communities, and from Syrian clergy Cosmas met in ports around the Erythraean Sea, he received information about Christians elsewhere: among the Huns, Bactrians, Medes and other people of Central Asia. Throughout Persia, there were uncountable churches and clergymen, and multitudes of Christians, besides monks, hermits and martyrs. North and west of Persia, among the Hyrcanians, Dalmatians and Illyrians of Eastern Europe, wrote Cosmas, the Gospels were already familiar. In Africa, among the Nubians and the people of the Libyan Desert, Mauretania and as far west as Cape Spartel in Morocco were communities of Christians, far outside the borders of the Roman Empire, or the Holy Land, or Europe.

Sailing down the western Indian coast, along the pepper country of the Malabar Coast, after meeting the Christians and bishops of India, Cosmas at last made his way south to what he called Siele Diva, the island of Sri Lanka which the Greeks called Taprobane. The island was an important way station for goods from Tzinitza (southern China) whose people, the Sinae, traded with India and the West. The island occupied a strategic maritime position and sailors from India, Ethiopia and China frequented its ports, as did Byzantine ships carrying grain and cotton.

Cosmas found Taprobane split in a civil war between two kings, one occupying the south and the other the rest of the land. The Alexandrian found Christians here as well, with a Persia-appointed bishop, a deacon and a complete ecclesiastical ritual. Cosmas was also informed that the Christians, though a stable community, were small in number compared to the heathens, which included the feuding kings.

Standing on the Lankan shore, looking out at the southern sea beyond which, as sailors informed him, there was no land, Cosmas contemplated the growing Christian world and the many nations among whom the believers had found a home.

Cosmas's reputation among later scholars was so indelibly tied with his visit to India that he became known as 'Indicopleustes', the sailor to India. Unfortunately, in his own time, Cosmas was relatively obscure, while later medieval scholars would dismiss his world view and the flat earth he so adamantly championed. In the ninth century, the great Byzantine scholar Photius, Patriarch of Constantinople, included *The Christian Topography* in his critical compendium, the *Bibliotheka*, which examined scholarly works from Antiquity and the Early Middle Ages on the sciences, philosophy and history.

Photius, alas, had a dim view of Cosmas and very little patience for his theories. The elderly Byzantine minced no words in condemning the work, remarking that its style was below mediocrity itself, its syntax was faulty and that Cosmas was clearly making up a lot of the scientific facts he mentioned. Photius concluded that there was very little to recommend *The Christian Topography* in the context of any subject to his contemporary scholars.[6]

This was in contrast to the commentaries of Macrobius or the writings of Ptolemy and Pliny, which were widely circulated and studied during the time of Photius, both among the Europeans and the Arabs and Persians of the Islamic Golden Age. In terms of scholarly consensus, Classical Greco-Roman astronomy and geography continued to be part of mainstream discourse in the Middle Ages.

Cosmas's flat earth theories became an object of ridicule for the Early Modern world. Indeed, critics who viewed Late Antiquity and the Early Middle Ages as a gradual slide by Europe and the Western world into darkness have frequently pointed to Cosmas as a classic instance of the erroneous ideas which early Christians championed. On the contrary, Cosmas was virtually unique among Christian writers of this period in his defiance of Ancient Greek and Roman learning. Among his own contemporaries, there were few who believed in a flat earth or disagreed with Ptolemy and classical Greek thinkers, at least as far as geography and astronomy were concerned. In the Middle Ages, as Photius's commentaries show, Cosmas and his theories, far from being accorded the status of mainstream ideas, were actually discarded. A lot of the infamy of flat earth theories today is therefore a by product of Early Modern evaluation of writers such as Cosmas, and not necessarily based on an accurate understanding of mainstream, respected medieval European scholarship.

But while Cosmas's flat earth and a literal 'vault of heaven' have been repeatedly condemned, his merits as a travel writer and chronicler of Christians in the subcontinent have slipped by unnoticed, and unfortunately so. For the world of which he writes was as much a product of the Greco-Roman age as he or his native city were. In his time, Christians had established themselves securely across the known world and were neither isolated nor out of contact with the great cities of Europe, Africa, Persia or India. In famous port cities like Alexandria, Berenice or Adulis in Africa, or Bharuch, Kalyan and Kannur in India, Greek, Roman, Ethiopian, Persian and Indian merchants could still meet and trade as familiar equals. There was even a very high likelihood that they were all Christians, even if by the sixth century, they might have been from different denominations.

That world would not last for much longer. As Byzantine and Sassanid rulers plunged their empires into a war of annihilation, 100 years after Cosmas's voyages, a new power would emerge and reshape the world.

The Middle Ages

The Forge of the World

In November 636, an Arab army numbering around 20,000 led by Abu Ubaydah ibn al-Jarrah, a 'Sahaba' or one of the Companions of the Prophet, laid siege to Jerusalem. The Arabs had already conquered Syria, destroying a Byzantine army at the Battle of Yarmouk three months previously. The whole of Syria, including Damascus, had fallen.

After six months of a grinding siege, the Byzantine Patriarch Sophronius surrendered Jerusalem to Umar, the second Rashidun Caliph. Within four years, three of the five great cities of the Greco-Roman world—Jerusalem, Alexandria and Antioch—were under Arab control. The Byzantine Empire had lost Syria, Palestine, Egypt and North Africa and was struggling to save Constantinople itself.[1]

The coming of Islam so fundamentally and permanently altered the world that it is difficult to reimagine the global situation before Arab armies emerged from the peninsula. It is difficult, for instance, to place in context the magnitude of the change that fell on the existing peoples, cultures and faiths.

By the time the Byzantine collapse began, Jerusalem had been under Greco-Roman rule in one form or the other for 1000 years since Alexander. So had Egypt, its greatest city established by the Macedonian himself. Across the cities and ports of the eastern Mediterranean and the Red Sea, there might have been an odd cult or two which detested Greek bread, but Latin and Greek languages were still the media of commerce, liturgy and scholarship. Apollo, Zeus or Ares might no longer have been worshipped in the western Fertile Crescent and Egypt, but Christian rites were still held in Greek.

In the major urban centres around the Mediterranean, Hellenism and its essentially Greek structure had grown stronger over the centuries. Patriarch Sophronius was a product of his times. Growing up in the thoroughly Hellenized and very Christian city of Damascus, Sophronius got a classical education and the title of 'sophist' for his proficiency in rhetoric. Between 578 and 583, he was in Alexandria studying classical Greek philosophy before becoming a monk.[2] Decades later, as he led the citizens of Jerusalem through the first wave of Arab attacks, he would contemplate the collapse of Roman rule, and Greek culture, in the East. The *theomachoi*—literally, 'god-fighters'—were everywhere victorious, he noted, perhaps because of the displeasure of Christ.[3] There was, as yet, no reason to believe the Arabs were there to stay. Greco-Roman culture had endured for hundreds of years. Even the mighty Persians had not been able to dislodge it from the eastern Mediterranean and Egypt. Who were the Arabs?

But they won, and they stayed. The coming of Islam was a retreat of the West across the Mediterranean. For the first time in 1000 years, direct contact between Europe and India was lost. In losing Egypt, the Byzantines had not just been denied their most agriculturally fertile province but also access to the Red Sea, India and China. But at least, miraculously and against all the odds, Constantinople had survived the first wave of Arab expansion. The Persians fared much worse. Their version of Egypt—Mesopotamia with its fertile plains and prosperous cities—was occupied by the Arabs at around the same time as the Holy Land, and the Sassanid imperial capital of Ctesiphon was conquered in March 636. By 651, the Persian uplands had been taken and Arab armies were venturing into Khorasan. The last of the great Persian nobles held out for a few generations in their mountain fastnesses, but Sassanid Persia had ceased to exist.

Denied state patronage, the Zoroastrian hierarchy crumbled. What Mani and his 'world religion' had attempted in a surgical palace coup, the Arabs with their Abrahamic faith had achieved by bringing the entire palace down. The religion of Zarathustra would never recover from the blow.[4]

In the great Mesopotamian cities which had centuries of practice at accommodating invaders carved into the very foundations, people quickly realized which way the wind was blowing. This was no Alexander breezing through on his way to conquer some other place, or the Romans seeking to rival him. The Arabs were there to stay.

The traditional polytheistic religions of Mesopotamia and Syria had steadily dwindled after the great religious churn around the beginning of the Common Era and the arrival of Christianity. In the sixth century, when the Byzantine-Sassanid wars became a religious conflict, these faiths had shrunk further. There was, it seemed, no place for gods without empires. By the time of the Arab invasion, these polytheisms were limited to pockets in the countryside and some urban centres. In the early centuries of the Islamic Age, they would wither away even more.

Christians, being People of the Book, found themselves exchanging the rule of the Zoroastrians for that of the Arab Muslims and became 'dhimmis', a protected minority, a status extended to Jews and Zoroastrians. Moreover, for the Christians of Syria, Persia and Mesopotamia, the coming of Islam brought a fundamental and very welcome change to their fortunes. It had to do with the nature of the early Islamic state.

In the decades after 661 CE, when Ali, the last of the Rashidun caliphs, was assassinated and Muawiyah I became the first Umayyad caliph, the Arab Islamic empire extended from the Atlantic to the Indus. Built on the crumbled ruins of Roman and Persian might, the Arabs had surpassed both great powers and indeed even exceeded the wildest dreams of the Achaemenid Cyrus and the Macedonian Alexander. This state in the first flush of its expansion was almost continuously at war. In eastern Anatolia, Arab armies were repeatedly clashing with the desperate Byzantines, a struggle which would turn the entire region around the Taurus Mountains into a depopulated wasteland. Between 674 and 678, Arab armies and navies had even besieged Constantinople. From north-western Africa, Arabs had crossed into Spain and conquered virtually all of it by 711, destroying the kingdom of the Visigoths established when the Western Roman Empire had been disintegrating. To the east, the Arabs had reached the banks of the Indus and captured Sindh in 715.

The early Islamic state was therefore an apparatus geared wholly for the prosecution of war. Within this 'jihad state', Arab armies were more preoccupied with expanding the borders and less with administering or settling the lands they ruled.[5] At best, they set up barrack towns outside the cities which already existed in the Middle East. These settlements, called *misr*s, were sectioned on Arab tribal lines. Arab settlers were paid to establish themselves at these *misr*s from the plunder gathered during military campaigns and from taxes obtained from local populations. The greatest of these cities were Kufa, near the old Sassanid city of Hira and Basra, adjacent to Perat de Maishan.[6] Basra would emerge as a key entrepôt for maritime trade between Persia and India in the Middle Ages and the foremost port in the Persian Gulf.

The Christians of Syria and Mesopotamia found that they had been left to their own devices for the time being, a welcome contrast to the bureaucratic administration of minority religions and the grim probing eye of the Zoroastrian clergy which had, for centuries, been fixed on 'foreign' faiths, particularly those from Roman Palestine. Even better, Christian prelates found that the borders were not as strictly manned as in earlier times. Where the Zoroastrians were mindful of what kind of religions and philosophies came in from other lands, or went out to them—as witnessed by the swift capture and return of a fleeing Mani 400 years before—the Umayyads were concentrating on expanding their new empire as rapidly as possible, and not much bothered about minority religions or their missionaries within Arab dominions.

The late seventh century thus saw an unprecedented series of missions by Nestorian Christians to spread their faith beyond the traditional boundaries of Persia. Some missionaries, such as John of Daylam, went to the Caspian Sea and parts north. Some chose to stay at home and concentrate on the polytheists of Persia, achieving considerable success. Others went east. By 781, Christian missionaries had erected an inscription at the Tang Chinese imperial city of Xi'an (now Chang'an in Shaanxi Province, north-western China) celebrating the establishment of the Eastern Church, which was heavily Nestorian by then, in those lands in 635. This means the Nestorian expansion had started almost immediately after the collapse of the Sassanids, or in the years preceding the Arab invasion of Persia, when Sassanid imperial power and the bureaucratic control of Zoroastrian priests had both become considerably weakened.

Eastern Christianity was not the only religion that benefited from this changed world. As Nestorian missionaries discovered on their journeys into Central Asia, the Manichaeans had already ventured into those parts and set themselves up after generations of persecution by the Sassanids. The new freedom of movement made it easier for the Manichaean churches in Mesopotamia and Central Asia to reunite and forge strong ties. The market for religion might have come upon a new-found freedom of movement, but competition between the products on offer was as intense as ever.

The free-for-all was not destined to last for very long. The Islamic state was engulfed by civil war, a period known as the Second Fitna, after the death of Caliph Muawiyah I in 680. The same year, Husayn ibn Ali, grandson of the Prophet, and his followers were killed in the battle of Karbala in central Mesopotamia. After five years of struggle between the supporters of the Umayyads and the followers of Husayn, who called themselves the Shia, the Umayyad Abd al-Malik managed to assert control over the empire. He then brought in perceptible changes in administrative policies, including a centralized government. The caliphate also started making public announcements as a clearly identifiable Islamic polity.

This profession of Islam as an imperial religion was even recorded on monuments such as the Dome of the Rock in Jerusalem and in coinage.[7] The Church of the East found itself once more restricted in terms of its ability to proselytize within the Umayyad empire or send missionaries beyond it, although their status as protected minorities continued and they had greater freedom to proselytize than they had had during Sassanid rule.

Gradually, inexorably, even the Arab expansionist juggernaut ground to a halt. Incredibly, the Byzantines had survived. On 10 October 732, a Frankish army under Charles Martel defeated an Arab force at Poitiers in France. Christians of northern Spain began what would become the 700-year-long fight to oust Islam from the Iberian Peninsula, the Reconquista.

In time, even the Umayyads had to go. In 747, a family descended from Abbas, an uncle of the Prophet, revolted against the caliph. The Umayyads were ousted after great slaughter, and the Abbasid Caliphate came to power. In 751, an Abbasid army met a force dispatched by the Tang dynasty of China. At the Battle of Talas, on what is now the Kyrgyz-Kazakh border, the Arabs bested the Chinese, and the region would henceforth be the border between these two cultures. Gradually, the shape and limits of the Islamic world was being forged and defined, at least for the time being.

In 762, the Abbasid Caliph al-Mansur directed the construction of a new city, which was to be the capital of his empire. As with the misrs of Kufa and Basra, the site for the new capital was just 30 km north of the old Sassanid Persian capital of Ctesiphon. The name of the new city was derived from that of an ancient Persian village on the site: Baghdad.

In time, Baghdad would become the greatest city in the world, a metropolis so legendary that Ctesiphon itself would be forgotten. The early Abbasid caliphs would settle down and consolidate the empire, promoting architecture, the arts and sciences. The Sassanids had always been influenced by Hellenism and the Abbasids inherited this tradition. The scholars of Baghdad studied classical Greek philosophers and mathematicians and advanced their works. The culture that emerged, a continuation of Persian scholarly traditions under Arab rule, would be called the Islamic Golden Age. From the ninth to the beginning of the twelfth centuries, Baghdad would be the unrivalled light of the world.

Eastern Christians in Mesopotamia and Persia too contributed to this period of consolidation in the history of Islam, with scholars writing several works on philosophy and participating in discussions on the sciences.

The centre of the world, it appeared, had shifted to the East after centuries of bipolar struggle between the Roman Empire and the Persians. This was reflected in how the leaders of Eastern Christianity began to see themselves. In 785, Timothy I, Patriarch of the Church of the East wrote a letter to his counterparts in the West where he pointed out that the East was the origin of civilization; that Christianity had first expanded in Syria and Persia after the Holy Land; and that Christ himself was descended from Abraham who was from the East. The Church of the East therefore deserved primacy among the many divisions into which Christianity had entered.

An ambitious idea, and it did not work. But Timothy was an extraordinarily influential figure in the history of Nestorian Christianity. A prolific writer, he was able to continue amicable relations between the Christians of the Middle East and the

Abbasids. He was also deeply involved in overseeing the fate of missions to the East. He appointed senior clergymen for ecclesiastical provinces in Central Asia including the Turkic people and for China, where Nestorianism had begun making steady inroads. He was also aware of Nestorian missions in Tibet, a region which he thought could have its own metropolitan (equivalent to an archbishop). By the late eighth century, India had become a region important enough for Timothy to separate it from central Persia—an arrangement which had survived from the time of the Council of Nicaea—and to appoint metropolitans for the subcontinent. The Eastern Church was flourishing and wealthy, and Timothy was so well connected in the Abbasid court that the Church could buy large plots of land in Baghdad, which was still under construction.

Due to the work of Church fathers such as Timothy, the Nestorians experienced a period of rapid expansion in Central Asia. By the middle of the ninth century, they had a significant presence in Tibet. Nestorian Christianity interacted with Tibetan Buddhism and produced some remarkable results. In western Tibet several crosses carved on to rock have been found. In Dunhuang area of Gansu Province in north-western China, a painting in a cave shows a Bodhisattva figure with a number of crosses on his necklace. At the beginning of the twentieth century, a sealed cave in the region was found to contain a treasure trove of Tibetan manuscripts from the fifth to the eleventh centuries, which reveal the impact of Nestorian Christianity on Tibetan Buddhism. One of the manuscripts, dated from the late eighth to the early ninth centuries, tells the reader to prepare for the End of Days, when 'the god known as Jesus the Messiah, who acts as Vajrapani and Sakyamuni' will return. This 'judge who sits at the right hand of God' will arrive and teach yoga to believers, who are told not to fear any demons or malevolent spirits.[8] At about the time when Barlaam and Josaphat were on their long journey to sainthood in Western Christianity, Christ was being internalized as Buddha Maitreya in Tibetan Buddhist eschatology. Significantly, in contrast to Revelation and Islamic eschatology with their prophecies of climactic battles, Christ in Tibetan Buddhism was expected to return on Judgement Day and fulfil the functions expected of the Maitreya as a teacher.

While Nestorian Christianity expanded eastwards, Western Christianity was trying to navigate changed circumstances in Europe. The Church of Constantinople was limited to the shrinking boundaries of the Byzantine Empire, with some missions to the north in what are now Bulgaria and its neighbouring countries. In Egypt, Coptic Christianity, which had emerged from the schism after the Council of Chalcedon, became a dhimmi religion under the Abbasids. As for the Church of Rome and Western Europe, India was just a dimly remembered legend from the Roman Empire, an era which had vanished. New polities had emerged in what used to be European Roman provinces. The Germanic Franks had carved out an empire in what had been Gaul, giving their name to the kingdom of France. By the eighth century, Anglo-Saxon kingdoms were contending among themselves in what had been Roman Britain. Christian missionaries were spreading the faith in western and northern Europe, but there were dangers in a world without imperial authority. Viking raids had begun along the coast in north-western Europe, Britain and Ireland. In Iberia, the Reconquista would leave a legacy of violence which would ultimately affect India in the Age of Exploration and the early colonial period. Ties with the East or even with Persia and the Holy Land were not a priority in those difficult times.

This period was at one point called the Dark Ages by early modern historians, an era when Europe was assumed to have been left stumbling in ignorance after the glories of the Roman Empire. As new evidence emerged and was examined, this idea has now been largely discarded. The period from the collapse of the Western Roman Empire to the beginning of the twelfth century was not as dismal or unproductive as was once thought. The knowledge of the Greeks and Romans endured. In monasteries and abbeys across Europe, Western Christian monks diligently copied manuscripts of classical thinkers, historians and writers. Most of the manuscripts of Antiquity which have survived today in the West were made during this period, and the Church was aware of them. Roman structure and military efficiency might have vanished, and Greco-Roman logic might have been tempered by Christian theology, but the Dark Ages were not as tenebrous as was once thought, nor was Europe beginning an inevitable slide into obscurity. Powerful leaders would emerge, while the Roman Church would seek to consolidate its influence among them and expand the boundaries of Christendom.

But it is undeniable that Europe had become localized. Indian emperors had once upon a time sent ambassadors and Buddhist monks to Hellenistic Egypt and Greece, while lesser kings were believed to have sent envoys to Roman emperors seeking alliances. The chances of a subcontinental ruler having such relationships with the newly emerging power centres in Western Europe were remote.

India too was going through a post-imperial churn. The Gupta Empire, which had ruled most of north and west

India, had disintegrated by the middle of the sixth century. Occasionally, a ruler like Harshavardhana would emerge. Harsha ruled from the close of the sixth century to the middle of the seventh over the Indo-Gangetic plain and his domain included the ports of Gujarat and extended to western Bengal. But, largely, northern and western India did not find an imperial replacement for the Guptas till the beginning of the twelfth century. In the south, the Cholas became India's first maritime power, leading campaigns in the twelfth century to Indonesia and Cambodia. The ports of Malabar were under them, but their imperial ambitions never extended to the Arabian Sea.

The coming of Islam had also changed the nature of trade in the Arabian Sea. The principal link language from Egypt to India, which had been Greek for more than 1000 years, changed to Arabic as Arab merchants expanded along the coast and set up communities from Berenice to Socotra and, ultimately, the ports of India. While the Arabs did not have a significant role in maritime commerce during the period of the *Periplus* and Cosmas, the coming of Islam also marked the arrival of Arabic as a key player on the international linguistic stage.

It was these Arab traders who first brought Islam to India, to the Malabar Coast. In the town of Methala in Thrissur district of Kerala is the Cheraman Juma mosque, which local tradition holds was built in the lifetime of the Prophet himself by Muslim Arab traders. The Muslims of the Malabar Coast therefore hold the distinction of being India's oldest Islamic community, thus making the region an important part of the history of all three major Abrahamic faiths.

By the eleventh century, the Abbasid Caliphate had reached a point of stagnation. The caliphs were not of the high standards set by al-Mansur, or Harun al-Rashid in the ninth century. Turkic people had converted to Islam and had begun eating away at Abbasid territory. Seljuqid and Ortuqid Turks had expanded along the Black Sea region into Anatolia and were menacing the Byzantine Empire. The Arabs were no longer the greatest foes of Constantinople.

In the middle of the tenth century, the Abbasids lost Egypt to the Shia Fatimid dynasty which had begun as a Berber rebellion against the caliphate. The Fatimids would proclaim their own caliph, and by the end of the eleventh century had become a key player in the geopolitics of the eastern Mediterranean.

In the late twelfth century, Muizuddin Muhammad, sultan of the Ghurid Empire which had taken over Persia from the Abbasids, invaded India, defeating a local Hindu king and occupying the city of Delhi. The origins of the Ghurids is a matter of some dispute, although they emerged from eastern Persia. Muizuddin left one of his trusted generals, a manumitted slave named Qutb ud-Din Aibak, in charge of the Indian conquests but was assassinated in Punjab while on his return from India. Aibak, born a Turk in what is Kazakhstan today, became Sultan of Delhi. His generals started campaigns in western and eastern India and very soon a substantial part of the subcontinent till the Deccan was under Islamic rule.

Aibak founded what would be known as the Mamluk dynasty, the first of several houses which would rule what is collectively termed the Delhi Sultanate. These houses, which were variously of Turkic or Afghan origin, would rule sultanates whose boundaries fluctuated rapidly, depending on the capabilities of individual rulers.[9]

The beginning of Mamluk rule over north India would also see the arrival of Sufism from Persia and Mesopotamia. Charismatic preachers brought a mystical Islamic philosophy to the subcontinent and contributed substantially to the conversion of Indians to Islam, particularly in Punjab and eastern Bengal. Muslim rulers also brought the concept of *dhimma* to the subcontinent. Originally referring exclusively to protected minorities of Abrahamic faiths, or the People of the Book, such as Jews, Christians and Samaritans, the dhimma would be extended to polytheistic Hinduism in India by the sultans of Delhi and other regions, a political compromise between orthodox Islam and the complex realities of the subcontinent.

As Abbasid control of Persia ended, Eastern Christians in Baghdad had to contend with political uncertainties. Although connections with Indian Christians remained, the Abbasid decline and actions of Turkic warlords in Syria and eastern Persia meant that the Nestorians of Mesopotamia were progressively isolated from their counterparts in Central Asia, Mongolia and northern China. These eastern Nestorians led an autonomous existence but were successful among the tribes beyond the Turkic sphere. And in Mongolia were a people whose time was to come.

The arrival of Islam on the world stage would lead to the formation of religious and cultural spheres that would survive to the modern age. Arabic culture and language expanded from the peninsula to north-western Africa, across the area known as the Islamic Maghreb. Syriac, a language which played a vital part in the early history of Christianity in northern Mesopotamia and influenced Arabic in the early Islamic period, was gradually localized and now survives as a liturgical language in Syrian Christianity, including in India. Zoroastrianism, once part of the Persian imperial power structure, steadily declined and today survives among a small minority in Iran and Azerbaijan, besides an extensive diaspora. Communities of Persian Zoroastrians would establish themselves in western India, particularly coastal Gujarat in the Middle Ages, becoming another of the many peoples who made their home in the subcontinent over the centuries. Islamic sultanates and kingdoms radiated across India.

In Western Europe, the successors to the Roman Empire would establish spheres of influence and occasionally nurse imperial ambitions, such as Charlemagne in the ninth century. The Roman Church would minister to the Christians of Western Europe while in Constantinople, the Byzantine emperors would continue the fight with the newly emerging Turkic powers. Both the Church of Rome and the Church of Constantinople were constantly aware that the Holy Land and Jerusalem continued to be in the control of a people who claimed their own prophet and who believed that they were the new Chosen People. A century before the Delhi Sultanate was established in India, it was the struggle between Turkic warlords and the Byzantines that would result in the re-emergence of Western Europe on the world stage and create a series of events that would eventually see Western Christianity arrive in India.

'Deus Hoc Vult'

The schisms and rifts that had divided the Christian world in the closing years of Antiquity had been about regions and cultures as much as they had been about ideas and doctrine. Arians, Nestorians, Copts and Ethiopians had all found geographical areas within which they tried to establish a secure home. These schisms had been unfortunate, but the heartland of what had been the Roman Empire was still doctrinally united. There was yet another rift which was to happen; the greatest schism that had ever occurred.

Murmurs of discontent had been heard for generations from the prelates of the Church of Rome and Church of Constantinople. Europe was thought to be divided into these two cultural and linguistic spheres from the days of the Roman Empire. West of the Dalmatian coast was the Latin Church's domain, east was that of the Greeks.

An ancient point of contention, dating back to the second century, was the claim of the Church of Rome to primacy among the churches. Before the Oriental Orthodox churches had split, on occasions when the churches of Alexandria and Antioch were involved in disputes, Rome had been called in to mediate.

But then came Emperor Constantine, and he built New Rome. The city named after him sought recognition as an equal among the great churches, and the bishop of Constantinople was held as second after the Pope of Rome in terms of honour. But after the Western Roman Empire collapsed and the Byzantines became the sole imperial remnants, the heads of the Church of Constantinople sought equality if not a higher status than the Pope of Rome. And there were areas such as southern Italy, the Balkans and Sicily over which both churches sought authority. It was the old story of empire as reimagined in ecclesiastical order. If Roman could slay Roman in civil wars at the height of the united empire many centuries earlier, bishops could be no less ruthlessly political.

There were differences in doctrine and practice too, though not as fundamental as those seen during the Arian or Nestorian crises. The Church of Rome, with exceptions among lower-ranked clergy, had increasingly opted for celibacy among clergymen, while among the Greeks, parish priests could at least marry. The Church of Rome had also inserted a clause in the Nicene Creed which said that the Holy Spirit came from the 'Father and Son', whereas the Church of Constantinople held that the Holy Spirit derived from the Father alone, and considered what Rome had done outrageous.

Original Sin was another point of contention. The Church of Rome had partially agreed to the idea of Augustine of Hippo, the former Manichaean of the fourth century, that the sin of Eve had been perpetually inherited by humans. The Church of Constantinople rejected this idea outright. There was also the debate over Mary. The Church of Rome taught that during the Immaculate Conception of Mary to her parents, she had been protected from Original Sin because she was to give birth to Jesus, not because of her specific merits.[1] The Church of Constantinople held that she had been chosen because of her purity and virtue.[2]

And then there was the matter of the bread. The Church of Rome had, since the ninth century, started using unleavened bread to celebrate the Eucharist. Constantinople thought this to be yet another western European innovation, and continued with leavened bread.

Bread, doctrinal discord and terrestrial ambitions. Of such are ecclesiastical schisms formed.

In 1054, after a series of bitter arguments, the Pope of Rome and Patriarch of Constantinople issued proclamations excommunicating each other, leading to what would be called the Great Schism. It was not a complete cessation of relationships. The general sentiment among the public in Rome and Constantinople mirrored the feelings of the clergy, but for the larger Christian world, it was a distant debate among clergymen. Feelings between Latins and Greeks would vary depending on immediate circumstances, sometimes leading to outright violence.[3] But the magnitude of the conflict would not be the same as that which Europe would see during the wars of the Protestant Reformation.

Over the centuries, both churches have attempted reunion, with varying degrees of success. In the modern era, ecumenism has been attempted and efforts have been made by popes and patriarchs to redress grievances. At the Second Ecumenical Vatican Council from 1962 to 1965, Pope Paul VI and Patriarch Athenagoras expressed regret for the actions by both churches during and after the Great Schism, and also lifted the excommunications of 1000 years earlier.[4]

During the difficult years after the Great Schism, the situation of the Byzantine Empire had become even more precarious with regard to the Seljuq Turks of eastern Anatolia. In 1071, Byzantine Emperor Romanos IV led an army east from Constantinople to recover the fortress of Manzikert, which had been taken by Seljuq Sultan Alp Arslan. The Byzantine army was not what it had been in the past and mainly comprised mercenaries from Georgia, Armenia, Bulgaria and even Frankish and English fighters, as well as Norsemen from the Varangian Guard. The campaign was poorly led and managed, and the Byzantines were annihilated. Romanos himself became the first Byzantine emperor ever to be captured by the Turks.[5] He would be ransomed, but would then be deposed by factions in Constantinople, exiled and ultimately blinded, dying of his injuries.

The Seljuqs then took an enormous swath of Byzantine territory, and it was several generations before the damage caused by the loss at Manzikert could be reversed. In 1081, Alexios I from the Komnenian dynasty became emperor in Constantinople and began the process of restoring Byzantine glory. It was not an easy task. Normans from the western French coast had invaded southern Italy and taken Sicily, beginning in 999. Alexios fought campaigns against them as well as the Seljuqs. In 1095, he sent emissaries to Pope Urban II in Rome, seeking some Latin Christian warriors to help him in his fight against the Turks.

Urban held a council that year at Clermont in the Duchy of Aquitaine, one of the numerous kingdoms and principalities ruled by Frankish nobility and monarchs in what would be

France and Germany. Urban asked the feuding nobles of Europe to set aside their mutual quarrels and to set out with common Christians for the East to battle the Turks and free the churches of the East. Urban characterized the coming struggle as a war in defence of the faith and a conflict that was righteous. Everyone who died on that long journey from Europe or in the field of battle was promised forgiveness for their sins, because this was a war commanded by Christ himself.[6] The audience, wrote chroniclers, were roused by Urban's speech and responded with cries of 'Deus hoc vult.' God wills it.

Pope Urban's plan was for a united army of Latin Christians to sally forth in August 1096. By then, clergymen and monks had spread his call among Christians in Frankish territory and elsewhere. Among these preachers was a monk named Peter the Hermit who travelled through what is now northern France and Belgium, rousing the populace, and so great was his oratory that some began thinking it was he who had called for a war against the Turks and not the pope. Peter ended up with a disorganized but still massive gathering, estimated to be nearly 40,000, poorly armed, inadequately trained or equipped peasants, who then set out to the East. Along the way, some of the mobs appear to have thought that they were going on a long journey to fight enemies of Christ whom they had never met, while the people who had crucified the Son of God lived among them.[7] In towns of what would become western Germany, mobs attacked and massacred Jews. The beginning of the crusading era was therefore also the beginning of a new kind of anti-Semitism in Europe, one which could not be controlled by the Church of Rome, which had previously prevented forced conversions of Jews by Christian kings.

Nor was this anti-Semitism limited to peasant mobs. Among the many noblemen who raged against the Jews of Europe was Godfrey of Bouillon, Duke of Lower Lorraine, who swore to go fight the Turks only after slaughtering Europe's Jews.[8] Holy Roman Emperor Henry IV had to personally intervene to save the Jews of the town of Mainz from Godfrey, who was later to play a prominent role in events in the Holy Land.

Amid these riots and massacres, Peter the Hermit set out with his army of peasants to wage war against the Turks. But it was not a military force so much as a mob with near unlimited potential for violence. Marching through Hungary, they rioted and burnt down the town of Zemun on the border with the Byzantine Empire, killing some 4000 of its residents after a petty dispute. They then reached Belgrade, whose citizens simply abandoned the city and fled, after which Peter's army burnt it down. After a battle with soldiers of the city of Nis (now in Serbia), in which 10,000 of Peter's forces were killed, the people's army somehow arrived in Constantinople, still numbering around 30,000.

The portents were ominous. Emperor Alexios, worried about this unpredictable mass which had manifested from the West, arranged for their transportation across the Bosporus. But he also told Peter and his lieutenants not to fight the Seljuqs till the professional Frankish armies arrived.

Peter's control over his forces was slipping, and he was no general. A faction captured a fortress from the Seljuqs, who in turn besieged and defeated them. Some of the captured German peasants converted to Islam. The rest were killed.

The remainder of Peter's army arrived outside the city of Nicaea, which had played such an important role in the history of Christianity. They were attacked by the forces of Seljuq

Sultan Kilij Arslan and routed. Only 3000 would survive in a fortress till a Byzantine relief force evacuated them. Peter himself escaped with his life, because he had returned to Constantinople before these battles.

This utter disaster was the first direct confrontation between the Franks and Muslim armies, and would come to be called the People's Crusade. To the more professional Frankish army that followed it shortly afterwards to Constantinople, the debacle would be a sobering lesson in not underestimating their unfamiliar enemy. If Christendom was to be at war with Muslims it would, while being a just war, also have to be a professional war run by people who knew their job.

This Frankish army had at its core the knights and nobility of Western Europe who had responded to Pope Urban's call. But there were also countless others—women, the elderly, the sick and peasants. The call to crusade appears to have tapped into the deepest wells of piety among Latin Christians. There was no particular pattern among the nobility either. Some of the aristocrats were second or third sons; in other cases, almost the entire family travelled east. It was a movement with no precedent in European history, and ultimately the Crusades would change the fate of Europe and the rest of the world.

But the First Crusade was still a professionally led and managed campaign. The crusaders travelled to Constantinople as four armies, one of which was commanded by Godfrey of Bouillon. Emperor Alexios was still recovering from the sight of Peter's rabble and was eager to see the crusaders across the Bosporus as soon as possible. He quickly declined leading the Frankish army but wished them the best against the Turks, and got them to swear that they would return to the Byzantine Empire all the land they recovered from the enemy. The

Franks then set forth for Nicaea and were joined by Peter the Hermit and what little remained of his peasants' army. The crusaders, with logistical support from Alexios, captured the city. Optimistic after this success, they set their eyes on the Holy Land and marched farther east. This was in 1097. It took them two years of fierce fighting through eastern Anatolia and Syria before they arrived at the gates of Jerusalem.

Along the way, the crusaders had made unexpected gains. Baldwin, son of the count of Boulogne—who himself had fought in the army of William the Conqueror at the Battle of Hastings in England three decades earlier—and brother of Godfrey had ventured east from the Taurus Mountains and reached Edessa, by then a city and province populated by Armenians. Baldwin found himself hailed as a hero, adopted by Edessa's lord, a former Byzantine administrator, and by 1098, had become Count of Edessa. The first of four crusader states to be established in the eastern Mediterranean, the County of Edessa was a large province, extending from west of the Euphrates to near the Tigris.

The main body of the crusading army had continued south, capturing Antioch after a gruelling siege during which the Franks defeated two Seljuq armies that had come to the relief of the city. The crusaders killed most of Antioch's population. As they continued farther down the coast, the Franks suffered an outbreak of plague. Their supplies ran out, and they killed Muslim locals and ate them.[9] The war in defence of the idea of a united Christendom had become a feast of cannibals, as far a fall from Christian values as can be imagined.

By the first week of June 1099, the crusaders had besieged Jerusalem. The holy city was under the Ismaili Shia Fatimid caliphs of Egypt, foes of the Seljuqs. The governor of Jerusalem expelled the Syrian and Greek Christian residents of the city, fearing treason. After a siege that lasted nearly six weeks, the Franks entered the city and slaughtered most of the Muslims and Jews in it.

Jerusalem had been retaken by Christians after more than 460 years. By the time the news reached Rome, Pope Urban II had passed away. The events he had set in motion would continue. The Franks chose Godfrey of Bouillon to administer their new possessions. By then the crusaders did not trust Emperor Alexios and believed he had not been a reliable ally because of events during their march to Jerusalem. Godfrey, who had two years earlier vowed to exterminate the Jews of Europe before setting out on the Crusade, chose a curious title. He would be neither king nor prince, but would govern as Advocate of the Holy Sepulchre.[10] His term of self-reference was more telling: 'princeps', the title used by Augustus and the early Roman emperors as an assurance to post-Republican Romans that they were merely first citizens. In their reimagining of the Holy Land and the place of Europe in the world, the Franks were still, consciously or otherwise, borrowing ideas from the Roman Empire, or inadvertently paying homage to it.

The First Crusade, the most successful of them all, was a turning point in the history of Europe. For the first time, the Franks and Western Europe had a direct presence in the Middle East. So far, their understanding of the East had been through a distant relationship mediated by the senior clergy of the Latin Church. The merchants of Genoa and Venice who traded from the Byzantine Empire to Egypt and Iberia had been their intermediaries. For nearly five centuries, the Byzantines had been 'Rum' for the Islamic world, the only Christian power worth treating with, but no longer. Out of the bloodshed and a conflict spanning centuries, the Crusades would create a different Europe.

The Frankish nobility already found itself in charge of a different political system and a much more complex society in the Holy Land than what it had been accustomed to in Europe. Surrounded by hostile Turks, Fatimids and Arab warlords, the four crusader states—the Kingdom of Jerusalem, County of Tripoli, Principality of Antioch and County of Edessa—had to create a stable structure if they were to survive. Their subjects were not merely Christians, Jews and Muslims but also from virtually every denomination of these faiths. Jerusalem was so fundamental to the Christian imagination that medieval European maps painted the Holy Land golden and placed it at the centre of the world. But the Franks had not expected such a profusion of variety in their own faith. Jerusalem and what had been Fatimid Palestine contained Latin Christian pilgrims, Greek residents, Nestorian Christians from Syria, pilgrims from Persia and India as well as Copts from Egypt and Ethiopian Christians, not to mention large populations of Armenians and Georgians with their clergy and churches. Where a Constantine would have perhaps called a council and sought some order, dividing the world into what was official belief and what was not, the Franks could not alienate their non-Latin Christian subjects, so they began by announcing tax exemption for all Christians in their territories. Differences in Christology or rites were matters which might have scandalized clergymen in Europe, but the Franks were soldiers first and could not afford to split such doctrinal hairs.

The Muslims, as the Franks found out, were hardly the reprehensible, faceless adversaries they had imagined, and had their own schisms. The crusaders had to understand the differences between Shia Fatimids to their south and the Sunni Abbasid caliphs in Baghdad.

Nor were the Jews a simple demographic to govern. North-west of Jerusalem were areas which had large populations of Samaritans, a Judaic people whose Scripture was the first five books of the Jewish Bible.

It was a time of western pilgrims arriving in greater numbers than before to Jerusalem. It was also the time of military monasticism, of the Knights Templar and the Knights Hospitaller, who participated in many battles against the Seljuqs and Fatimids and maintained strongholds in the crusader states.

The Frankish model was based on arriving at some kind of provisional understanding with the local populations. It was not benevolent, and the crusader states were never fully stable or secure, but over generations, Franks born in the Holy Land would acquire a different, more accommodative philosophy with regard to their neighbours of other faiths and denominations than crusaders newly arrived from the West.

The relative positions of these Franks born in the Holy Land and the Muslims who lived in the region in those times can be witnessed in the works of two remarkable men. William of Tyre was a Latin Christian born in Jerusalem in 1130, who would become Archbishop of Tyre and begin the discipline of Crusade history. He studied under noted scholars of his time in the great educational centres of Paris and Bologna, before returning to the Holy Land. He chronicled the politics and the lives of Frankish leaders of his time, providing an intimate glimpse into how the crusader states functioned and how the Franks viewed the Turks and Arabs. Besides his ability to set aside Latin biases and make an attempt at being fair to the

Byzantines, William often commended those Muslim rulers and generals he found worthy.[11]

Among the most striking insights that can be gained from William's chronicles is his deep love for the land of his birth. Jerusalem and the region around it was significant for him not just because of its holiness but because it was his homeland in a way that far-off Europe was not. In this, William would be a precursor to the many Europeans in the colonial period who were born and lived far away from the land of their ancestors. The Crusades were building the first generation of international Europeans of the Middle Ages.

And then there was Usamah ibn Munqidh, an Arab nobleman born in the Syrian town of Shaizar, which his family ruled. Usamah, born three months before Pope Urban preached crusade to the Latin kings, was a man of many parts: soldier and mercenary, amateur zoologist and dedicated hunter, poet and compiler of verse on walking sticks, aesthete, friend and occasional foe of the Franks. Through his eyes one can see how some Arabs of the Islamic Golden Age in Palestine and Syria saw the Franks. He admired crusader courage in battle but was appalled at their primitive ideas of medicine (and was baffled when it sometimes worked) and was bemused by their apparent sexual liberation which contrasted so much with his fellow Arabs' ideas of male and female infidelity. He too noticed how Franks born in the region were easier to have a dialogue with than those who had recently arrived.

Usamah would frequent Jerusalem, and whenever he went to the grand Al-Aqsa Mosque, the Knights Templar who had occupied it and who were his friends would vacate the smaller mosque next to it—which they had converted into a church—so that Usamah could pray. One day, a Frank interrupted the aristocratic Arab in the middle of his prayers. Lifting Usamah bodily, the crusader turned his face to the east instead of the south, saying that was the correct direction of worship. Usamah's Templar friends rushed in and dragged the Frank away twice, apologizing and explaining to the Arab that their fellow Christian had recently arrived from Europe and had never seen anyone pray in the direction of Mecca.[12]

But despite his friendships with the Franks and his numerous reverses from his own people, including his uncle who exiled him from his considerable inheritance, Usamah was at home in Syria and Palestine. One of his Frankish friends, who called Usamah 'brother', offered to take the latter's fourteen-year-old son to Europe and give him some proper Western lessons in chivalry and the knightly life. Usamah would have none of it, but was polite and claimed he could not send his son away because Usamah's mother—a battle-hardened aristocrat herself—would be sad at parting from her grandson. The Frank understood and said that Usamah should certainly obey his mother.

Among realistic and fair-minded people like these, there could be dialogue and accommodation across religions.

But the crusader states were never stable enough to have long-term prospects. The first to fall was Edessa, conquered by the Turkish warlord Imad-ad-Din Zengi in 1144. The victorious Turks would ravage the city, and among the many old buildings to be destroyed was the tomb of the apostle Thomas, one of the most important pilgrimage sites for Syrian Christians till then. The apostle's relics, brought from India, would be taken away by the Franks and find separate resting places around the Mediterranean. The fall of Edessa would lead to the launch of the Second Crusade, which failed in its objectives but led to a new focus for Europeans: Egypt.

As the crusaders expanded their conquest into the deserts south of Jerusalem and reached the Red Sea at the beginning of the twelfth century, they witnessed the other side of a maritime trade route which they knew only at its European end. Ships from India carrying goods from countries in the far east of the world would sail up the Red Sea along that ancient route to ports from where overland caravans would take the goods to Alexandria and Cairo. Increasingly, the Fatimids of Egypt more than the Turks were seen as the real strategic hurdle to Frankish supremacy in the Holy Land. It would be a very short step from that realization to an understanding of what the source of Egyptian wealth and power was, and which people were responsible for it.

The fortunes of the Kingdom of Jerusalem ebbed and flowed with the calibre of the kings and their advisers, until 1187, when King Guy de Lusignan was lured into an ill-advised march against Salah ad-Din, the Kurdish Sunni who had ousted the Fatimids and established his own dynasty, the Ayubbids, in Egypt. Salah ad-Din was a brilliant strategist and had steadily chipped away at the crusader states, reconquering Syria. At Damascus, Salah ad-Din had spent thirteen years preparing to retake all the Frankish territories, while spending his leisure time at Usamah's poetry gatherings and trading ideas on military theory with the old warrior.

At Hattin near the Sea of Galilee in Israel today, Salah ad-Din's army routed the forces of Guy, and took Jerusalem shortly afterwards. In contrast to the slaughter by the Franks when they had conquered the holy city, Salah ad-Din's entry was relatively peaceful, although many Franks who were not ransomed were enslaved. Usamah died a year later, lamenting his old age and his body 'rusting like a sword of Indian steel in its scabbard'.

The gains of the First Crusade had been squandered, leaving Europe scrambling to organize other crusades, with varying degrees of success. In 1228, Ayyubid Sultan al-Kamil surrendered the city to Holy Roman Emperor Frederick II during the Sixth Crusade, but Jerusalem was lost to a Turkic army from the Khwarezmian Empire in Persia sixteen years later. The Khwarezmians had themselves been displaced by a new force which had erupted in Central Asia and which would, much like the coming of Islam, reforge the world.

One of the problems with assigning numbers to the Crusades or considering them only from the perspective of the conquest of Jerusalem is the inadvertent result of localizing the Crusades both in geography and time. War in defence of Christendom had become an integral part of the western European way of life. There was the Albigensian Crusade in the thirteenth century, which went nowhere near the Holy Land but was instead directed against heretical Cathars in the Languedoc region of France. There was the perpetual Reconquista in the Iberian Peninsula, which continued to be fought throughout the crusading era. There were also the Baltic Crusades by Latin Christians against the pagans and Slavic Orthodox Christians of western Russia, Poland and the eastern Baltic coast.

The main crusades, or the Mediterranean Crusades, were also not limited in time: the later Crusades from 1274 to the end of the sixteenth century were no less significant. From that first call by Pope Urban, the crusading paradigm would seep into other aspects of how the Europeans saw themselves. In time, the mantle of the crusaders would be inherited by Portuguese seafarers of the Age of Exploration.

The Crusades were a coming of age for Europe so long after the Roman imperial retreat of the 630s. For the Muslim world, the Franks became so synonymous with western Europeans that 'firang', derived from 'Franj'—as Usamah and his contemporaries called the crusaders—which entered Indic languages through Arabic and Persian, refers to Europeans of all nationalities even today. Medieval European kings from the thirteenth century onwards would have diplomatic relationships with their counterparts in Egypt and North Africa. The pope and his counsellors would consider the complexities of the Middle East in discussing the situation in the world. And Europeans would continue being yet more aware of the vast maritime and land network that connected the world from Portugal and England to far-off lands they had been hearing of—India and China.

Western Christianity had never travelled that far to the East. At the beginning of the Nestorian Schism in the fifth century, it had been limited to the territory of the undivided Roman Empire. After the rise of Islam, Western Christianity had neither the political will nor missionary apparatus to spread eastwards. Nor had there been a direct connection to India and China. But now, at the beginning of the thirteenth century, Western Christian scholars knew from crusader experiences in the Holy Land that Nestorians had spread to the eastern corners of the world. There was, as yet, no reason to expect Western Christianity to journey to those mythical lands.

But the apparatus that would take Western Christianity to the East was beginning to emerge in the twelfth century. As Europe's awareness of the world grew and trade networks became stronger, Western cities prospered. So did the Church of Rome, which acquired greater land and wealth than ever before. For some clergymen, this prosperity and political power was at odds with the life of Christ and the old ideals of poverty and simple piety. Towards the end of the twelfth century, pioneers of a new monastic tradition emerged in pursuit of these ideals. These would be the mendicant orders.

Francis of Assisi, son of an Italian merchant, military veteran and sometime prisoner of war, turned away from his family's wealth and became a wandering monk at the beginning of the thirteenth century. After seeing divine visions, he decided to form a monastic order dedicated to following the example of Christ. Founded in April 1210, the Order of Friars Minor would rapidly expand, opening an order for nuns called the Order of Poor Ladies, whose members were better known as the Poor Clares after the aristocratic young woman from Assisi who started it. The Friars Minor would in time be better known as the Franciscans.

Francis wanted to go on missions beyond Christendom and tried to sail to the Holy Land, only to be prevented by a storm. After an abortive attempt at journeying to Morocco, Francis visited Egypt in 1219 during the Fifth Crusade.[13]

Missions abroad became a key activity of the Franciscans. In the years after, the order would be known as a kind of conscience of Latin Christianity, sternly watching the Church and on occasion rebuking the pope and senior clergymen if they strayed from what were true Christian values: moral rectitude, piety, compassion and a humble earthly existence. In time, the Franciscans who would travel east would view their experiences through the lens of these virtues.[14]

The other significant monastic movement was started by Dominic, a Castilian Spaniard. A student of the humanities and theology in his home country, Dominic journeyed to the Massif Central in 1205 to preach and debate with the Cathars, that heretical sect which was to face the Albigensian Crusade.

Twelve years later, he founded the Order of Preachers, whose members in time would be called the Dominicans.

Like the Franciscans, the Dominicans also quickly became known for sending missionaries beyond the boundaries of European Christendom, while those who stayed on in the Continent opened schools and houses where they devoted themselves to study and contemplation.

Between the Franciscans and Dominicans, the Church of Rome found two groups devoted to the twin ideas of Christian values and the conservation and propagation of knowledge. Several members of both orders would become noted scholars and be counted among the early humanists of the Middle Ages and Renaissance.[15] And their missionaries would spread across North Africa, the Byzantine Empire and the Holy Land.

But east of Jerusalem, the highlands of Persia, Central Asia, India and China were still regions that Western Christianity had not hoped to venture into. There were just too many kingdoms and empires, many of whom were not familiar, as the Muslim rulers of North Africa, Syria and Egypt were, with Latin Christian missionaries. There was no political structure that would create conditions favourable enough in the Middle East for the mendicant orders to venture out.

That conducive political apparatus was about to arrive. Neither Western Christians nor the Muslims of the Middle East ever expected the sequence of events which would overturn the existing global structure. At about the time when the Dominican and Franciscan orders were being established, far to the east were emerging a people who would shatter nations and rebuild the world.

The Hammer of Dajjal

Great Khan Chinggis, ruler of the people of the felt tents, was angry. His sons Jochi, Chagadai and Ogedei had recently brought down the formidable city of Urgench in the Khwarezmi Empire, but in dividing its many treasures, including its people, had failed to set aside a portion as was due for Chinggis. The Great Khan of the Mongols had words to say to them, and refused to meet them for three days. His generals humbly begged him to at least talk to his sons, and so finally he relented. They were the sons of Borte, his great love, after all.

But the young men had to be chastised, and chastisement from Chinggis could have dire consequences. Entire cities in China and Central Asia had been annihilated by the armies of the Mongol ruler. For his sons, however, Chinggis used 'old men's words, ancient words' of admonition so strong that the fearsome young men were paralysed and almost sank into the ground.[1]

His generals intervened again, saying, 'Why do you reprimand your sons, and constantly dishearten them? We fear that they, being afraid, will become careless. Our enemies extend from East to West. When you incite us, your sheep-hounds, to go out against the enemy, our one wish is to bring you gold, silver and people. If you ask: which people? We reply that the presence of the Qalibai-soltan of the Baqtat people is reported in the West—let us go to war against him.'

The Secret History of the Mongols, which records this bit of domestic disturbance in the tent of Chinggis, is the oldest surviving work of literature in Mongolian and one of the keystones of their culture. Written sometime after the Great Khan died in 1227, it narrates in strikingly intimate language how the Mongol people, led by the searing vision of Chinggis, were transformed from an obscure semi-nomadic people west of China into rulers of the largest contiguous land empire the world has ever seen. The account is also remarkable in its matter-of-fact narration about great events. It chooses not to mention geographical distances or time frames, as if the vast regions covered by the armies of Chinggis were immaterial to the narrative or the magnitude of the deeds of the Mongols.

Chinggis, waiting in his tent outside Urgench, was at the pinnacle of his achievements and was beginning a process that would lead, long after his death, to the demolition of the old order in Eurasia and the beginning of a new era. He was on the most remarkable campaign of his life. And it had begun with a diplomatic misunderstanding.

After his victories against the Jin Empire in China, Chinggis looked to the west and sent diplomatic overtures to the sultan of the great Khwarezmian Empire which extended from the Persian Gulf to southern Kazakhstan, a formidable dominion which had some of the most prosperous and vibrant cities of Central Asia. Sitting astride the Silk Road, the Khwarezmians controlled trade between China and India and the West.

After some initial progress, Chinggis's attempts at diplomacy and trade agreements ran aground. The culprit appears to have been Inalchuq, governor of the Khwarezmian city of Otrar in southern Kazakhstan today. Inalchuq, suspecting the members of a caravan sent by Chinggis to be spies, arrested the lot of them, numbering around 500, and seized their goods. Chinggis then sent diplomats, two Mongols and the third a Muslim, to the Khwarezmian emperor, Shah Ala ad-Din Muhammad, to complain about the incident, demanding that the caravan members be set free, and that Inalchuq be handed over to the Mongols for punishment.

The emperor, not accustomed to what he considered rulers of mere nomadic people making requests like this to him or treating him as an equal, ordered the beheading of the Muslim ambassador, while the Mongol diplomats had their heads shaved. And then, Ala ad-Din ordered the execution of every single member of the caravan, just to send a message to Chinggis. The Great Khan then suspended diplomatic relations with Khwarezmia, gathered intelligence and his troops and, in 1219, invaded the Khwarezmian Empire.

The Mongol army numbering 30,000 and led by Jochi and the great general Jebe that crossed the Tian Shan range into what is now Kyrgyzstan in the dead of winter was no mere rabble of nomads on horses. Chinggis's campaigns in China had led to the addition of the most sophisticated siege technology in the world to his already formidable arsenal. His troops were now familiar not just with combat on the field but also with besieging hitherto impregnable fortresses. Defenders of cities could no longer hope to bar their doors and wait for the besiegers to leave.

Jochi's army was a diversion for the main Mongol invasion force. Dividing his army into three sections, Chinggis sent two to engage, separately, the Khwarezmian imperial army, which though mighty was divided into smaller units and garrisoned across the land to prevent coups. Attacking them piecemeal, the Mongol armies broke the Khwarezmian forces in a campaign lasting a mere six months. No invader had dismantled an empire at the height of its power and might with such ruthlessness and speed in the history of the world. The conquest of the entire empire and defeat in detail of Khwarezmian remnants and holdouts would take two years.

The third section of the invasion force, meanwhile, had been given just one task: find Ala ad-Din. The emperor was forced to abandon his capital and flee. Cities across Khwarezmia received an ultimatum from Chinggis: surrender immediately and you will be spared. Shelter the emperor, and you will not be. Ala ad-Din, knocking fruitlessly on the doors of his own cities, would realize the limits of imperial power in the face of a truly implacable enemy.

In six months, the Khwarezmian Empire had ceased to exist. Many of its finest cities, including Otrar, Nishapur—birthplace of the great eleventh-century mathematician and poet Omar Khayyam—Bukhara, Samarkand, Urgench, Merv and even Bamiyan far to the south in what is now Afghanistan were sacked, their populations decimated. Cities like Otrar never recovered. Ala ad-Din, fleeing to a tiny island in the Caspian Sea with a few guards and his son Jalal ad-Din, died of what could have been either pneumonia or, on witnessing the loss of his empire, a broken heart.

As for Inalchuq, the governor who had brought the wrath of Chinggis down on Persia was captured during the siege of Otrar, which began with the invasion of Khwarezmia and lasted six months. The Mongols, who valued symbolism in all matters, told him that his greed for treasure should be suitably satisfied and poured molten gold down his throat and ears.[2]

At Urgench, presiding over this demolition of the Khwarezmians, a sulking Chinggis, as *The Secret History* shows, was calmed down by his generals and reminded that there were yet more enemies to be conquered. The 'Qalibai-soltan of the Baqtat people' was the Abbasid caliph of Baghdad and now, with Persia under the Mongols, Chinggis was the caliph's new neighbour.

By the thirteenth century, the Abbasids were no longer masters of the world. Parvenus in the shape of Turkic warlords had taken away their possessions in northern Mesopotamia, Persia and Anatolia. The front ranks of the long war with the Byzantines were now manned by Muslims from Central Asia, not Arabs. The Maghreb had been lost to Berber upstarts, who themselves were being pushed out of al-Andalus by the resurgent Christians of the Spanish Reconquista. Egypt, lost in the tenth century to the Fatimids, was now under the Mamluks. The Holy Land, the caliphs were aware, had been recovered from the Franks not by an Arab from Baghdad but by a Kurd from Syria, brilliant though Salah ad-Din might have been.

The Islamic Golden Age was over. In the courts of the caliph, there had not been many discussions on philosophy or the pagan Socrates, Plato and Aristotle ever since the eleventh-century scholar Mohammed al-Ghazali wrote the *Tahafut al-Falasifa* (Incoherence of the Philosophers) which conclusively demonstrated, to the Islamic world, the errors in rationalism and Ancient Greek ideas that medieval Islamic intellectual giants such as Ibn Sina and Ibn Rushd had championed. In contrast to *ijtihad* (independent reasoning), the watchword in the Islamic world after al-Ghazali would be *taqlid* (imitation, conformity to precedent).

In terminal political and intellectual atrophy, Baghdad could only look to the West, at Constantinople and Alexandria, to understand what these cities, once the greatest in the world, had felt on contemplating their decline.

Baghdad endured, with its palaces, mosques, markets and libraries. Mesopotamia was still fertile, fed by the Tigris and Euphrates. But it was a precarious existence. By the early thirteenth century, menaced by the Khwarezmians to the east, the Abbasids even considered treaties with those new people which, they had been told, had erupted from the steppes on the far side of the world.

And then the unthinkable happened, and Khwarezmia fell. Great Khan Chinggis always listened to good advice from his generals, so on being told of the caliph to the west, Chinggis ordered his armies to raid Abbasid territory in northern Mesopotamia.

Eight years after chastising his sons in Urgench, the Great Khan died in 1227. His third son, Ogedei, was elected Great Khan and swore to honour his father by completing unfinished conquests. The raids into Abbasid territory continued, although some, notably the ones in 1238 and 1245, were repulsed by the Arabs.[3]

Meanwhile, in the far north of the world, trouble was brewing for Europe. The northern conquests of Chinggis had been given to his firstborn Jochi to administer. A gifted strategist and commander, Jochi would have been the logical successor to his father if it were not for the circumstances behind his birth. Borte, the great love of Chinggis's life, had been kidnapped by rival tribes from the Merkit Confederacy when she was seventeen, shortly after she came to live with him as his wife. Chinggis was sixteen and led a raid to rescue her. Sometime afterwards, Borte gave birth to Jochi and although he was close to his father and a true Chinggisid, whispered comments about his paternity always followed him. Borte would become the Grand Empress of Chinggis's dominions, and he would not hear of questions about the circumstances behind Jochi's birth.

But the words and insinuations lingered. As Chinggis was about to set out on his great campaign against the Khwarezmians, says *The Secret History*, he was reminded by a Mongol noblewoman that he was no longer young, and needed to nominate a successor. Chinggis admitted that he had been remiss, although, as he reminded his court, he did not have any precedent to guide him, because there had never been a Great Khan for all the Mongols. Then he asked Jochi for counsel.

This provoked Chagadai to ask his father if he wanted to nominate Jochi as his successor. 'Are we,' said Chinggis's second son, 'to be governed by a bastard of the Merkits?'

Jochi caught hold of Chagadai's collar, and asked why he had always discriminated against Jochi, when Chinggis did not treat the two any differently. 'Only in stupidity are you superior to me,' said Jochi. 'If you beat me in long-distance arrow shooting, I will cut off my thumb. If you beat me in wrestling, I will not get up from the earth.'

Serious words from a Mongol, and Chinggis sitting on his throne noted it. His solution was to nominate neither of them, choosing Ogedei, his third son. After the destruction of Khwarezmia, Jochi went north to govern the lands he had been given, which extended west to the Ural Mountains in what is now Russia. There he sulked and refused to meet his father, despite several summons to appear before him. In 1226, when Chinggis was preparing to march out himself and discipline his eldest son, he received news that Jochi had died.

Jochi's vast lands were divided among his sons, and from them would emerge the fearsome Golden Horde. They would agree to the nominal rule of the Great Khans that succeeded Chinggis, but the memory of that scuffle between Jochi and Chagadai would fester on among the descendants of Chinggis, and would ultimately directly affect the history of Asia and Europe. In time, the Mongol Empire would be divided among the heirs of the four sons, and their rivalries would ensure the empire never expanded in the way it had at the beginning.

One of the reasons why India did not suffer a full-scale Mongol invasion was this fragmentation of the empire. Khwarezmian Shah Ala ad-Din's son Jalal ad-Din, in mounting a resistance with the remnants of his army, was chased by Chinggis across the Indus, after which he sought refuge with Iltutmish, the third Mamluk sultan of Delhi. This was the moment which could have triggered an invasion by Chinggis. As it turned out, Iltutmish refused to shelter Jalal ad-Din, who spent some years pillaging Indian provinces before returning to a doomed campaign to retake Persia from the Mongols. In the years to follow, the united Mongol Empire had other campaigns to fight and did not consider an invasion of India. By the time they did, it was not a united empire but a small fragment of it which nursed ambitions in India, and would not be up to the task.

While the Middle East awaited the Mongols' next move, the heirs of Chinggis were eyeing Europe as well. In 1235, Ogedei, now Great Khan, after defeating other steppe tribes of

Eurasia, began a campaign against another western power: the Kievan Rus', who were to give their name to Russia. By 1240, the Mongols had decimated all resistance and reached Kiev in what is now Ukraine. Russia was under the Golden Horde. Armies under the great general Subutai and Batu Khan, son of Jochi, marched into the wide plains west of Kiev. The Mongols were at the gates of Europe and the fractious countries of the West belatedly woke up to them.

Europeans were familiar with barbarians. The learned in the Middle Ages were doubly familiar with barbarians who won battles, and who could not be bought off, or coerced, or outfought or out-thought. Scholars were even familiar with that rarest of barbarian breeds—the patient ones. But the Mongols were something apart from the Goths or Vandals who had sacked Rome ages ago, or the Vikings who had plagued France and Britain, or even the Magyar and Arab raiders of later times.

In battles two days apart, as an incredulous Europe watched in trepidation, the Mongols destroyed the armies of Poland and Hungary in April 1241. Soon after, Transylvania lay in ruins. The Mongols were at the gates of Vienna. Beyond lay the whole of Europe.

But then the Mongol armies received news of the death of Great Khan Ogedei in December 1241. All the descendants of Chinggis, 'princes of the blood', had to be at the capital of Qaraqorum for the election of the new Great Khan. Europe got some breathing space. The invincible enemy, which had appeared as if conjured from the very air, melted away into the East. Although the Mongols would return, and the Golden Horde would make several attempts at invading Europe, 1241 was when the West was in greatest peril.

But what of the Middle East? After a decade of relentless, almost annual raids by Ogedei's armies, the Abbasids had become weary and started sending tributes to the Mongols, and envoys at the coronation of Ogedei's successors Guyug and, eventually, Mongke in 1251 at Qaraqorum. Guyug, son of Ogedei, had told Caliph al-Mustasim to submit to Mongol rule formally but had been refused.

Mongke, son of Chinggis's youngest son Tolui, looked to the Abbasid Caliphate and decided to bring those lands under his direct rule. He gave the task to his brother Hulagu. In 1257, Hulagu, after the customary gathering of intelligence that Mongol generals were so adept at, assembled his invasion force for the march west.

It was by all accounts a formidable force, numbering between 100,000 and 150,000. The most powerful elements of the vast Mongol Empire had been brought into play. There were Mongol horsemen and the pick of Mongke's Chinese siege warfare specialists and a new kind of expert: gunpowder artillery men. There were soldiers from Turkic nations which had been brought under the Mongol heel, and there were Persians from what had once been Khwarezmia. There were also Christian allies. King Hethum I of Armenia had come, as had King David VI of Georgia, among the oldest Christian kingdoms of the world.[4]

Generations later, as the remains of the Arab world considered with horror the destruction that the Mongols wreaked on venerable old monarchies and dynasties in the Middle East, their chroniclers would struggle to frame the magnitude of the catastrophe in terms that could be comprehensible to their descendants. Words, it appeared, simply failed them. Ibn al-Athir, the noted thirteenth-century historian, could only compare the Mongols of his time to Dajjal, the Antichrist whose coming was believed in Islamic eschatology to herald the End of Days. The Arabs were not alone in this. At the time of the first Mongol invasions of Eastern Europe, Latin Christians had begun thinking of the invaders as the Antichrist.

Armageddon was indeed coming to the Middle East. But first, Hulagu dealt with the Nizari Ismailis, a splinter group of Shia zealots who had since the eleventh century carved out a fearsome reputation for fanaticism and targeted assassinations. Under the command of their leader Hasan-i Sabah and his successors, they had seized several fortresses in a line extending from Persia to the Syrian coast, including the impregnable stronghold of Alamut, 'the Eagle's Nest' in the mountains of northern Persia.

The long list of assassinations by the Assassins was also an eclectic one. On the afternoon of 28 April 1192, days after being elected king of Jerusalem, Conrad of Montferrat, a capable nobleman related to royal houses in Austria, France and Germany, was stabbed to death on a street in Acre. It was murder for hire, and various personages have been accused of it, including the English king, Richard the Lionheart. Forty years prior to that, Raymond II, count of Tripoli, was murdered in that city by them. But the Assassins also murdered a Seljuq prime minister, various generals and even two Abbasid caliphs. Legend also sees their hand in the murder of Muhammad of Ghur, who invaded India and captured Delhi at the end of the twelfth century. This is unlikely to have happened, but the Assassins were certainly a political force in the Middle East that other powers did not care to cross.

The Assassins were also shrewd political operators more than anything else, and by 1238, they had realized two things—first, that the Mongols could not be stopped by any single kingdom or empire in the world and second, that these conquerors from the East would, inevitably, pass through Assassin dominions to seize the Middle East, including the whole of Mesopotamia. In that year, the Assassin grand master, Ala al-Din Muhammad, convinced the Abbasid Caliph Al-Mustasim—no mean feat this—to seek an alliance with the Christian rulers of France and England against the Mongols. Such an alliance, unprecedented and possibly unimaginable in a world before the Mongols burst into it, never materialized in any case, and all the players of the Middle East were left to fend for themselves against the coming storm.

And then, sometime in 1253, Ala al-Din Muhammad sent his men to murder Great Khan Mongke in Qaraqorum. Mongke survived, but the die had been cast. The Assassins had made their last error. The great Mongol army that marched into Persia was also tasked with making an end of the accursed sect.

One after the other, the invincible citadels of the Nizari Ismailis, of which the people of the Middle East and the entire Muslim and Christian world spoke in hushed horror, collapsed. One after the other, the diehard Assassin defenders of these forts were captured and killed. At last, on 8 November 1256, Hulagu's great army snaked up a tortuous mountain path, stood before Alamut, and began bombarding it with gunpowder artillery. Assassin Grand Master Rukn al-Din, son of Ala al-Din, surrendered. Travelling in great humility to Qaraqorum, the leader of the deadliest group of zealots in the Islamic world prostrated himself before Great Khan Mongke and swore he would order the remaining Assassin holdouts in Persia and Syria—there were several—to surrender. Mongke nodded and

The Mongol sack of the dreaded Assassin fort of Alamut became a subject of Islamic art afterwards, even in Mughal India

appeared to agree, but on the way back to Persia, Rukn al-Din was executed.[5] The remaining Assassin forts were eventually brought down and the sect was, for all intents and purposes, wiped out, although isolated bands appeared at various places occasionally for years afterwards, and were blamed for a few actual assassinations as well.

Hulagu led his men westward. Mongke had told his brother to get a solemn assurance from the caliph that the latter would formally submit to the Mongols and pay tribute. This was supposed to be an expedition to pacify an already conquered land. The Assassins had been uprooted. Mesopotamia, already under the Mongol heel, would now know peace.

Or so Mongke had thought. Incredibly, Caliph Al-Mustasim refused to show submission to the Mongols. The sequence of events, considering the aftermath, is a little opaque but, apparently, the caliph's chief adviser Ibn al-Alkami successfully assured the Abbasid ruler that the Mongol invasion force was not much of a problem and anyway, if Baghdad was besieged, the whole of Dar al-Islam would empty into the plains around it to defend the greatest Muslim city in the world.

Al-Mustasim should have consulted the many books in the libraries of Baghdad, which would have shown him the folly of his chief adviser. The caliph should have looked to the tremendous absence of any such rallying by the forces of Islam after Jerusalem fell in 1099. And if the slaughter that followed the sack of Al-Quds could not rouse the House of Islam and fill it with outrage, would the siege of Baghdad have any effect at all? Al-Mustasim gambled on the hope that it would, that a great victory and deliverance would occur and Baghdad would be saved.

But the allies the caliph was looking for, the stalwart champions of Islam, would not come. The Mamluks had seized power in Cairo just a few years earlier in 1250, toppling the descendants of Salah ad-Din, who had fled to Damascus. The Mamluks were not particularly enamoured with Al-Mustasim's behaviour, which they found patronizing. To the north and west of Baghdad, the grizzled Turkish warlords of Syria, veterans of battles against Christian foes and arguably the most experienced allies the caliph could have counted on, saw the writing on the wall very clearly. The Mongol tide would shortly sweep into their dominions. All they could do was begin preparing their own strongholds for siege. The steward of the Prophet was alone.

By the end of January 1258, Hulagu had reached and deployed his massive force around the walls of Baghdad. The defenders are estimated to have numbered a little more than 50,000, including 20,000 cavalrymen. Compared to the besiegers, Al-Mustasim's forces were neither well-trained nor well equipped, and they were defending one of the largest cities in the world. Hulagu's forces, in contrast, included the latest in sophisticated siege engines and massive catapults built and manned by Chinese specialists who had practised their skills on the dozens of stoutly defended Assassin forts to the east which had fallen on the march to Baghdad.

The result was inevitable. By the middle of January, Al-Mustasim had sent out his cavalrymen, who were then swiftly trapped—the defenders had to learn the errors of being surrounded in open combat by Mongol horsemen. Hulagu's Chinese experts destroyed the intricate system of dikes and levies which for generations had channelled the waters of the Tigris to Mesopotamian farmlands. The great river flooded the plains around the city, trapping the Baghdad cavalry, and the Mongols surrounded and annihilated them.

By 5 February, the situation in Baghdad had become desperate. No help was going to arrive, it was clear. Al-Mustasim made his last play. He decided to give Hulagu, and ultimately Mongke, what they wanted—submission and a truce. Hundreds of Baghdad's elite, the cream of Arab and Abbasid nobility, marched out and sought to negotiate terms with the Mongols. Hulagu sent a single message to Al-Mustasim, waiting inside his palace—there would be no truce. The Arab aristocrats were rounded up and put to the sword.

On 10 February, Al-Mustasim signalled the surrender of the great city. Its massive doors, battered by Mongol siege engines, were opened. But Hulagu held back. For three days, Mongol cavalrymen marched and wheeled around the stricken city while the terrified residents watched them from the broken ramparts.

Finally, on 13 February, Hulagu's Mongols, with their Armenian and Georgian allies, marched into Baghdad and began sacking it. As the horrified Dar al-Islam watched, the residents of the greatest city ever built by the Arabs were slaughtered, and the many palaces and fine houses ransacked for more than a week.

Al-Mustasim was cornered in his palace and brought before Hulagu. Mongol law was very specific about the treatment of captured royalty. It was believed by the sons of Chinggis that the earth would never forgive them if the blood of royals touched it. So on completing a conquest and capturing kings and princes, Mongol generals had to be inventive in interpreting the restriction. Arab chroniclers wrote that Al-Mustasim was rolled up in one of his more sumptuous carpets and trampled to death by Mongol chargers. The Venetian Marco Polo would later record a somewhat different tale. Al-Mustasim, he said, was imprisoned in one of his treasure rooms and there starved to death surrounded by the riches of his lost kingdom.

In either case, Al-Mustasim before his passing witnessed the magnitude of the horror that had descended on his people. The extended Abbasid family was virtually wiped out, including the line of succession. But not entirely. Abu al-Qasim Ahmad Al-Mustansir, an uncle of the caliph and a prominent Abbasid, was in prison during the siege of Baghdad and managed to escape during its fall. Al-Mustansir fled the ravaged city and escaped into the Syrian Desert. Three years later, he arrived in Cairo, where the Mamluks promptly set him up as the next caliph. The Abbasid line might have been uprooted from the city its ancestors had founded but it would continue, much diminished in earthly powers but still claiming the stewardship of the faithful, in Egypt.

For the other hapless citizens of Baghdad, however, there would be no escape and very little mercy.[6] The canals of the city, and the Tigris, ran red with the blood of more than 100,000 people, perhaps nearly a million. Many were caught trying to escape, brought back to the city and slaughtered. Mixed with the red, wrote chroniclers, was black. The thirty-six famed public libraries of the Abbasid capital and the numerous private collections of its nobility and scholars were ransacked; hundreds of thousands of priceless works on the sciences, philosophy and literature were thrown into the Tigris. The invaders would cart away the gold and treasure of the great city but not the books.[7] It may not have been the demise of the Islamic Golden Age, but was certainly its funeral.

In a week, Baghdad had been reduced to a smouldering shell, while the fertile plains around it had been denuded of farmland and people. The devastation was so thorough, it was later said, that Mesopotamia never recovered from the loss of the intricate network of canals which fed it. And thus Arab rule in Mesopotamia ended.

The destruction of a great city has a metaphysical impact that goes beyond the immediate and the visible. As the Islamic world witnessed the unthinkable unfold in front of it, it was as if a force of nature, an implacable elemental entity, had been unleashed to remake the world. The warlords of Syria and the Mamluks in Egypt waited for the next hammer blow from the armies of Dajjal.

Far to the West, the potentates of Europe, including the pope, the Holy Roman Emperor, and the kings of France and England, heard of the cataclysm that had befallen the Muslim world. For them too it was unthinkable. For 500 years, Baghdad had been the light of the world. The most significant city the Arabs had ever built in the first flush of their arrival on the world stage, the demise of Baghdad was the passing of an era. The Mongols would later repopulate and garrison it, and a city by that name has existed there and survived other invasions, but it is not the city that it had once been.

The Europeans were already familiar with the devastation Mongols could bring in their wake. Vienna and the German plains had only recently earned a reprieve. But the pope and the kings had also been informed of an interesting phenomenon—that among the Mongol hordes which had erupted into the Mesopotamian plains were Georgian and Armenian Christians. What manner of new world was this, thought the European powers, where Christians allied with barbarians?

And then, from the shambles of what had once been Arab power in Persia and Mesopotamia, came further, more incredible news. The Latin Church had known for a while that some of the Mongols were Nestorian and had sympathies for Christianity, if not more. There had been much speculation on the faith of Great Khan Mongke, with some in Europe convinced that he was Christian. Now it was being said that the general of the Mongols, the great Hulagu about whom Muslims were whispering in horror as far as Spain, was a Christian too, and that he had spared the lives of the Nestorians of Baghdad and had even built a church for them after garrisoning the city.[8] It was just possible that Western Christianity had found the great ally it had been seeking in its struggle against Islam.

Our Khan in Persia

Among the many remarkable members of the house of Chinggis, the lives of two women deserve special mention, because their deeds would help shape medieval Eurasia. The first was Borte, wife of Chinggis and mother of his four favourite sons. The second was Sorqaqtani, a woman so influential in the court of the Great Khans that she was referred to in the years after her passing simply as 'Beki', the Mongol honorific for 'lady'.

Sorqaqtani was the daughter of a chief from the powerful Kereyid tribal confederacy, which by the early thirteenth century had been subsumed by Mongol power. Sorqaqtani's father was, at least in the early part of Chinggis's life, a committed ally of the Great Khan, and she was married to Chinggis's thirteen-year-old son Tolui when she was fourteen. Sorqaqtani, even by the standards of Mongol women and daughters-in-law, was an extraordinarily capable political operator.[1] Through a series of adroit moves, she lived to see her eldest son Mongke become Great Khan in 1251, months before she passed away. Hulagu, her third son, would sack Baghdad and Mesopotamia for his elder brother. And Sorqaqtani's second son Qubilai would eventually be Great Khan too and found the Yuan dynasty of China.

Sorqaqtani set her sons on the path to greatness virtually from the moment they were born, and among the steps she took towards this was to get them trained in particular languages and cultures of the vast empire. Culture, language and ways of life: these, as Chinggis had told his sons and daughters, were the keystones of running a multi-ethnic dominion.

Religion was a somewhat different matter. By the eleventh century, the Kereyids appear to have converted entirely to Nestorian Christianity, and Sorqaqtani was brought up in that faith. On her death, she would be buried in a Nestorian churchyard in north-western China with all the elaborate ceremonies of her faith, and would be eulogized by Nestorian prelates. But her sons were not Kereyid, they were Chinggisid.

The Mongol Empire has been the subject of considerable generalization, and with understandable reasons. It was so vast and so influential that, in several matters, arriving at a nuanced view is a difficult task. Popular imagination often considers Chinggis and his people genocidal barbarians who were somehow consistently successful on the battlefield, perhaps because of pure bloodthirstiness. This view does not take into account the sophisticated nature of medieval warfare, or how proactive the Mongols were in incorporating advances in military technology. This view also ignores their diplomatic capabilities, which were formidable, and their ability to adapt to local social conditions, which was impressive.

Mongols have lately been considered an example of a pre-modern secular state. It has been claimed that successive Great

Khans pursued a policy inherited from Chinggis, of separating the state apparatus from ecclesiastical systems or religious structures, predating similar Early Modern models in the West by more than 600 years.

As with other parts of the Mongol mythos, the truth here is a little more complicated. The waters were muddied by the claims of representatives of virtually every single religion that came in touch with them that the Chinggisids, and the house of Borjigin to which Chinggis and his family belonged, favoured them above everyone else. Ata-malik Juwayni, the Persian historian and chronicler of the Mongols, said that even Sorqaqtani, despite being a devout Nestorian, donated liberally to Islamic seminaries and Muslim mendicants in Persia. Mongke, wrote Juwayni, favoured Muslims the most in his acts of beneficence, while Minhaj Juzjani, who chronicled the life of a Mamluk sultan in Delhi, claimed that Mongke on his ascension as Great Khan recited the 'shahada', the Islamic profession of faith. At the same ceremony, Buddhist chroniclers from China claimed Mongke had announced that all the faiths of the world were to Buddhism what the fingers were to the palm of the hand. Meanwhile, the official Ming dynasty history of the Mongols in China, the *Yuanshi*, claimed that the Chinggisids were without exception devoted to the shamanism of their ancestors.[2]

The truth is the Chinggisids were not secular in the modern Western sense by any measure. Nor were they enamoured by all religions, believing them to be equally worthy of reverence as the modern Indian state defines secularism to be, although some Great Khans such as Mongke would occasionally proclaim this. The Chinggisids treated religions and religious leaders without distinction, keeping them in good humour through whatever means, because this was necessary for governing the people. This was no version of secularism but merely the pragmatism of world conquerors who intended to keep their dominions. But there was another, perhaps unintended, reason.

In 1253, the Franciscan friar William of Rubruck, who had accompanied King Louis IX of France on the Seventh Crusade, was asked by the king to travel to the court of the Great Khan in Qaraqorum. William would bring back to Europe one of the earliest and clearest accounts of the Mongols and their polity. And while at Mongke's court, watching the Nestorians, Buddhists, Muslims and shamanists jostle for imperial favour, William had a tremendous flash of insight that had apparently escaped the other religious leaders.

'He believes in none of them . . . and yet they all follow his court as flies do honey, and he makes them all gifts and all of them believe that they are on intimate terms with him and forecast his good fortune,' wrote the Franciscan.[3] For the Great Khans and the other rulers of the house of Chinggis, the only identity worthy of having was that of a Mongol. Everything else was just policy.

Nevertheless, the first rumours of Nestorian and therefore Christian influence on the Mongols were received enthusiastically by the Latin Church and the kings of Western Europe. In 1248, two Nestorian Christians had arrived at the court of King Louis IX bringing him a letter from Eljigidei, a general of Great Khan Guyug, cousin and predecessor of Mongke. Eljigidei, who was campaigning in Persia, wanted to wish the French king good fortune on his impending crusade. The Nestorians claimed that the Mongol general had been baptized and that Guyug too was a Christian. That was the beginning of the Latin Church and European kings' persistent belief that the Mongols were destined to be the great Christian allies from the East who would help the West vanquish Islam. Louis then sent his own envoys to Guyug, but they discovered that the Great Khan regarded their embassy as a tribute from the French king.

Owing to this misunderstanding, Louis told William of Rubruck that the Franciscan was to present himself as a man of God and not as an ambassador. In Qaraqorum, an Armenian monk told William that he had told Mongke that if the Great Khan became Christian, the whole world, including the French king and the pope, would submit to him. That was apparently the only enticement that the Great Khan would understand, not doctrinal niceties like Salvation and the afterlife. The Armenian helpfully advised William to tell Mongke the same thing. William was horrified, and had to be content with telling Mongke that the West would consider him a friend if he ever got baptized.

In 1258, Hulagu's forces swept westward beyond Baghdad and reached Syria. Prince Bohemond VI of Antioch, which was one of the last remaining crusader provinces in the Holy Land, placed his Frankish troops at the disposal of the Mongols. The Ayubbid ruler of Damascus just fled the city, which fell in March 1260. Hulagu then headed southwards, raiding Jerusalem but not occupying it, sacking cities like Nablus and conquering Kerak. And then Great Khan Mongke died, at the siege of a city in China in August 1259. Hulagu retreated to Central Asia, quite possibly because he saw himself as Mongke's successor.

In any event, a much smaller Mongol force remained in Syria and it was this army, led by the general Kitbuqa, that met a Mamluk Egyptian army under Baybars at a place called Ayn Jalut in Galilee. The result was a complete victory for the

Egyptians, and Kitbuqa was killed. The Mongol campaign in the Holy Land was in jeopardy.

Hulagu never carried on with the campaign from where he had left it. By then, the unity of the Mongol Empire was in peril. The old feud between the sons of Chinggis over Jochi's parentage had returned to haunt the royal court. Two brothers of Mongke, Arigh Boke and Qubilai, staked claim to the throne. Arigh Boke was supported by Berke, son of Jochi. Hulagu, who did not like Berke, naturally supported his brother Qubilai. After four years of tension, the Qubilai faction triumphed and he became Great Khan, establishing his capital at Khanbaliq (modern Beijing) in China and founding the Yuan dynasty. In the process, the Mongol Empire was compartmentalized into four provinces. Qubilai ruled in China. The family of Chagadai got Central Asia up to India. Berke of the Golden Horde kept his father's dominions in the north, including what would be Russia and Eastern Europe. As for Hulagu, he became Ilkhan or 'junior khan', ruling over Persia and the Middle East. These khanates would be united only in name under Qubilai and his descendants, and would pursue their own policies. The divisions would increase as time passed.[4]

From its beginning, the Ilkhanate was at a state of war, or at best a wary peace, with the Golden Horde to the north because of the ancestral grouse, personal dislikes and the infighting that occurred after Mongke died. To the Ilkhanate's north-west were the Turks of Anatolia. To the east were the Chagadayid Mongols, who over time became close to the Golden Horde because the former had problems with the Yuan dynasty. Qubilai's descendants would be friendly with the Ilkhanate, but too distant to be immediate allies in military affairs. To the south of the Ilkhanate were the Mamluks, victors at Ayn

Jalut and, for the moment, heroes of the House of Islam. The Ilkhans needed friends.

They turned to Europe, whose kings were also open to the idea of an alliance with an eastern power against the Mamluks. King Louis IX of France had lost against the Mamluks in 1250 and had been captured and ransomed for one-third of the entire annual revenue the French royal treasury earned in a year. In 1270, still dreaming of glory in the Holy Land, Louis went on the Eighth Crusade accompanied by the then Prince Edward of England, who would go on to be King Edward I.

The Eighth Crusade was an utter disaster. At Tunis near the site of Carthage, the ancient city and birthplace of Hannibal Barca, the crusaders were struck by disease and Louis died of dysentery. The remnants under Prince Edward sailed out and made contact with the army of Abaqa, who had succeeded his father Hulagu as Ilkhan. Abaqa advised Edward to coordinate his proposed attack on Mamluk possessions with a Mongol force that would separately attack the Egyptians. Although this coordination was effectively initiated, the Mongol army was limited to a raid on the cities of Harim and Afamiyya before retreating under Mamluk attrition, while Edward's attack on the Mamluk fortress of Qaqun was similarly ineffective, and both armies were unable to complement each other to Mamluk disadvantage.

This would be the strongest military campaign launched by a European-Mongol alliance against Egypt. But the Ilkhans remained receptive to the idea of further ventures. Orghun, who succeeded Abaqa, was the most enthusiastic of the Ilkhans in seeking an alliance with the West. In 1285, he wrote to Pope Honorius IV suggesting that between Latin Christian kings and the Ilkhanate, they could isolate Egypt and defeat the Muslims.

Two years later, he wrote to King Edward I of England, King Philip IV of France and Pope Nicholas IV and got a lukewarm response. In 1289, he wrote again to Edward and Philip, offering Jerusalem to the West if the crusaders marched on to Egypt. Three years later, he sent another emissary. By now the Latin Christians were becoming aware that the few remaining crusader holdings in the Holy Land, such as Acre, were in grave danger from the Mamluks. Pope Nicholas wrote back, saying King Edward I was preparing to leave on crusade. By the time the reply arrived in Persia, Orghun was dead.

These three decades, from the arrival of the Mongols in Syria to the death of Orghun, comprised the finest opportunity for Latin Christianity to triumph over the Mamluks and secure the Holy Land. Both secular leaders and popes were aware of how vital a Mongol alliance could be. In 1260, as Hulagu's forces erupted into Syria, Jacques Pantaleon, Latin Patriarch of Jerusalem, observed the dismantling of Muslim kingdoms and principalities. A year later, Pantaleon was elected as Pope Urban IV. 'I was,' he admitted in a letter to a French count who participated in the Seventh and Eighth Crusades, 'dazzled by the opportunities on offer.' But the opportunities never resulted in substantial achievements beyond cordial diplomatic exchanges.

For the Franks of the Holy Land, the coming of the Mongols would result in renewed hostilities with Egypt. The Mamluks would begin a series of campaigns to end crusader presence in the region, viewing them as a perpetual menace which might launch joint campaigns with the Ilkhanate or with crusading armies from Europe at any time. But for the kings of Europe and the Church of Rome the Ilkhanate was the first kingdom in the Middle East which was open for alliances, cordial diplomacy and a steady partnership.

This proximity was not just for strategic reasons. The Ilkhans continued the old Chinggisid policy of equal treatment of all religions, matched by a private disdain for the doctrinal specifics of all of them. The result was occasional bemusement among the representatives of these faiths who still had not been able to grasp the Mongol approach to religion. Hulagu seems to have assured an Armenian traveller and chronicler that he had been a Christian since birth, because of his mother Sorqaqtani, whose Nestorian credentials were unimpeachable. But Christian representatives at Hulagu's capital Maraga (now Maragheh in north-western Iran) were scandalized to find he had built a temple where idols of someone called 'Sakmonia' were worshipped. This Sakmonia was Sakyamuni, and the Buddhists were happy that Hulagu would pray there and spend time with them. But when Hulagu died, he was buried on an island in a lake not too far from his capital in traditional Mongol fashion. When his widow Doquz, another formidable Mongol lady, asked Christian clergymen to celebrate Mass for him, the Armenians, who felt betrayed that he had turned out not to be Christian after all, refused. The Nestorians, who perhaps understood the Mongol mind a little better, did celebrate Mass.

Orghun, the Ilkhan who most actively sought an alliance with European kings, was no less successful in baffling religious leaders. A Dominican missionary, viewing Orghun's moral composition with disapproval, would call him an egregious villain capable of anything, but also a friend of Christians. The same Orghun once went to the shrine of a noted Persian Sufi mystic to seek, or so he claimed, divine intercession in a campaign against the Golden Horde, which persuaded local Sufi Muslims into believing he favoured them above others. And he could be seen in the company of Buddhist lamas too;

he ultimately died after taking a mysterious medicine which the lamas had assured him would prolong his life. His son and successor Oljaitu was in turn a Nestorian Christian, a Buddhist, a Sunni Muslim who subscribed to the Hanafi and then the Shafi schools and then, getting annoyed with the continuous feuds among Sunni schools, became a Twelver Shia. He was apparently baptized in 1291, which caused celebrations in the West, particularly in the court of Pope Nicholas IV, who was told Oljaitu had taken on the Christian name of Nicholas in honour of the Holy Father.

Actually, the Ilkhans had by then understood a fundamental truth about ruling such a vast empire. The heads of the four Mongol divisions were all ruling people of different faiths, and perhaps it was advisable to ensure stability by embracing one of them, at least for public consumption. Surrounded by enemies, each division of the empire needed to ensure internal cohesion if it wanted to survive. If religions were interchangeable, this ultimate goal of internal political cohesion could be achieved by such a symbolic gesture. It wasn't conversion born of faith, but of the necessity to appease. Ghazan, eldest son of Orghun, was raised a Buddhist but, like Ilkhan Oljaitu, converted to Islam in 1295 to appease a powerful general in his court. He never informed the pope or his fellow kings in Europe of this and it did not matter with regard to foreign policy. He still continued the Ilkhanate's hostility to Mamluk Egypt, and in many ways was a more committed enemy of the Mamluks than his predecessors were. Oljaitu, his younger brother and successor, was Muslim when he received a letter from King Edward II of England in 1307, congratulating him for his intention to destroy Islam. Oljaitu also did not let religion come in the way of his foreign policy.

As a result, Persia under the Ilkhans became a place where Christians could be free to practise their faith without either being treated with the suspicion of Zoroastrian mowbeds in the old Sassanid Empire, or being forced to live like heavily taxed dhimmis under the Abbasid Caliphate. The Yuan Empire in China would have a similar policy towards Christians, while taking care to be seen as protectors of traditional Chinese polytheism and Buddhism.

Ilkhanid Persia gradually became a staging post for Latin missions to the rest of the Middle East and beyond, an unprecedented development in the history of Western Christianity. Persia had always been one of the conduits for ideas and goods from East to West and in reverse. Now Dominicans and Franciscans began arriving at the new Ilkhanid capital of Sultanieh, approximately 240 km north-west of Tehran today. Sultanieh was established in 1306 by Oljaitu, then in his final religious phase as a Shia, and soon grew into a major metropolis and prospered from Silk Road commerce. Between Tabriz and Sultanieh, the fulcrum of political power in Mesopotamia and Persia in the Mongol era had shifted to the north from Baghdad.

By the late thirteenth century, Latin Christian missionaries had begun travelling through Persia to the Far East and China. Successive popes sent emissaries to the Ilkhans and through them to the Yuan emperors. Western Christianity had received an opportunity unimagined till then, to proselytize in the East. The Mongol approach to religion and the relative stability of the Ilkhanate had opened the world to the Latin Church. Constantine and his fellow Roman emperors had never been able to give Christianity a friendly power in Persia. There had been no possibility of such an arrangement with the Sassanids.

Under the Byzantines, the Greek Church had proselytized in Eastern Europe and what would be Russia west of the Ural Mountains, but never in the Middle East. But the Ilkhanate, as long as it lasted, would be a new home for Latin missionaries. And for those who were appointed to the task or sought it, the Yuan emperor in far-off China awaited.

There was trouble within the Church of Rome. Pope Boniface VIII in 1302 had declared papal supremacy over earthly kings, which was disputed by King Philip IV of France whose Italian allies then took over the Vatican and beat Boniface to death. Three years later, Pope Clement V shifted the seat of the papacy to Poitiers in France. Rome had become unsafe because the French king's friends were locked in a violent conflict with Italian noble families who had lost their influence in the Vatican. In 1309, Clement established himself in Avignon, beginning what would be known as the Avignon Papacy which would last till 1378. But Clement and his successors continued to be interested in the political situation in the East and the work of the missionaries.[5]

The Avignon Papacy also saw a significant development in the Church of Rome's understanding of its position in the world. In 1302, Boniface issued the papal bull named *Unam Sanctum*, which would influence later popes in their approach to non-Latin Christians.[6] Later changes in understanding of Western Christian canon law would lead other Avignon popes to believe that they held responsibility for the spiritual uplift of all people, even non-Christians, which would give a significant impetus to missions abroad from Persia.[7]

By 1318, the Dominicans and Franciscans had established missions in Persia in significant numbers. At Sultanieh, Tabriz and Basra, there were Latin Christian churches and convents of both the mendicant orders and a respectable number of converts. In that year, Pope John XXII declared the establishment of the Archbishopric of Sultanieh, with the Dominican Francesco of Perugia as the first archbishop. The geographical extent of Sultanieh's ecclesiastical territory would far exceed that of any other archbishopric under the Church of Rome. To the north, it extended to the Ilkhanate's borders with the Golden Horde in the Crimea and the Caucasus. In the south, it included the region east of the river Jordan. In the east, it spread to Khorasan and Central Asia. East of the Ilkhanate were the Chagadayids and, depending on how amicably the two Mongol factions were behaving towards each other, missionaries could venture to the great Silk Road cities in those parts as well. A little more than a decade after Francesco, during the time of his successor archbishop Giovanni of Cori, the bishopric of Samarkand was added to the areas under Sultanieh. Latin missionaries were to come across Nestorians in Central Asia and, like William of Rubruck three-quarters of a century earlier, would realize how far Eastern Christianity had spread in the centuries since the coming of Islam.

But there was yet another land where Eastern Christianity had arrived long ago. Unlike Central Asia or China, an apostle had brought the faith to that land and had been martyred there. Through the Ilkhanid court's understanding of Central and South Asia, Latin missionaries at Sultanieh were aware that Islam had arrived in India. But it was such a vast and relatively unknown land that it had till then been predominantly peopled in Western imagination by myths and legends surviving from Antiquity and the Early Middle Ages, from dimly remembered fables of Roman imperial times and theories of classical Greek scholars.

India had been a place where pagan heroes like Alexander had reached. It was the home of the fabled unicorn, and the Latins still had old manuscripts like those of Cosmas, which talked about Christians in India. There was no reason why the Latin Church could not be established in that land. It would not travel there as an imperial embassy. There was no Roman Empire to seek dominion overseas and no Yuan emperor interested enough in Western Christianity to invite papal legates. It was not being carried by colonizers with a larger strategic plan or accidentally by merchants. In the closing years of the thirteenth century and the beginning of the next, Western Christianity would be brought to India by members of mendicant orders devoted to humble Christian values; by scholars who were just as interested in the lives and beliefs of the people they travelled among as they were in preaching Christianity to those people. The idea of India that would emerge in Europe in this period was thus a reflection of the intellectual heritage of these mendicant orders as well.

And so, carried along by a complex current of geopolitics in Eurasia, Western Christianity found itself poised to travel to India through the missions that were emerging from Sultanieh. Almost 700 years after Hellenism and the last vestiges of Greek language and culture had died out from the Arabian Sea region, the West was about to return to the subcontinent, carried by a succession of very remarkable men.

The Pioneers

In 1291, Giovanni of Montecorvino, a Franciscan friar, was directed to travel to the East from Persia. The forty-five-year-old, a Campagnese by birth, was already far from home and accustomed to preaching among those unfamiliar with Western Christianity. By the late thirteenth century, the Franciscans' reputation as missionaries and ecclesiastical diplomats of the Latin Church was formidable.

Giovanni himself was particularly suited to the task of journeying to the East. Nineteen years prior to his greatest mission, he had been entrusted by the then Byzantine emperor, Michael VIII Palaiologos, with a diplomatic mission to the court of Pope Gregory X. The objective: nothing less than a reunion of the Greek and Latin churches.[1] In 1274, a council was convened at Lyons in France under Pope Gregory X. In attendance were envoys from Emperor Michael as well as Mongol diplomats from the court of Ilkhan Abaqa. The churches of Rome and Constantinople agreed to a union. The Great Schism, it seemed, was over.

But it was not to be. Michael's son and successor Andronikos would repudiate what Greek clergy saw as compromises with Rome and the union would be dissolved.

A year after the council, in 1275, Pope Nicholas IV sent Giovanni to Persia to preach Latin Christianity in that newly opened land. For thirteen years, Giovanni lived among the Persians of the Ilkhanate and was ideally placed to understand the tremendous complexities of the Mongol Empire.

Three years after Giovanni went to Persia, Pope Nicholas III sent the first real religious mission to the courts of Abaqa and Great Khan Qubilai. The embassy comprised five Franciscans: Gerard of Prato, Antony of Parma, John of St Agatha, Andrew of Florence and Matthew of Arezzo. They appear to have travelled overland to China, but did not reach Qubilai's court in Khanbaliq.

In 1286, Ilkhan Orghun, grandson of Hulagu, wrote to Pope Nicholas IV with a suggestion. Orghun's grand-uncle Qubilai in China was encouraging towards Christians, so perhaps the pope could send an official mission to the court of the Great Khan.

For this task, Nicholas turned once more to Giovanni. Five years after Orghun's letter, Giovanni set out with a younger Dominican friar named Nicholas, other monks and lay merchants familiar with parts of the route. Starting from the city of Tabriz nearly 350 km north-west of Sultanieh, Giovanni travelled to the Persian coast and then by sea to India.

Giovanni's travels would result in two celebrated epistles, both written from the court of the Yuan emperors in Khanbaliq and addressed to the pope.[2] Decades afterwards, a Dominican friar named Menentillus chanced upon a fragment of the first epistle composed by Giovanni about his stay in India. Together, these comprise the first account of the subcontinent by a Western Christian missionary.

Making landfall at Thane and then travelling by sea to Kollam, Giovanni eventually reached the tomb of the apostle Thomas. Although he does not specifically identify the site, it is likely to have been at Mylapore in what is Chennai today, where Christian tradition holds the apostle was first buried after his martyrdom. At this sacred site, Giovanni officially established the Latin Church in India. Thirteen centuries after the arrival of Thomas, Western Christianity had finally come to the subcontinent.

From Mylapore, Nicholas was to set out as papal envoy to the court of 'the king of kings' in India. Giovanni does not identify this monarch, but from the Ilkhanate's understanding of the political situation in India, it is likely to have been a reference to Jalal-ud-Din Khilji, Sultan of Delhi and founder of the Khilji dynasty, who had recently supplanted the Mamluks. The mission was never completed, with Nicholas falling sick and passing away shortly after starting his journey north. This would be the only official papal legation to the sultanate, and indicates that Pope Nicholas IV wanted his missionaries in India to seek diplomatic relations with the most powerful monarchs in the land, on the lines of legations to the Yuan court. Later missionaries would concentrate on the coastal areas and not be sent as envoys to Delhi, perhaps in consideration of Ilkhanid advice about the fluctuating fortunes of sultans in that city.

Giovanni spent thirteen months in India preaching among Syrian Christians, whom he found in abundance along the western coast, and the Hindus. He made, the first epistle notes, approximately 100 converts and established Latin rites among them.

Giovanni travelled extensively in India, particularly along the coast, and made in his words 'inquiries about the rest' of the land, partly out of missionary curiosity but also out of scholarly interest, for he knew there were many questions which the Church fathers and scholars of Europe had about the mysterious East. Did it in fact measure up to the accounts left by the legendary travellers and writers of Antiquity?

Giovanni's impressions of India and its people are warm, bordering on effusive. 'It would be most profitable to preach to them the faith of Christ, if the brothers came,' he wrote. But there were hidden attractions for the unwary among the mendicant orders. The land was very fertile and abounded in wealth and aromatic spices. Only missionaries of the most impeccable character were to be sent to these parts, so that they could practise their vows of poverty and the simple life without distraction.

Giovanni, unlike Cosmas Indicopleustes, was not a merchant, so the epistles do not indicate he was interested in specifics about India's commercial relations with the West. Because of the climate, the people went about dressed in the merest of loincloths, therefore Giovanni did not see much possibility for European tailors to make a profit if they were to visit the land. This was the only observation he had to make of a mercantile nature.

Noting that he was far to the south of the world, because the Pole star could hardly be seen near the horizon and there was no winter to speak of, Giovanni wrote about his impressions of the Deccan. As with other travellers from the West, beginning with Herodotus, the Franciscan was struck by how extensively populated the land was, with many great cities (although he declined to list them, given the brevity of his epistles). In contrast to the grand buildings of the great and powerful in these cities, the houses of common people were made of mud and roofed with thatched leaves. He found rivers of varying sizes and noted the abundance of wells. However, he warned, the traveller should stay away from drinking well water, because it loosened the bowels. Instead, the local custom was to dig water tanks and drink accumulated rainwater, which was always safer.

Giovanni found that Indians mostly did not keep horses, which were always owned by royalty or prominent nobility. Although flies could be seen sometimes, he noted that fleas were not to be found at all.

In the India of Giovanni's epistles, beards were very popular and baths were frequent, but leavened bread and wine of the type drunk in his native land were not to be found. Sugar, honey, and what can be inferred to be toddy were to be found abundantly and were cheap. Toddy was very popular, the friar found. Crops were cultivated in all seasons and spices, naturally, were also commonly produced and consumed, although some spices were expensive and difficult to get, even for locals. One of these was cinnamon, which was imported from an island off the coast. This was the first time that cinnamon was associated with Sri Lanka in European imagination. Ginger and various kinds of gourd were also grown and eaten customarily. Giovanni noted the popularity of rice and milk and wrote with considerable disapproval of the Indian custom of eating with hands, and the apparent absence of cutlery. This was an observation that other early visitors from the West too were to make.

But Giovanni was primarily a student of society, and he turned his keen eye repeatedly on the people of the land and their customs. He noted that cattle were sacred (he did not specifically refer to cows). The people did not eat the flesh of cattle at all, although milk and its products were commonly used and bulls, oxen and buffaloes were used in the field just as in other parts of the world.

People worshipped idols, and at first glance appeared not to have an observable moral code which had been written down and could be compared to systems in Western Europe. Books were not in common circulation either. The Indians did have an alphabet, but this was used to write scripture or prayers to the local gods. The means of writing too was different. Paper was not used at all, with Indians preferring leaves of palm trees and other means. In Giovanni's time, the written word appears to have been used only for trade or liturgy by Indians.

As a Latin Christian preacher, Giovanni found considerable differences with the Indian idea of morality. He noted that they had no idea about the nature of sin, particularly of carnal sin. Just as Usamah ibn Munqidh in the Holy Land had been bemused by the Franks' blasé approach to sexual relations, the Franciscan missionary found his views on sin were conservative compared to those the Indians held.

Worship took place at all times of the day at temples, where each individual was free to visit and offer prayers as convenient. Giovanni also noted the frequent number of festivals and fasts of the Indians, although there was no fixed day for a fast either in the week or month. Weddings he found to be taking place only during a certain time of the year, and widows would not marry again.

By the time Giovanni arrived in India, Islam had been present on the Malabar Coast for 600 years. In the north, Afghans and Turks had begun making inroads a century previously. Giovanni did not find significant numbers of Muslims in the interiors. On the coast, he did find them in influential communities: a governor of the Coromandel Coast at that period was a Muslim, although the Franciscan does not specifically refer to him. Native Christians and Jews, although present, were not in comparable size and did not have widespread administrative powers.

Giovanni also found that Christians and those who had 'Christian names' were persecuted by the local authorities. This is mentioned in a single instance, and no details are added, which makes this a curious inclusion. In the later part of his travels, when Giovanni came across long-entrenched persecution of Christians in other parts of the world and suffered it himself, he did mention details, but chose not to in the matter of India, even though he was writing to the pope and seeking missionaries for the subcontinent. It is possible that he was referring to specific instances by the authorities, and did not find that this persecution was carried out by the common people. This too was an observation about India that early Christians had made while composing *The Acts of Thomas*. The world had not changed much, in that respect. Persecution still flowed from the trappings of power.

Giovanni found the strange and the curious in everyday events. He noted the funeral rites of Indians, particularly the procession to the burning ghats accompanied by music and song. And yet, he wrote, the relatives of the dead also showed grief as much as other people did.

In the many kingdoms and principalities of the subcontinent, among the multitude of languages and customs, Giovanni noted that most Indians were polite and friendly, but spoke little as a rule and conducted themselves with dignity. In their mannerisms he found little to differentiate between ordinary Indians and European peasants.

In his travels, Giovanni found peace and a general sense of security in the land, both on the coast and in the countryside. There were few robbers and miscreants to be found. But the people did have to pay a lot of taxes. Interestingly, the friar also noted the relatively fewer numbers of craftsmen and artisans compared to the cities of Europe, which was odd considering the flourishing trade in Indian crafts of that period. It is possible that he spent most of his time in the great ports of Gujarat, the Konkan and Malabar coasts and saw mainly merchants, scholars and, inland, farmers.

Giovanni made a passing reference to the Indian way of war, noting how men would go into battle in their loincloths with sword or dagger, although he also wrote of mercenary Muslim bowmen in the employ of regional kings.

The friar was apparently most familiar with the Malabar and Coromandel coasts, noting the approximate distance from the Strait of Hormuz in Persia to the Malabar Coast and onwards through the Gulf of Mannar to the Coromandel Coast, including Mylapore. He marked the way for European pilgrims who wished to travel from Persia to the tomb of the apostle Thomas. Giovanni also apparently classified Sri Lanka with the islands of Lakshadweep, a conflation that was to be repeated by other medieval visitors, both Christian and Muslim.

The main idea of India then prevalent and popular among European laymen and scholars was that of a magical and mysterious land which was at the same time a source of trade and wealth. In response to those in the West who thought of India in terms of a small and homogenous geography with minute differences, such as in Italy, Giovanni wrote that India contained vast realms and many more languages than had been assumed. He also confirmed that he had made many inquiries and tried to find out himself about the mythical creatures and the Garden of Eden which was supposed to lie somewhere in the subcontinent, but had come to the conclusion that these tales had no basis. The first Western Christian missionary in India was also the first to begin demolishing the fantastic associations that European imagination had made with the subcontinent, although these associations would endure into the Early Modern period in subtle forms. The India of Giovanni Montecorvino was not exotic by any means and more complex than he could hope to describe.

Around the time that Giovanni was composing his account of India, Marco Polo was travelling along the Malabar Coast on his way back from China. If the two, being fellow Italians in a distant land, ever met at some point, neither Giovanni's epistles nor Polo's *Il Milione* mention this.

The Latin Church might have officially come to India, and Giovanni might have been greatly interested in its growth in the land beyond his 100 converts and in the fate of India's resident Eastern Christians, but his first task was to travel to China, a land which, as he wrote in his first epistle, was much different from the subcontinent.

No apostle had ever gone there, nor had any of the early Christians. Instead, the Franciscan found that Nestorians had already made deep inroads at the Yuan court and, either through influence or outright bribery, managed to persecute him several times. These persecutions were severe enough for Giovanni to begin his first epistle, written thirteen years after he arrived in China, with a complaint to the pope about the 'perfidious Nestorians'. At various points, Giovanni seems to have been accused of being a spy and even an impostor masquerading as an innocent friar and ambassador of the pope. He was accused of murdering the actual ambassador somewhere in India and was even tried by Qubilai's court, but found innocent.

For eleven of those years, Giovanni led an isolated existence, devoting himself to the spread of Latin Christianity in China while awaiting assistance from the West. It took him seven years to build a church in Khanbaliq, and by the time of his first epistle in 1304, he had baptized 6000 Chinese subjects. If it hadn't been for Nestorian interference, he hastened to add, he would have baptized five times that number.

Giovanni was apparently unfazed by the linguistic differences between Mandarin and Latin. In fact, he wrote, he had made arrangements for 150 little boys who had not received any particular religious training, and taught them Greek and Latin. He then formed a choir group and wrote that by the reign of Timur, grandson of Emperor Qubilai, the Latin choir was very popular with the emperor and his court. The Yuan emperors, both Qubilai and Timur, favoured Buddhism just as much as Christianity in keeping with true Mongol policy and Giovanni could not convert them, although that was the first task to which he devoted himself immediately upon arrival at Khanbaliq. His failure was emblematic of the Church's relationship with the Mongols: thus far could they go, but no further.

But Giovanni was also determined to render unto the Nestorians what they had been making him go through, and among his triumphs, he was happy to tell the pope, was the conversion of one George, khan of the Mongol Ongut confederation, who had been brought up a Nestorian. Giovanni thought George was from the family of the fabled Prester John himself, whose realm was said to be in India. Prester John's myth had become very popular in Europe and was a subject of considerable speculation among visitors to the East. The 'India' associated with Prester John was a nebulous region and over time, the great ruler was thought to be located in eastern Africa, which in the Middle Ages as in the closing years of Antiquity was considered to be part of India. Alternately, Prester John was supposed to be from Eastern Mongolia at some point.

This George then got a considerable number of his people to convert to Latin Christianity, despite being called an apostate by the naturally scandalized Nestorian Church. Near the banks of the Hwang He, a journey of twenty days from Khanbaliq, George built a large church.

Giovanni was delighted with this turn of events, but George died some years afterwards, and the Nestorians converted his subjects right back. The Franciscan, sitting in the capital by himself, was unable to intervene. Could it not be possible, he urged the Holy Father, that some worthy men of God be sent over to journey either by land or by sea to China and help him spread the true word of the Lord?

After eleven lonely years, Giovanni got reinforcements in the form of a friar from Cologne named Arnold. The Franciscan was still starved of news from Europe. The vast distance meant he had to rely on whatever sources could turn up, such as an unnamed physician from Lombardy. This person somehow arrived at Khanbaliq and apparently proceeded to spread an enormous amount of patently false and misleading ideas about the pope, Latin Christianity and the Franciscan Order, causing much indignation to Giovanni.

Sometime towards the beginning of 1306, a delegation from Nubia in eastern Africa appears to have arrived at

Khanbaliq, where they asked Giovanni to visit them and preach.

A year later, Pope Clement V received Giovanni's epistles and was informed of Latin Christianity's success in the Far East. The Franciscan was declared Archbishop of Khanbaliq, and a legation of seven bishops was sent to China to assist him. Three of them—Peter of Castello, Nicholas of Apulia and Andrutius of Assisi—passed away sometime after arriving in India. A fourth, William of Villeneuve, either did not start on the journey for unknown reasons or turned back much before the embassy reached the subcontinent. The other three bishops—Andrew of Perugia, Gerard and Peregrine—travelled to Mylapore and then arrived at Khanbaliq and consecrated Giovanni as archbishop. The three bishops then set out on their own missions, in time settling in the port of Zayton, identified with the city of Quanzhou on the Taiwan Strait today. Zayton would become an important centre for Latin Christianity in China and would also see a thriving community of Genoese merchants establish themselves over the next few decades. Some years later, western Europeans apparently heard rumours that Giovanni had succeeded in converting the Yuan emperor himself, so Pope Clement sent three more bishops, Peter of Florence, Thomas and Jerome. Peter would later become bishop of Zayton as well.

The epilogue to these early years of Latin Christianity in the East comes from Andrew of Perugia. By 1326, he was the last remaining survivor of the 1307 delegation of seven bishops. He was old but healthy, and looked forward to many more years in China. Writing to the warden of his old Franciscan house in Perugia, he was doubtful the letter would reach that Italian city far to the west. He wrote of his arrival at Khanbaliq and his first few years in the imperial city. The Yuans had continued to be kind to the Latin missionaries, and Andrew received the equivalent of 100 golden florins a year*, a grant called 'alafa' by the Yuan court. Gerard, his fellow bishop, had at first taken charge of the mission at Zayton, and on his death Andrew had declined it, so the choice fell on Peregrine. Andrew had travelled to Zayton in 1318 and established himself there, devoting his energies to the construction of a church and a mission station, which had grown into a spacious residence which could accommodate twenty-two friars. The Latins also had four apartments in the city fit for a senior bishop or even an archbishop. The mission was located about a quarter of a mile from the centre of Zayton. Giovanni elevated the church at Zayton to the rank of cathedral, and the port city became the second-most important centre of the Latin Church in China, after the Yuan capital. In 1322, Peregrine too passed away and Andrew became bishop of Zayton.

Andrew had a comfortable life at Zayton, dividing his time between his official residence and the mission station. The missionaries were doing well, but there were points of dissatisfaction too. The Yuans, Andrew had discovered, persisted in believing that any person could be saved regardless of his sect, while most Han Chinese did not feel the need to make a break with their traditional beliefs and formally convert to Latin Christianity. People did convert, but for Andrew they were not satisfactory enough in their devotions

---

* Equivalent to £116,000 or Rs 1.07 crore in today's currency. Andrew did not know much about currency exchange rates prevalent in his time, and wrote that the Genoese merchants of Zayton calculated the amount for him.

or understanding of Scripture and rites. Among the Jewish and Muslim communities of the port, the Latin missionaries had had very little success despite considerable efforts.

Western Christianity had indeed arrived in the East, and had begun engaging with it. There were successes beyond expectations, such as in Khanbaliq, and frustrations, such as the continued insistence of the Yuan emperors not to convert. The number of lay converts had increased and the missions had expanded. The prelates looked forward to the future with anticipation.

As far as India was concerned, these early missionaries wrote home of the complexities of their host societies and expected people like themselves to follow in their footsteps to the east. The Indians were welcoming towards any faith and were a reasonable people. This, the first contact by the Latin Church with Indians, would be an indicator of the kind of wisdom and reasonableness that the Dominicans and Franciscans brought in their journeys to India, and would reflect how the Latin Church considered these missions in the subcontinent in those times.

But a new era of scholarship was dawning in Europe, and would soon arrive in India in the form of a most remarkable man who had formulated an unprecedented idea. This was the time of pioneering missionaries, but it was also the time of the Later Crusades, and the time of strategists.

The Source of All Evil

A round the time when Giovanni Montecorvino arrived on the Malabar Coast, a Mamluk Egyptian army under Sultan al-Ashraf left the Nile Delta and struck out north across the Holy Land. On 5 April 1291, they reached Acre in what is Israel's Haifa Bay today.

It had been a quarter century of misfortune for the crusaders. After the Mongol debacle at Ayn Jalut, the Mamluks had turned their attention to European possessions in the Holy Land, taking the Principality of Antioch in 1268. The response from the West had been underwhelming. The Eighth Crusade, launched by King Louis IX in 1270, was aimed at reaching the Holy Land via the island of Cyprus. Despite Ilkhan Abaqa also attacking Egypt, it achieved nothing, beyond the death of Louis.

The royal courts of Europe, it seemed to observers, were just not able to put together a campaign to rival the tremendously successful First Crusade. Six years after the death of Louis, Henry II, claimant to the lost throne of the Kingdom of

Jerusalem, left the Holy Land and settled down in Cyprus to await deliverance from the West. For generations, Europeans had been referring to the Holy Land as *outre-mer* or 'beyond the sea'. Now, the kingdom built by the First Crusade had literally become an offshore venture.

More reverses ensued. In 1278, the crucial Syrian port of Latakia was lost. In 1289, the Mamluks took the County of Tripoli and its eponymous capital city, a feat that would rival if not exceed the taking of Jerusalem by Salah ad-Din 100 years previously.

The Mamluk army's siege of Acre in 1291 was therefore a defining moment in medieval history. The Franks were defending their last major city in the Holy Land, but apart from a few sailors from the Italian cities and a band of knights sent by King Edward I of England, the West did not come to their aid. By the evening of 18 May, Acre had fallen.[1] Some of its notable defenders, including King Henry II of Jerusalem, had fled back to Cyprus. Others, including the Hospitaller and Templar garrisons of the city, had perished. Among the dead was William of Beaujeu, Grand Master of the Templars. The Mamluks had completed the Muslim reconquest of the Holy Land.

Europe had seen it coming for years, and yet the loss of Acre and the erasure of crusader territory in the Holy Land had a profound impact on the political and intellectual environment of medieval Europe. The question in the papal and royal courts now was: How should the Crusades be conducted? What needed to be done?

In the Second Council of Lyons in 1274, where Pope Gregory X laid out the proposal by the Byzantine emperor, conveyed by Giovanni Montecorvino, of a reunion between the Greek and Latin churches, another matter was also discussed. Suggestions were sought for strategy manuals to outline campaigns against Muslim powers, aimed ultimately at recovering Jerusalem. Gregory personally asked the Franciscan friar Fidenzio of Padua for a proposal for such a campaign. Fidenzio was extensively travelled and familiar with Mamluk armies in Egypt. In 1290, he submitted what would be the first crusade proposal of its kind. These proposals would, in their entirety, constitute the single largest body of strategy manuals written during the Middle Ages, a remarkable feat of intellectual effort by European scholars.

Fidenzio's plan, which called for a campaign by land through the Balkans, breaking out into the Byzantine Empire and making landfall on the Mediterranean coast north of the Holy Land, was too late for the Siege and Fall of Acre.[2] By 1291, the situation had become dire and Pope Nicholas IV would call for more such proposals.

Scholarly opinion in the early twentieth century held that in this period, the crusade proposals became an outlet for European inability to check the advance of Muslim forces in the Middle East. The fourteenth century was generally referred to as a time of 'sterile projects' with very little activity on the ground.[3] Subsequently, these writings were also considered a form of medieval propaganda, with scholars pointing to the fact that the period with the greatest concentration of proposals was also characterized by an absence of campaigns on the ground, in contrast with later decades of the fourteenth century which witnessed Latin Christian campaigns at places like Nicopolis and Smyrna but did not see many proposals.[4] The implication was these treatises were a medieval form of theory as a substitute for effective action.

There has been a reappraisal of these proposals since then, indicating that crusading continued to be a vital endeavour for Europeans in the early fourteenth century. The shadow cast by Acre, however, was long and deep. The complete loss of the Holy Land became an apocalyptic event, presaging the End of Days. There is also the view that these writings were 'refined literature' of a sophistication unusual in European works of the Middle Ages.[5] Traces of the humanism and scientific method that are apparent in Renaissance literature too can be found in these proposals.

Of this vast body of work (there are at least a dozen significant proposals which bear a look), the most extensive came not from the Franciscans and Dominicans, who had already achieved a well-deserved reputation for scholarship and wide-ranging travel. Marino Sanudo Torsello came from a different background. An actual merchant of Venice, Sanudo had sailed across the Mediterranean and seen the last of the Frankish holdouts in the Holy Land. He had been to Alexandria and was familiar with the economy of Egypt, still the powerhouse of the Muslim world. Possibly the only definition that fits him is 'mercantile humanist'; he was a self-taught scholar of Christian thought and military strategy in equal measure. Although not regarded among the prominent early humanists such as Dante, Petrarch or Boccaccio, the manner in which he presents information, the use of tables and maps (made by the Genoese master cartographer Pietro Vesconte) to build on his ideas and his overall treatment of the concept of knowledge dissemination elevates him from the ranks of most crusade advisers to that of a humanist.[6] He was perhaps what Cosmas might have been if that Alexandrian merchant had not taken his war against classical Greek scholarship so seriously.

Sanudo's crusade proposal was a mammoth exercise: written in three parts over fifteen years between 1306 and 1321, the *Liber Secretorum Fidelium Crucis* (Book of the Secrets of the Faithful to the Cross) leaves no aspect of the idea of crusading out of its ambit. Sanudo digresses too, in a gentle meandering manner. A lot of the proposal involves a recounting of the biblical geography of the Holy Land, and he even finds it necessary to include a particularly salacious biography of the Prophet Muhammad which seems to have been taken from a tract then in circulation in Europe and which reflected popular Christian prejudices in the West against Islam during that period.

To every amateur historian, no matter how gifted, there must be granted one bugbear, and for Sanudo it appears to be the Italian city states which traded in the Mediterranean. He gave his native Venice, as can be expected, a primary role in a campaign he proposed to be directed against Egypt. Take Egypt, said Sanudo, and you take the economic heart of the Muslim world.

Sanudo called for a naval expedition up the Nile, helmed by Venetian expertise and supported by troops which would make landfall in northern Egypt. Aware of the divisions within the Mongol Empire and the enmity between the Ilkhanate and the Golden Horde, Sanudo warned that the latter might intervene in case of an invasion of Egypt. So an alliance with the Ilkhanate was to be pursued by all means, for the road to keeping and holding Jerusalem lay through Egypt.

But what was the secret to Egyptian prosperity? True, the Nile Valley produced, as it had for centuries, foodgrain and cotton which were exported across the Mediterranean. But the Egyptians also benefited from geography. An enormous part of their 'honour, revenue, profit and reputation' (for the Venetian these were interchangeable attributes) came not from what they produced themselves, but from trade with India.

Sanudo identified the port of Khambat (in Gujarat today) and the Malabar Coast as the principal points of origin for Indian shipping to Egypt. He was not very familiar with Indian maritime topography, because he called the Malabar a single port. From India, goods were transported to four major ports in the Muslim world. Three of them—Hormuz, the island of Kish in the Persian Gulf and Basra—were under the Ilkhanate. The fourth, noted Sanudo, was Aden from where the goods were shipped onward by sea and land to Cairo and Alexandria. Of these four, Aden received the bulk of shipping from India.

Almost all the goods that ultimately arrived in Europe from India passed through Egypt, and Sanudo calculated that one-third of the income the Mamluk Sultanate earned came from taxes on these goods. Europeans, meanwhile, were exporting silver, bronze, tin, lead, mercury, oil, wool, woven cloth and other products to the Mamluks, who were selling whatever they did not use to the Indians and making, from European labour, a tidy profit which was then being used against Christendom. If the European merchants who so readily flocked to Alexandria to trade with the Egyptians showed only a little more restraint and prudence, wrote Sanudo, here was a marvellous opportunity to bring the economic edifice of the Mamluks crashing down. The merchants could instead be induced to trade with the Ilkhanate, which would in turn become the new fulcrum of maritime commerce with India. The Ilkhanate already had three perfectly viable ports, and flourishing inland centres such as Tabriz which received goods along the overland route from China and India. The Persian Gulf ports could very swiftly replace Aden as principal entrepôts for Indian goods. The Ilkhanate would prosper while the Mamluks would decline, and Europe would reap the benefits. In Sanudo's plan for a crusade, therefore, European strategic security and the Ilkhanate's economic prosperity went together.

The economic structure of the Muslim world, noted Sanudo, could therefore be compared with a tree, the trunk being the Mamluks and branches being their allies, including the Turks of Asia Minor, the kingdoms of the Maghreb and, to the north, the Golden Horde. The roots were the maritime lanes which converged on Cairo from the East. But the source that watered this tree was the sea. And the life-giving nutrition that flowed along the roots, the very source of Mamluk strength which kept Europe from reclaiming Jerusalem, was trade with India whose fruits 'are so good that they are appropriately called goods'. The term 'goods' as reference to commodities actually derives from European usage during this period.

There was, wrote Sanudo, very little that Europeans limited to the Mediterranean could do about Indian Ocean trade. Any active measures would depend on the Ilkhanate. But Europeans could take some measures of their own. European navies could patrol the Mediterranean and enforce an embargo on Mamluk shipping. They could even be authorized, by papal decree if need be, to police European shipping and punish those merchants, including from Italian city states, who would still trade with Egypt.

This embargo was not to be limited only to cargo from Egyptian ports. No goods from India, including spices and sugar, and no Egyptian cotton or other material was to be allowed to enter Europe from the smaller ports of Tunisia and the rest of the Maghreb, and even from those parts of Spain still under Muslim control. There was to be a boycott of Indian goods, and penalties were to be levied on any European who imported any item from these lands. If Jerusalem was to be recovered, Europeans were to be induced to do without Indian goods, at least till such a happy time when the Ilkhanate would replace Egypt as the nerve centre for trade with the East. As a substitute, the Venetian pointed out that sugar was even then being produced in Cyprus, Rhodes and other Mediterranean islands. Sicily, which he recommended as another site for the product, had actually been producing sugar for a long time. Silk, another European import from which the Mamluks were making a lot of money, could be produced in Italy, Romania, Sicily, and even on Crete. Six hundred years before the Indian nationalist movement called for a boycott of British goods and urged self-reliance, Sanudo was suggesting a boycott of Indian goods and a sophisticated campaign of economic warfare if Europe was to prevail over Islam.

Sanudo completed Book 2 (*The Ways and Means by Which the Holy Land Can Be Recovered*) of his magnum opus in 1312. Five years later, while he was working on Book 3, a Dominican missionary named William of Adam submitted his crusade proposal to Raymond of Farges, cardinal deacon of the church of Santa Maria Nova (now Santa Francesca Romana) in Rome. William did not give his manuscript a title, but subsequently it came to be referred to as *Tractatus Quomodo Sarraceni Sunt Expugnandi* or 'How to Defeat the Saracens'. As a crusade proposal, it is quite distinct from the rest and not merely because its title talks not of recovering the Holy Land but an outright defeat of Islam. Arguably the least known of that vast body of strategy manuals, William of Adam's proposal also ventured farther afield than the rest.

William was born c.1275 in south-west France, and by 1302, might have studied theology at the Dominican house in Condom in the department of Gers in that country. A trained writer of some talent, his work shows a flair for complex sentences, wordplay and even some medical knowledge, judging from his references to diseases and their cure. In 1307, he was in Constantinople and for the next decade, he travelled through Persia to India as a preacher. Certainly, of all the proposal writers, William had the most detailed knowledge of India. In 1316–17, he was back in Rome. A year after he submitted the *Tractatus*, he was appointed as one of the six bishops of the archdiocese at Sultanieh. Sometime later, he was made bishop of Smyrna (now the city of Izmir in Turkey). In October 1322, William was appointed Archbishop of Sultanieh. Two years later, he became the Archbishop of Antivari (now the city of Bar in Montenegro). Returning to France in 1329, he stayed till 1337, when he was asked by Pope Benedict XII to leave for Antivari again. William passed away in that Adriatic city in c.1339.

A widely travelled man, William himself mentioned that he had seen from one end of Persia to the other, large parts of coastal India, the Balkans, the Red Sea coast and even Ethiopia. Although he was familiar with Egypt, it is unlikely that he ever visited it, and he was not very familiar with either the Greek mainland or the Holy Land.

The *Tractatus* in comparison to Sanudo's work is concise but reaches the same conclusion that the key to retaking Jerusalem lay in neutralizing the Mamluks. William enumerated five ways of achieving this. Like Sanudo, he wrote that the first step would be to enforce a naval embargo against European merchants crossing the Mediterranean to Egypt. The cargo they brought—particularly wood, weapons and enslaved children, Christian as well as pagan, from the Balkans and the Black Sea coast—were used by the Mamluks for military purposes. 'There will not be a spade or a lance in Egypt,' said William, if European merchants were not colluding with the Mamluks. Calling this slave trade 'damnable to Christianity', the Dominican said that if it were not for these children, the population of Egypt and the size of its army might never increase. European merchants who still continued to treasonously carry out commerce with the Egyptians and participate in the slave trade were to be excommunicated and their assets seized.[7]

The second task necessary for a successful crusade was to stop the flow of Christian pilgrims to the Holy Land through Mamluk territory, because the pilgrims, by paying taxes, were adding to the wealth of the enemy.

William was a vitriolic critic of the Byzantines, because of the legacy of bitterness between the Greek Church and the Latins after their failure to repair the Schism. Some elements within the Church of Constantinople, opposed to a union between the Greek and Latin churches, were no great admirers of the Dominican Order either, whose representatives in the Byzantine Empire had been trying for years to reunite the churches. This mutual distrust was one reason why William had to resign from the order before taking his appointment as one of the bishops of Sultanieh archdiocese.

The third task that William set for a crusading campaign was the conquest of Constantinople. The Greeks, he said, were a more immediate enemy of the West than the Muslims themselves. Just as a father on failing to discipline a wayward son must be forced to take strong measures, Europe must invade and occupy Constantinople to save the Greeks, said William, because the Byzantines were clearly incapable of doing this on their own and were very likely to come to the aid of the Mamluks against a crusading army.

In implying that the Greeks would betray the Christian cause and ally with the Mamluks, William was perhaps being too harsh, because the Byzantines had to carry out a delicate balancing act between the Europeans and the Egyptians. But William also said that the Byzantines were tremendously weak and must be taken over, because there was another enemy to contend with. In his travels, he discovered how the Greek Christian world of Anatolia and Asia Minor had been devastated by Turkish incursions. In Tabriz alone, William calculated that there were 1,50,000 enslaved Greek Christians, brought to that Persian city by Turkish raiders from Anatolia or the Black Sea coast, sold and eventually converted to Islam.

In the slave markets of Tabriz were to be found pregnant women or those with children, who regretted giving birth because of the life their offspring were condemned to. William wrote of a female slave who had just given birth and, in front of him, was prepared to kill her baby boy. On seeing William and his fellow monks, she brought her child to them for a secret baptism, afraid of being punished by her master. The monks were in two minds, fearing the baptism might cause more harm to the woman and her baby than good, but ultimately chose to go ahead with it, hoping for the best.

Such, wrote William, was the fate of Greek Christians from what used to be the former great Byzantine Empire which had been almost completely overrun by the Turks. The Greek emperor was clearly unable to defend the faithful, so it was the task of the Latin Church to convince European kings to conquer Constantinople again (it had been sacked and conquered by the Latins in 1204, forcing the Byzantines to relocate to neighbouring dominions before they retook the city in 1261). That great city, warned William—prophetically, as it turned out—was about to fall to the Turks otherwise, and with it would fall Greek Christianity.

William, like Sanudo and other crusade proposal writers, was quite familiar with the complex internal politics of the Mongol Empire, and also recommended strengthening the alliance with the Ilkhanate, which would be necessary to protect the flanks of a crusader army if the Golden Horde and the Turks of Asia Minor came to the defence of Egypt.

But it is the fifth part of William's crusade proposal that makes it unique among all the treatises on this subject. In his travels along the coast of eastern Persia through Sindh and western India, William met indigenous Christians. Once thriving communities, these had fallen on difficult times since the advent of Turkic invaders in South Asia. He noted with perplexity how Eastern Christians who had—either voluntarily or through coercion—been newly converted to Islam persecuted Christians with greater ferocity than those who had been born Muslim.[8] After one of them attacked William in India, the Dominican reproached him for renouncing Christianity and, worse, for being so cruel afterwards.

Chastised, the Indian asked what other option was available to Eastern Christians when the Lord had turned his back on them. With no chance of being free of the yoke of the invaders, with no great empire or champion to come to their aid, people of these broken communities could only choose among conversion, slavery or death. In Persia and southern Mesopotamia, reported William, there were many such Christians who still hoped for deliverance.

William appears to have been a basically decent man of learning—his principal objection to Islam was what he thought of as doctrinal error in that religion—and bore very little malice to actual people, regardless of faith or denomination. He was genuinely pained, for instance, by the trade in young slaves, pagan and Christian alike, from Central Asia to Egypt or Greek Christian slaves in Persia. He had a great deal of admiration for Ethiopians, and hoped to travel among them again whenever, as he hoped, he was called upon to do so by the Church. There is very little in his mindset, like those of his contemporary scholars, to suggest racial or ethnic bias.

Somewhere along his journey to India, William began to understand the principal weakness of Eastern Christians in Persia, Central Asia and India. These small communities, without the patronage of a kingdom or empire consistently sympathetic to them, had always been at the mercy of changing times. In India, as polytheistic rulers were being replaced by monotheistic ones, the first to be affected were minority faiths dependent on an identifiable clergy for their religious sustenance. The Syrian Christians of Persia and Mesopotamia under the Ilkhanate had temporary respite, but their position too could not have been as secure as that of Christians in the West. Among the fragmented communities along the Persian Gulf and Arabian Sea, William could see trauma which was quite distinct from that suffered during war or temporary unrest. He knew that these vestiges of an older world would soon fade away.

Perhaps because of these insights, William did not consider a crusading campaign to be merely limited to recovering the Holy Land for Western Christendom. It was true that Jerusalem, city of the Christ, was still the focus of his faith, but there were other ways of achieving its liberation than just in the Mediterranean. From Africa to India, everybody was involved.

Trade from India being manifestly the source of Egyptian wealth, William made an analogy as vivid as Sanudo comparing this seaborne commerce with a tree. Just as food entered the throat from the mouth and then passed into the stomach from where it went to the rest of the body, wrote the Dominican, valuable cargo came over the Arabian Sea from India, passed through the port of Aden and then up the Red Sea to Egypt. '*India omnium malorum que supra posui materia sit, non casualiter nec occasionaliter sed ueraciter effectiue*,' wrote William. India is, not casually or occasionally, but truly and effectively, the source of all the evils.

In this case as well, William bore no malice towards Indians, although he was not an admirer of subcontinental merchants who traded with Mamluk Egypt. The evil of which he spoke was the wealth that this trade generated for the Egyptians. The remedy to this disease lay in cutting off the head, upon which the body of Egyptian commerce would perish.

But while Sanudo focused on Mediterranean trade embargoes and domestic alternatives to Indian products, William advocated a daring and unprecedented plan: a fleet of ships to police the maritime trade route from India.

The Dominican is aware of how fantastic this idea would sound to his readers in Rome, so he hastens to assure them that although no other proposal writer had ever made such a suggestion, it was merely because he alone among them was familiar with India and Persia.

The second reason why this idea might sound absurd, he said, arguing against himself, was because the sheer volume of

Indian and Arab seafaring traffic would be difficult to control or thwart by a relatively small task force.

And the fleet that William had in mind was indeed astoundingly small. Three or perhaps four 'galee' (galleys) should be enough for the task, manned by 1200 sailors, and there were two ways to build the fleet. The first was if the Church were to pay the expenses to a suitable man who would be in charge of the enterprise. If the Church was unable to pay this money, the expenses could be obtained from 100 merchants who would have been excommunicated—following his earlier suggestion—for trading with Alexandria, in exchange for pardon from the Church. This was, William said, the easier and cheaper option.

There were, in fact, two precedents to the kind of naval campaign that William was suggesting east of Egypt. The first, of which he appears to be unaware, was in 1182, when Baldwin IV was King of Jerusalem and the crusaders still held the Holy Land minus Edessa. Reynauld of Chatillon, lord of the crusader province of Oultrejourdain (now southern Israel and Jordan), got men and construction material for five ships transported over land from the fort of Kerak to the Gulf of Aqaba in the northern Red Sea. Building the ships, his men and he set sail down the Egyptian coast, attacking towns, ports and ships sailing up from India, before shifting to the Arabian coast. Salah ad-Din dispatched a fleet which fought Reynauld's forces and sank two crusader ships. The men from the remaining three landed in Arabia and fled inland towards the Holy Cities of Mecca and Medina. It was the only time that crusaders came close to the two holiest sites of the Islamic world. While Reynauld somehow escaped and returned to his dominions, his men were captured and, on the orders of an incensed Salah ad-Din, put to death.[9]

The second instance, that William mentioned, was in 1290, during the heady days of Ilkhan Orghun. In response to his request for European assistance for an invasion of Egypt, only 800 Genoese turned up in Persia. Casting about for ideas on how to effectively deploy them, Orghun tasked the experienced Italian sailors with building galleys and, like Reynauld of Chatillon, sailing down the Red Sea, attacking Mamluk shipping. That campaign was an even more dismal failure than Reynauld's. At some point during the boat-building process, the Genoese, being from the opposing Ghibelline and Guelph factions which had been at each other's throats in their home city for generations, fought a miniature civil war on the Red Sea's shores and perished. Nothing less, noted William, could be expected from the customarily fractious Italians.

But aside from his strategic insight, William had inside knowledge about the region, having spent twenty months sailing around the Arabian Sea, of which he spent nine months on Socotra alone. The merchants of Aden who were such an important part of Egyptian commerce traded at every port up to India, except those in the Persian Gulf—which were under the Ilkhanate and which therefore did not welcome Arabs—and some islands off the western coast of India, whose indigenous merchants apparently did not like those from Aden. So the ships for William's proposed fleet could be made at these ports. There were three such areas that also had an abundant supply of high-quality timber with which the ships could be built. The first was the port of Hormuz in Persia. The second were the islands of Diu in Gujarat. The third were the Indian ports of Thane, Khambat and Kollam. The rulers of these ports would be quite willing to assist the Europeans—if not for their shared dislike for the merchants of Aden, then perhaps for wealth. And despite the previous debacle in the Red Sea, the task of building the ships should be given to the Genoese, because they were the best at this. William reported that the Genoese were already present in strength in Indian and Persian ports, designing and building ships.

Once deployed, the fleet could find safe harbour at Hormuz or Kish (modern Qays) in Persia and if the Ilkhanate withdrew its protection, the Europeans could certainly find safety in Diu. The fleet would then patrol the Arabian Sea and attack Egyptian shipping. They could expect other allies, for William seems to have discovered some islands near Aden itself, where lived a community which preyed on ships from that port. Among these islands was also a kind of pirate base, which at any time had around 600 cut-throats, all of whom heartily disliked the merchants of Aden. There were yet other communities of pirates at Thane and farther down the Indian coast, all of whom could also be induced to ally with the European sailors.

Such were the maritime allies that William had in mind. And he had no illusions about the kind of venture he was suggesting. It was piracy, pure and simple, and piracy for the sake of the Holy Land.

The campaign suggested by the Dominican, covering a 3000-mile arc from the Indian coast to eastern Africa, would have been the most ambitious naval expedition ever attempted had it been launched. In imagining an alliance among Mongols, Persians, Europeans and Indians against Egypt, with the blessings of the distant Yuan emperor in China, William was suggesting a complex military venture, a war extending much beyond the traditional geography of the Crusades. The Dominican was suggesting a war involving the known world. One could, perhaps, call it a world war.

Signs and Marvels

The India of the late thirteenth century which the Latin Church was discovering and engaging with was also changing in fundamental ways. In February 1299, three years after he became Sultan of Delhi, Alauddin Khilji, son-in-law and successor of the king who had nearly received a papal emissary, marched on the Hindu Vaghela Kingdom of Gujarat ruled by Karnadeva. The ports of that kingdom, including Bharuch and Khambat, were key links for maritime trade between India and Egypt and the fertile countryside contributed much to the wealth of the Vaghelas. Khilji wanted this maritime access. Islam had already been present on the Gujarat coast, converging from two directions: Sindh to the north-west, which had by then been under Muslim rule for 500 years, and the sea route from the Persian Gulf and the Red Sea. The ports of Gujarat had well-settled Muslim communities of merchants, clerics and learned men of law.

Khilji's army of 24,000, true to the Turkic model, had a cavalry of nearly 14,000, making it remarkably mobile. Half of

Khilji's army manoeuvred from Sindh eastwards to Jaisalmer in the desert of what is now the state of Rajasthan. The second half marched south from Delhi, and the two elements met in Mewar region north-east of Gujarat. At Ashaval (now the city of Ahmedabad), the Khilji army defeated Karnadeva.[1] Sometime in June of that year, Alauddin had a second victory at Somnath, on the southern coast of Saurashtra. The great Shiva temple in that town, which had been destroyed or damaged by invaders earlier, was destroyed again. Khilji's men gathered considerable spoils from the ports of Gujarat, and a large number of captives. The campaign was significant enough for an Ilkhanid chronicler to record it.[2] At Khambat, one of the captives was Malik Kafur, born a Hindu. Taken to Delhi, the slave and eunuch would become one of the most noted generals in medieval India and would considerably expand Khilji dominions in the Deccan. Kafur would eventually rise to become a likely successor to Alauddin before he was assassinated by elements in the Khilji court.

The Gujarat campaign was not a glorious triumph for Khilji, however. During the march back to Delhi, at Jalore in today's south-western Rajasthan, a section of his army mutinied over the division of plunder. The mutineers seem to have mainly comprised new Central Asian converts to Islam, many of whom were Mongols.

Defeated, the rebels later joined forces with Karnadeva, who seems to have recovered some of his kingdom from Khilji. The sultan could only complete his conquest of Gujarat in 1304, when Karnadeva was finally defeated and fled to a neighbouring kingdom.

These events were noted with considerable interest and in great detail by the Ilkhanate. Alauddin Khilji was the subject of a great deal of curiosity in Persia, because he was dealing with his own Mongol problem in the north. In the previous century, Chinggis had come to the western banks of the Indus in his pursuit of the son of the last Khwarezmian emperor, but had never crossed into north India. Mongke had been preoccupied with Europe, China and the Middle East, although there were a few raids in Punjab over the years, including the sack of Lahore in 1241. Six years prior to that, the Mongols had taken Kashmir, which remained within their empire till the end of that century, although there were occasional disturbances, such as a revolt in 1255 during which the Mongol governor of Kashmir was killed by the subordinate local king.

Increasingly, the internal politics of the Delhi Sultanate had to accommodate the might of the then-united Mongol Empire with all its implications. In 1251, Ala ad-Din Masud, Mamluk sultan of Delhi who had been ousted by his nobles, convinced Mongke to help him recover the throne from his cousin Nasir ad-Din. Mongke's generals made a tentative foray and wrested western Punjab from the sultan, and gave the province to Masud to rule as a client. In 1257, a year before he marched on Baghdad, Hulagu had responded to an offer of a similar relationship from the Mamluk governor of Sindh by sending a force into Multan. But beyond these forays, and the conquest of Kashmir, the united Mongol Empire never planned a conquest of India. From these and later small-scale conflicts would emerge the Mongol prisoners of war who would be settled around Delhi and serve in the sultanate's armies and, eventually, rebel against Alauddin during his Gujarat campaign.

By the time of Alauddin Khilji, the Mongol Empire was too divided to launch an India campaign of the type or magnitude that had devastated Khwarezmia and the Abbasid Caliphate.

The Delhi sultans now had to deal with the Ilkhanate and the Chagadai Khanate. The latter by the time of the Khiljis still extended to the Delhi Sultanate's borders. Of the four divisions of the Mongol Empire, the Chagadayids were militarily the least inspired or successful. In 1299, a Chagadayid army invaded India and fought an indecisive battle near Delhi before retreating. Four years later, Alauddin Khilji survived the siege of his fort at Siri, although the Mongol army razed the surrounding settlements and countryside before retreating westwards. This led Khilji to reform the Delhi Sultanate's revenue system to fund a stronger army and improve Delhi's fortifications.

For the Chagadayids, this series of inconclusive campaigns rankled. Shortly afterwards, there was a detente among the four Mongol khanates in 1304 and the Chagadayids suggested to the Yuan dynasty a possible joint invasion of India in strength. Such a campaign did not happen, but the Chagadayids made their strongest foray into India in 1305. Bypassing Delhi, where Siri Fort by now was heavily defended, the Mongol invasion force of 30,000 was defeated by Khilji's army at Amroha on the Gangetic plain. This victory, and the subsequent massacre of Mongol prisoners, was the basis for Khilji's reputation as scourge of the Mongols. His chroniclers, however, appear to have inflated the figures of the invasion force. It would thus be a bit of an exaggeration to term Khilji a defender of India from the Mongol threat. From the Chagadayids, India had not faced a threat of the magnitude of Chinggis, Mongke or Hulagu, but a succession of uninspired raids led by generals of far inferior abilities. The only time India faced the very real threat of a full-scale Mongol invasion was when Chinggis stood on the western bank of the Indus and awaited news of the fugitive Khwarezmian prince Jalal ad-Din.

The Mongols did not return in similar strength after Amroha, although the Qaraunas, a Turkic people under the Chagadai banner who had settled in Afghanistan and who comprised the bulk of Chagadayid invasion forces in India from the middle of the thirteenth century, continued independent raids in the years to come.

Because of this recurring conflict with the Chagadayids, the Delhi sultans found the Ilkhanate in Persia more cordially disposed towards them. Diplomatic correspondence would continue intermittently between the Ilkhans and the Delhi sultans of successive dynasties including the later Tughluqs. The last correspondence was between Ilkhan Abu Said and Muhammad bin Tughluq in Delhi. Residual suspicion of all Mongol factions remained at the Delhi court over the early fourteenth century, but Persia was not considered a threat.

The Yuans of China, being even more distant, were also favourably viewed by Delhi sultans such as Muhammad bin Tughluq, who appointed Ibn Battuta as an ambassador to the Yuan court in 1341.

By 1307, the Chagadai menace to the Delhi Sultanate had ceased to exist and there was no likelihood of a joint Mongol invasion of India—the rift between the four divisions of the empire was too deep and irreversible. Alauddin was free to pay attention to the rest of the subcontinent and reasserted control over Gujarat and the northern Konkan.

This was the situation when William of Adam travelled in India before writing the *Tractatus*. It is possible that the Dominican, in his quest for Indian allies against Egypt, was referring to Vaghela loyalists on the Gujarat coast. It is more likely, however, that William thought the Delhi Sultanate, which by 1317 was firmly in control of Gujarat's ports, could be such an ally. The Ilkhanate, and by extension Western observers in Persia such as William, might have considered the Delhi Sultan an ally after his defence against the Chagadayids.

It is unlikely that either the Vaghelas, if they had ultimately triumphed against the Delhi Sultanate or Alauddin Khilji, after his victories in Gujarat, would have been interested in an alliance with the Ilkhanate. The idea of any military campaign which would affect the lucrative trade network with Egypt would have caused considerable anxiety to Khilji, who spent a lot of effort in stabilizing his kingdom's finances with considerable success.

As Muslim rule spread in peninsular India in the wake of Alauddin's campaigns, the nature of experiences by Latin Christian visitors to India and the accounts they wrote back to Europe also underwent a change.

Alauddin Khilji passed away in 1316, and his successors were not of his calibre, although his son Mubarak Shah, who ruled for four years after Alauddin's death, made some successful forays in the Deccan.

While Mubarak Shah was trying to put down rebellions within the Delhi Sultanate and William of Adam was in Rome finishing the *Tractatus*, Jordanus Catalani, a Dominican friar from southern France, was travelling in the Middle East.

The city of Tabriz and its 2,00,000 residents was flourishing under the Ilkhanate. The Latin missionaries had a large church for themselves and a flock of 1000 believers. At Sultanieh, Latin Christians were half this number. But the market of religion in Persia, as newly arrived European monks discovered, was extremely competitive. There were Persian Muslims and those of the Mongols who had converted to Islam, but there were also proselytizing Greek Christians, Syrians, Armenians and Georgians. There was also Persia's long-established Jewish community, although small in number. Jordanus had found the right place to begin his study of the East. An intensely curious man, he travelled not just to preach the faith but also to see for himself the people of the world and how they lived.

The Persians appear to have failed to impress him. They were undeniably prosperous, and he was fascinated by their irrigation system which did not rely on the scant rainfall at all. But there was also this insistence of theirs to eat while sitting on the ground and share from the same utensil where all the food was mixed and, moreover, to eat with their hands. This was the custom in Central Asia and India as well, although Indians did not share utensils and were not as messy, wrote Jordanus.

The term 'India' in European imagination by then referred to three regions. 'India the Lesser' began in Sindh and extended to the Narmada. 'India the Greater' began with the Deccan—what had been 'Dachinabades' in the time of the *Periplus*—but included Sri Lanka and the Indonesian islands. And there was 'India Tertia' (the Third India), which was how Europeans referred to the east African coast.[3]

Jordanus travelled to Hormuz in the company of three Franciscans—Peter of Siena, James of Padua and Thomas of Tolentino—to preach among the residents of that Persian Gulf port. Accompanying them was Demetrius, a layman. The group appears to have had little success in Hormuz and decided to travel onwards to India. Bad weather at sea drove them to Thane. The Franciscans and Demetrius met the Syrian Christian community of Thane while Jordanus went north, intending to preach at Bharuch. However, he had only managed to reach Suppara when he was informed that his companions had been arrested.

It appears to have begun when the Syrian Christian man at whose house the Franciscans were staying beat up his wife after a domestic quarrel. The woman complained to the local qadi against her husband and added that she had four male witnesses to the crime, monks from Persia, no less. The qadi called for the Franciscans and Demetrius, and they went, while Peter of Siena stayed at home to mind their few belongings.

The hearing then seems to have digressed into a religious debate between the qadi and other learned men present there, and the Franciscans. The qadi asked them what their view was of the Prophet, at which Thomas made some derogatory remarks against him. The court declared them guilty of blasphemy and they were sentenced to death. While James, Thomas and Demetrius were executed on 8 April 1321, Peter, who had stayed at home, was arrested later and executed on 11 April. What had begun as a case of domestic violence had ended in death.[4]

Jordanus arrived too late to save the four men, but he took their bodies to a church in Suppara and buried them. He was helped in this by a Genoese youth, one of several present in Indian ports at that time. This young man accompanied Jordanus on the Dominican's travels along the western Indian coast.

The Four Martyrs of Thane, as they came to be called, were the most noted of historical Christian martyrs in India in the Middle Ages, and over time, they acquired considerable renown in Europe. Astounding miracles were attributed to them, particularly to the relics of Thomas of Tolentino, and later travellers would tell of miracles that occurred during their martyrdom. Jordanus, it is said, once cured his young Genoese fellow traveller of illness by using one of Thomas' teeth.

By the fifteenth century, while the Barlaam and Josaphat legend was on its way to becoming one of the first bestsellers of the Age of Printing, the Four Martyrs were considered saints in their own right. The Catholic Church would officially recognize the cult that emerged around the martyrs in 1809, when Thomas was beatified. The Feast Day of the Four Martyrs falls on 9 April.

After this tragic beginning to his stay in India, Jordanus was left to himself, and in two letters to his order at Sultanieh in the succeeding years, he wrote that despite some harassment by the authorities, he was largely allowed to travel as he pleased. His condition remained dire: he had very few resources or local help to call on, his tattered monk's robes were soon cast away and he was frequently hungry. The climate was not easy and Jordanus, in his forties by then, suffered illnesses and afflictions.[5]

Jordanus ultimately reached Bharuch, from where he travelled along the Bay of Khambat and preached, among other places, at the town of Goga (now Ghogha in Gujarat's Bhavnagar district). Despite his physical problems, Jordanus continued to display a remarkably keen mind and a willingness to inquire into and understand a world full of marvellous sights. Where the strategist William of Adam saw naval campaigns, fleet bases and potential allies, Jordanus, an amateur naturalist and sociologist, saw the land and its people with an unexpected depth of detail and empathy.

The people of India, who had a darker complexion than those of Persia, would dress in the scantiest of loincloths, observed Jordanus. They ate rice at all times and did not bake or eat bread at all. Like Giovanni of Montecorvino, Jordanus made no mention of the unleavened rotis predominantly eaten in northern and western India, including Gujarat today. It is possible that in the early fourteenth century, rice was still the staple in Gujarat, at least in the coastal areas.

Cattle were used for almost all purposes, including as pack and draught animals. The land was rich in fruit, of which Jordanus found the jackfruit, which sometimes grew so big that it could feed five persons, fascinating. And he tasted the amba, a fruit so delicious that he did not have words to do justice to it. Jordanus the Catalan friar had found the mango. On the coast, he also came across the coconut and noted in detail how the tree was grown and its various uses. Like Giovanni, he saw the perennial popularity of toddy. He noted with wonder the banyan and its intricate branches, and the animals of India which visitors before him had marvelled at—lions, whose range then extended beyond Gujarat into central India and the Deccan, leopards and the tenacious Indian lynx or caracal. And he found the rhinoceros, which was also widely distributed in the subcontinent and was described by the Dominican's contemporary, Ibn Battuta. Jordanus seems to know about the medieval European debate regarding the rhinoceros, because he categorically said that this animal, although possessing a horn on its nose, was not the unicorn of legend.

The Dominican's interests and passions are palpable. While he took great care to describe virtually every single bird, tree and animal he came across, he had just a few scattered observations about objects of wealth. He was content with saying that several kinds of precious stones could be found across the land and that the diamonds of India were the best and biggest he had ever seen anywhere in his travels. Indian diamonds would continue to be famed in the West till the discovery of superior deposits in South Africa in the nineteenth century.

Jordanus found that the men of India went to war in their loincloths, with a small shield and a spear, an observation made by Giovanni before him. He appears to not have met or studied the great armies in the interior, nor does he seem to have been interested in the formidable arms and armour of indigenous soldiers or Turkish cavalrymen, or the flourishing export trade of Indian steel for swords and other weapons to the Middle East.

When a member of the nobility or a prominent man died, they were cremated. Jordanus did not describe the funerals of the poor, but he did witness the custom of sati, which was also noted in some detail by Ibn Battuta. The widows who entered their husbands' funeral pyres 'with joy as if they were going to their wedding', observed the Dominican friar, were the most respected among the women who performed sati. He wrote of funerals he attended where as many as five wives of the dead man entered the fire at the same time.

Jordanus was also the first European to meet and observe the Parsi community of India along the coast of Gujarat and the northern Konkan region. Speaking of the different kinds of funerals in the subcontinent, he talked of these people who neither burnt nor buried their dead but cast them into massive towers without roofs, where carrion birds would eat the bodies. Jordanus had many discussions with the Parsis, and learnt of the Zoroastrian faith from them. Apparently, he did not meet the indigenous Zoroastrians of Persia during his stay there and was thus unfamiliar with the religion in its land of birth.

The Dominican also met the Dumbri, people of the 'Dom' caste, who worked at cemeteries, did menial labour and ate the flesh of carcasses. The Doms of Jordanus's time did not have a deity of their own, at least none that he could come to know of. But he was aware of their subservient position relative to others.

In general, Jordanus formed very favourable impressions of the people of western India, commending the cleanliness of their feeding habits. They were truthful and honest in their public dealings, whether it was with strangers or among their own. Justice and fairness were important virtues for them. It was also a stratified society, and the people took care to preserve these distinctions which they had inherited from their ancestors. The Dominican did not note much else about the caste system, such as specifics about the varna hierarchy or endogamy within castes.

Most Indians were idol worshippers, although Jordanus found that Muslims had made considerable inroads from Sindh just prior to his arrival. He wrote of numerous Hindu temples and Syrian Christian churches which had been destroyed or converted into mosques.

Jordanus seems to have visited many Hindu temples and held discussions with the priests about their beliefs. The discussions were amicable and instructive enough for him. The most common Hindu method of making offerings to the gods was presided over by a priest dedicated to an idol. The priest usually had a designated assistant for his tasks. The priest would then advance with the eatable offerings on a tray which would be adorned with lit incense sticks, and place one of them on an outstretched hand of the idol. The priest would then eat a part of the remaining offerings.

Jordanus was fascinated by the multitude of Hindu gods and their forms, and the kinds of idols worshipped in the land. But above all these gods, there was supposed to be a single, all-powerful deity, according to what he was told by his sources. Jordanus was also told by Hindu scholars that the age of the world, by their reckoning, was 28,000 years, which was considerably lower than what the Puranas composed in the Middle Ages hold, but was still longer than the same according to biblical reckoning.

Jordanus found the Hindus welcoming towards Christian missionaries and never feared for his safety while preaching among them. In fact, missionaries would be treated with warmth and respect by Hindus across the land, and their safety would be ensured. Whenever a Hindu chose to be baptized, the people or the authorities would not create any hindrance or persecute either the convert or the missionary. This freedom, said the Dominican, was common to Hindu and Mongol societies and among other people east of Persia in his time.

Across the subcontinent, the one constant of practised Hinduism was the sacredness of cattle of both genders. While all Hindus honoured cattle like their own parents, most also worshipped them with the reverence seen for their gods. In most regions, the act of slaughtering cattle was considered as terrible a crime as parricide. A person who had murdered five men was more likely to receive a mitigated sentence than someone who had killed a cow. The status of cattle derived from their role in virtually every aspect of these societies, from agriculture to sources of dairy products, but whereas the cow was important for all agricultural societies in the known world, in India, cattle were the economic basis of the entire society and therefore crucial. Eminent men from the nobility or royalty would, before beginning their daily activities, await visits from the fattest cows in the area, touch the animals and then rub their faces with their hands in the belief that this act, at the beginning of the day, would shield them from disease.

Jordanus also observed something curious enough for him to write it down: Indians' attitude towards skin colour. For the darker the complexion of a man or woman, the more beautiful and respectable he or she was considered. Seventy years prior to Jordanus, William of Rubruck had noticed a similar belief among the Mongols, among whom women with the flattest noses were considered the most attractive.

Somewhere along the Saurashtra coast or in northern Konkan, Jordanus was told of a prophecy the Indians had: that the Latin Christians would, one day, rule the world. It was an isolated remark, and Jordanus merely mentioned it in passing. Nor does the Church appear to have noticed it or found it significant in any way. The idea that the West, or Western Christians, would have political domination over the world would not have been important for Europeans in the fourteenth century. But the question about the source of this 'prophecy' remains. Indians could hardly have been expected to be familiar with Latin Christianity, which had arrived in the subcontinent only three decades previously. It is possible that Muslim accounts of the Crusades and confrontations with European forces had percolated into India and the Hindus had responded to Muslim invasions by finding, in the Latin Christians of these stories, either allies or benefactors. In either case, Jordanus did not make much of the prophecy but merely noted it and moved on.

The Dominican's impressions of India's indigenous Christians were mixed. There were indeed Syrian communities in Gujarat and the north Konkan, which had churches where Jordanus visited. But he also found isolated and very fragmented communities of a people about whom he could not make much sense. They told him that they too were Christians. But beyond that declaration of faith, they appear to have had absolutely no knowledge of Christian beliefs and had not been baptized. On further inquiry, Jordanus was told they believed that the apostle Thomas had actually been Christ. It is possible that these were still surviving heterodox Syrian Christians who, starting from the docetic idea of Christ and Thomas being twins, had conflated the two figures over the centuries. Jordanus was quite certain that these were not Syrian Christians, so there might have been multiple schisms over the years due to doctrinal disagreements about which there is little historical record.

On the Gujarat coast and the region north of today's Mumbai, with slow labour, Jordanus baptized 300 Syrian Christians, Hindus and Muslims before crossing the Narmada into Greater India. By then Jordanus had already collected enough material, 'down to the worms', which would have taken him a year just to narrate. Sailing down the southern Konkan Coast to Malabar, Jordanus found that although there was this long-standing geographical division between the two Indias, there was not much to distinguish the people in terms of appearance. They were not as distinct from each other as the Indians in general were from the Persians. The wildlife too was similar, although he immediately noted the presence of the elephant, which was to be found in great numbers in the Deccan.

The Dominican was quite impressed with the size, majesty and intelligence of the pachyderms and noted how they were employed in tasks of great significance, or in battle, where they had a fearsome reputation. Apart from his specific interests in the humanities, Jordanus was familiar with warfare in general, and said that till his time in India, he had always held that there were two things an army could not protect itself against

By the time Jordanus crossed the Narmada into south India, he had more material than he could write about in a year

on the field: lightning bolts (being forces of nature) and siege equipment. The elephant, with armoured tusks and men mounted atop on howdahs, was the third such irresistible force he had ever seen: well-trained and docile, following the commands of the mahouts, an animal that could not be compared with any other in the world. Among the other marvellous animals found in southern India were flying squirrels and bandicoots, and Jordanus also observed that there was more variety among birds in the Deccan than in the north and west.

The Lakshadweep Islands and Sri Lanka were included in the definition of Greater India. On Silem (Sri Lanka) were to be found the greatest variety of gems, precious stones and pearls. Between the Indian coast and Sri Lanka, for three months in a year, fishermen would go out in boats numbering more than 8000 and dive for pearls.

The king of Sri Lanka was a powerful man whose wealth derived from this trade in precious stones and spices such as cinnamon, and his personal collection of gems was astounding. In particular, he had two very large rubies, one of which he wore as a pendant on his neck and the other on a ring on one of his fingers. The king was in the habit of touching his face and rubbing his beard with the ruby, for no particular reason that Jordanus was able to understand, but he found it an impressive sight nonetheless. The rubies of Sri Lanka caused a great deal of astonishment to another traveller during the same period. Ibn Battuta, on finding a large ruby carved into a saucer, which the king used for keeping aloe oil, expressed his amazement, at which the king told him it was not a great matter, because he had many rubies far bigger than that.[6]

Jordanus did not venture into Greater India beyond Sri Lanka, but he did hear of other marvellous and even fantastic places beyond the sea, such as an island whose people were completely naked and were said to use gold dust as money. But Jordanus was also dedicated to the scientific method and mentioned that he had never been to these fantastic places but only heard of them.

East of Sri Lanka was the great island of Jaua (Java), which had its own share of wonders. Jordanus was no historian of the spice trade, but he did confirm that the finest spices known in the West, excluding pepper, actually came not from India but from Java. In discovering this he came very close to understanding the origin of most of the spices barring pepper which were sold from India to the merchants of Egypt.

But Java was not just the home of the best spices, the place of origin of clove and nutmeg trees. There was a part of it where islanders would capture, kill and eat visitors, particularly if they were fair-skinned and fat—a very specific culinary preference, but Jordanus was unable to find out why.

In what is now the state of Kerala, the inheritance laws of the residents were also a subject of inquiry for the Dominican. The sons of the household, even of high nobility or royalty, would not inherit the parents' wealth. This would instead go to the sons of the daughters. The reason for this system, Jordanus was told, was the uncertainty about a man being the biological father of a child, but there could be no doubt about the woman.

There was also the custom of voluntary sacrifice among the Hindus. If a person were to suffer misfortune or a serious illness, he would seek deliverance from a god. If he became well again, he would start eating food to fatten himself up over a year or two. During a festival, the man would proceed to the temple decked in flowers and wearing a crown of white flowers, following the idol while it was carried in a procession through the streets. The man and others like him would participate in the procession carrying long two-handed swords, and at the end of the procession, after participating in the singing and dance, would cut his own head off from the back of the neck. Such customs were observed on the Malabar Coast and as far off as Cambodia by other travellers, including Ibn Battuta.

Jordanus also found that the length of the days and nights were more equal this far south in the subcontinent. Stars could be seen in multitudes and the night sky, he said, was several times clearer than anywhere in the West. In short, southern India was a good place for an astronomer to study the heavens.

The land was too vast not to still have legends and fables of fantastic creatures. But for Jordanus the true wonders of India were the people and societies he met and the natural world he discovered. There were snakes of all varieties, and a kind of termite with teeth so hard it could bite through the strongest wood and was even said to chew through stone; wasps that hunted large spiders, and a particularly villainous species of kite which seemed to subsist entirely on fish it would snatch out of the hands of fishermen. What mythical creatures could compete with a real world as diverse and marvellous as this?

But there was also India Tertia, far across the ocean in eastern Africa, and although Jordanus never travelled there, he heard of the many wonders in that land: fantastic creatures, including the giant roc, a bird that could carry away an elephant in its talons. The friar's source for this was some person he met at Kollam who claimed he had actually seen the bird. India Tertia was also the home of the true unicorn: no mere rhinoceros, but the actual creature of legend. Somewhere between the Third India and Ethiopia was the Garden of Paradise with its four famed rivers.

Jordanus did meet people from eastern Africa at Indian ports and learnt of African natives who regularly hunted, on foot with primitive weapons, leopards and even lions. And he heard of a strange kind of wild ass with black-and-white stripes all over its body, which he said must be very beautiful to look at. Somewhere in the vast sea between the Second and Third Indias were islands populated solely by women, or by men, and the men could not live for extended periods on the islands of women, and conversely. But for about a fortnight a year they could visit, and from these, children would be born, and segregated by gender to the respective islands. Even more marvellous were some islands where the men had the heads of dogs, but the women were said to be very beautiful. This seems to be a retelling of visitors' impressions of the Andaman Islands, whose native men according to Marco Polo had a decidedly canine appearance.

And there are other lands about which Jordanus heard from his sources in India: of north-eastern Arabia, a barren land chiefly known for myrrh; of the Ethiopian highlands; and of Central Asia, which by then had become very famous because of the Mongols. The Yuan dynasty in China, he said, ruled over a land four times as vast as France and very well-populated. There were at least 200 cities in that empire, each equalling the population of Toulouse. The people of that land were famed for their cleanliness, good manners, courtesy and hospitality to strangers.

It was a rich and fertile country, with an indigenous religion which had monastic orders, sermons and pontiffs who wore red hats. By the time of Jordanus, Buddhism had disappeared from almost the entire subcontinent. If it had persisted, it would be interesting to know what Jordanus would have made of them and their doctrine, instead of hearing from occasional sources about Chinese Buddhism.

And there were yet other lands stretching to the north and west: the Black Sea coast and mountainous northern Mesopotamia. There was, truly, no end to the places that could be visited. But Jordanus stayed on in India, and preached in the north and south. From his travels would emerge the monumental *Mirabilia Descripta*, arguably the most detailed account of India in the Middle Ages, in which he recorded his impressions of the land, pausing to explain to his prospective readers that he was trying to summarize his observations because there was just so much to tell.

In 1328, Jordanus travelled back to Europe through Sultanieh, and his reputation and travels in India preceded him. Pope John XXII expressed admiration for the friar's work, and in August 1329, announced that Kollam, where Jordanus had been based for around five years before he left India, would be the seat of the first Latin Christian bishopric in that land. Jordanus was appointed the Bishop of Kollam, tasked with the responsibilities of the Latin Church for the entire subcontinent and reporting to the Archbishop of Sultanieh.

Through the work of Giovanni Montecorvino nearly forty years earlier and of Jordanus, the Church had become intimately aware of the long history of Syrian Christians in India. Accordingly, the papal bull titled *Venerabili Fratri Jordano* which confirmed the appointment of Jordanus was addressed not only to the Latin Christians of India, but also to Syrian Christians, urging that the ancient schism between the two Eastern and Western denominations be repaired.[7]

The beginnings of the Latin Church in India in the late thirteenth and early fourteenth centuries were therefore amicable enough, in part because of the willingness of the Avignon popes to consider their responsibilities to non-Latin Christians as well as non-Christians, but principally because of the nature of the people who brought Western Christianity to India. Giovanni Montecorvino, the founder, and Jordanus Catalani, the first Latin Bishop of India, were not just men of probity and virtue; they were also students of the human condition, willing to understand and empathize with the people among whom they lived regardless of their denomination or faith. It is not surprising that while Jordanus was accepted by the Hindus, Giovanni lived for the rest of his life to considerable acclaim among the Chinese. The people of both lands in turn were accepting of Latin Christian missionaries and accommodated this new denomination of a faith already present among them. The papal bull was a sign of the optimism that accompanied the missionaries to the East.

The Courts of the Morning

As Jordanus was travelling down the western Indian coast, far to the north, the Delhi Sultanate was passing through another dynastic change. Khusro Khan, a general of Alauddin Khilji, had killed one of the sons of the sultan and usurped power in 1320. The other Delhi nobles then invited Ghazi Malik, the Turkic governor of Punjab, who defeated Khusro and became sultan of Delhi in the same year. With the throne, he acquired a new name: Ghiyath al-Din Tughluq. In 1325, he was succeeded by his son Muhammad, who would become the longest-ruling sultan of the Tughluq dynasty and would host Ibn Battuta, who passed a restive six years with the erratic monarch before leaving for the Yuan court as an ambassador of Muhammad.[1]

Odoric of Pordenone, a Franciscan born in north-eastern Italy, was around thirty years old when he began his travels to the East in 1316. He was not as well educated as Jordanus or William of Adam, and his approach to gathering information cannot be compared to Sanudo's. He accepted a lot of the myths and fantastic stories of the East as the literal truth, making it necessary to be critical about a lot of his account. His travels were, nevertheless, an impressive feat.

Travelling east from Italy, passing through the Byzantine Empire and Armenia, where he saw from a distance Mt Ararat, the fabled resting place of Noah's Ark, Odoric reached Tabriz in the Ilkhanate of Persia. The Franciscans had two houses in that city by then. From Tabriz, Odoric travelled to Sultanieh, a journey which took him ten days. Odoric then joined a caravan headed for Lesser India, reaching the city of Cassan (now Kashan in Isfahan province) in central Iran. This too was part of biblical geography, being considered the home of the Three Magi. Odoric calculated that the distance from Cassan to Bethlehem would take at least fifty days to cover and marvelled at how the three wise men had made that journey so quickly on hearing of the birth of Christ.

Passing through eastern Mesopotamia in a caravan bound for India, Odoric went east along the Persian Gulf coast and after many days reached Hormuz, from where he sailed to India. The Shatt al-Arab in south-eastern Iraq was called 'Near India' by the locals, although it was quite far from where Persia transitioned into India. The Arab historian al-Masudi, writing in the tenth century, had mentioned that in the pre-Islamic period, this region, which now has Basra and its suburbs, was simply called 'The Land of India'. It is possible that this name came about because, being a departure point by sea to the subcontinent, for the people of Mesopotamia it was literally a gateway to India.

From Hormuz, Odoric travelled down the Persian Gulf on a ship made entirely of wood called a 'jase' (from 'jahaz', Persian and later Urdu and Hindi for 'ship') on a voyage of twenty-eight days along the coast to Thane. The legend common among Europeans in Persia was that Thane was the capital of King Porus of Antiquity, who had fought Alexander at the Battle of Hydaspes. The historical Porus had actually ruled Punjab and had no connection with the northern Konkan, but by the early fourteenth century, there was a conscious attempt by Europeans to connect great cities of medieval India with those of Antiquity about which they had read.

Odoric found himself immediately surrounded by the strange and the marvellous. He noted the presence of rats so big that they could only be hunted by dogs because cats were not up to the task. And he observed a peculiar wedding ceremony among the locals. Indian women, he said, were in the habit of going about virtually unclothed. At weddings, the groom and bride would sit on a horse and would wear almost nothing except tall hats on their heads adorned with white flowers. The groom would hold a knife to the bride's throat, and accompanied by women singing and dancing, the procession would head for the groom's house. The Franciscan did not record the name of the community which practised this ritual.

Odoric arrived in Thane sometime in 1321, shortly after the martyrdom of the four companions of Jordanus. His account of the final moments of the martyrs included many miracles of which he came to hear, including how the Franciscans emerged unscathed from a fire after they had been cast into it, and how they were put to death by the authorities afterwards.[2]

But Odoric also heard of a singular epilogue to the incident. One of the administrators of Thane, who had been instrumental in the execution of the four Europeans, dreamt of the martyrs arrayed in bright clothes and armed with swords. On waking up and asking the qadi for advice, he was told to perform an act of charity, so the remaining Christians of Thane who had been arrested—Jordanus presumably among them—were freed. That administrator, or malik, later ordered four mosques to be built in honour of the martyrs, Odoric was told.

Meanwhile, Sultan Ghiyath al-Din Tughluq in Delhi himself heard of the Thane martyrs, and ordered the malik to be arrested and brought north to the capital and severely interrogated. The malik told Ghiyath al-Din that the Europeans had blasphemed against the Prophet and had to be put to death. The sultan retorted that the malik and the Muslim clerics should have seen, from the miracles during the execution, that these were holy men of God who should not have been harmed. The sultan then ordered the execution of the malik and his family. The qadi of Thane, on hearing of this, fled the city and was never heard of again.

This was a satisfactory end to the story of the Four Martyrs, and one that was heard and circulated in Europe to a considerable degree when Odoric's account of his travels reached his native land. The needs of justice had been met by an Eastern potentate, Muslim though he might have been. Satisfying, but unconvincing. Ghiyath al-Din had been on the throne of Delhi for less than a year by then, and was trying to stabilize a perilous position while planning a re-enactment of the campaigns of Alauddin Khilji. His reign was marked by near-continuous campaigns in the Deccan (where his son and eventual successor defeated the Kakatiya Kingdom of Warangal) and Bengal. The distance from Delhi to Thane was 1400 km over restive territory. It is unlikely that Ghiyath al-Din, veteran of the Battle of Amroha, suspicious of the Ilkhanate and the Mongols in general, would have taken a particular interest in the martyrdom of four European

Christians from Persia and executed the malik of a key port, regardless of the miracles he might have heard of.

But this account by Odoric also contains information about the Syrian Christians in Thane, for the Franciscan said there were fifteen households of the community in that city during his visit.

On hearing of the martyrs, Odoric went to their grave at Suppara and dug up the bodies, intending to take them back to Europe. During his travels, he believed he was an eyewitness to several miracles caused by the martyrs' relics. In an unidentified town north of the Narmada, while the Franciscan was sleeping at the house of an Indian, some Muslims, alleged Odoric, set fire to the place. While the rest of the house burnt down, Odoric clutched the relics and the roof above him held till he could safely escape, after which the entire structure collapsed. Later, as he travelled down the coast to Kollam, his ship was becalmed after the wind died, and the captain told Odoric bluntly that if they got no wind in their sails, he would personally throw the martyrs' bones into the sea. Odoric and a companion then prayed, and cast one of the bones into the waters, after which a wind arose and drove the ship to Kollam.

Odoric, unlike Jordanus, William or Giovanni, was quick to see a Muslim conspiracy behind his travails, and quicker still to see divine intervention when he was saved. Neither a scholar at heart nor as well educated as the other missionaries, he also found it difficult to forget that the Syrians of India were schismatics who subscribed to Nestorian ideas. In fact, for him schismatics were not too different from heretics or non-Christians. As for understanding local customs and beliefs, he was quick to condemn the unfamiliar or view the exotic with distaste. But barring the arson, and the threat of losing his holy cargo, Odoric could not claim that the Syrians of India or the Hindus were ungracious hosts or troubled him in his journeys. In this, at least, he agreed with his preceding Latin missionaries.

Despite his flaws as a chronicler, Odoric did make an effort at recording the sights he saw, and these provide a very detailed picture of India and Latin Christianity on its arrival in the East.

From Kollam, after collecting the head of Thomas of Tolentino from the Latin mission there, Odoric sailed south to what he calls the 'empire' of Malabar, where he found a forest, stretching over a journey of eighteen days, in which pepper grew. Along the coast were two cities named Flandrina and Cynglin. Flandrina had a large number of Christians and Jews, and there was frequently civil war between the two communities, and of course the Christians would always win. The two cities have not been conclusively identified. While the Jews of Malabar must have been more numerous in that period than later, there is no record of any city in India where Jews and Christians were ever at war with each other, or with Hindus.

Odoric added to the growing European awareness of two uniquely Indian practices: cow worship and sati. Cattle were made to work for six years, and in the seventh year, they would be retired from all labour and set free at a designated public spot in towns and villages across the land. The animals would then be treated with veneration.

Each morning, wealthy Indians would take two basins, one of gold and the other of silver, and in this would collect the urine and dung of cows. They would then wash their faces with the cow urine and mark the middle of their foreheads, their cheeks and the middle of the chest with the dung. This act, the Indians believed, meant they were ritually purified for the day, and so great was its significance that everyone from common people to royalty would do it.

Odoric also came across an idol which was part-man and part-bull, which was believed to speak and utter commands and required the blood of no less than forty virgins. Odoric was told that many Indians promised their own sons and daughters to this god.

The Franciscan also discovered that if a woman had living sons when her husband died, she could choose not to commit sati. If a man's wife died, however, the man was not required to die in her funeral pyre and could marry again, which he more often than not did. Odoric condemned sati in strong terms and classed it among the more terrible things he saw in the East.

But he also found that it was more usual for women to drink alcohol of all kinds than for the men among the Indians, and the women would often be seen with their foreheads shaved, while most men preferred to grow a beard.[3]

Odoric then journeyed ten days around Malabar to the Coromandel Coast, where he found cities to rival those on the western side of the subcontinent. At Mylapore, he visited the church over the site of the martyrdom of Thomas the apostle, a building filled with statues built by Syrian Christians. He also found fifteen households of Syrians adjoining the church.

Odoric then ventured farther northwards, entering lands where Europeans had not previously reached, and came at last to a great city famed throughout India for the massive statue of a god. The idol was built of solid gold and was seated on a golden throne. The temple too was walled and roofed with gold, and the idol had a necklace of priceless gems.

The temple was a centre of pilgrimage and Hindus journeyed from far across the land to visit and pray there. The pilgrims were a no less astounding sight, for some would travel with knives stuck into their arms, and the weapon was never removed till they reached the temple, by when the arm would be quite infected.

Others would walk three steps, and on the fourth, would prostrate themselves on the ground, light an incense stick and then take three steps again. And if they had to do some work while on the pilgrimage, they would stop and mark the spot from where they had stepped aside and would return and begin the process from there when they were ready. Not surprisingly, it took a long time for these pilgrims to reach the temple.

Near this temple of gold was a lake into which pilgrims would throw offerings of precious metal and gems, and whenever the temple or the idol needed to be renovated, the people would dive for the treasure and use it to finance the project.

Once a year, the giant idol would be placed on an intricately carved chariot of proportionate size and the king and queen, accompanied by the people, would draw the chariot from the temple with songs and music, with young women singing melodious hymns to the deity. And some pilgrims would even fall before the chariot and were crushed by its wheels. Every year, at least 500 people would die in this manner at the festival.

Some of the pilgrims would announce long before the festival their intent to sacrifice themselves, and their relatives and neighbours would have a feast for them. The man would wear a necklace of five knives and be taken to the temple, where he would cut off a piece of his flesh and throw it at the deity and then kill himself, after which his body would be burnt.

Odoric would be the first medieval European to venture so far up the eastern Indian coast and witness the Rath Yatra at the temple of Jagannath in Puri, in the state of Odisha today. Accounts of the festival by Europeans of the colonial period would contribute the word 'juggernaut' to the English language. What is interesting here is Odoric's account of human sacrifice at a temple dedicated to a form of Vishnu. In succeeding centuries, the Jagannath Temple would become an important part of the Vaishnavite movement with its emphasis on mystical devotion to Vishnu and his avatars, particularly Krishna, and to other principles like vegetarianism and the absence of blood sacrifice at rituals.

From coastal Odisha, Odoric voyaged through South East Asia, passing by the islands of Indonesia, and he was the first European to identify the island of Sumatra by its name, which he calls 'Sumoltra'. He heard of cannibals in the interiors of Java and Sumatra (but not whether they still preferred the flesh of fat white men, as Jordanus was told). On the island of Java, he visited and marvelled at the great palace of the king with its steps and floors paved with gold, and was told the Yuan dynasty in China had invaded the realm several times but had been repulsed.

Passing through the land of Champa (in South Vietnam today), Odoric eventually reached China. In the cities he passed through, he met Nestorians, some Latin Christians as well as Muslims, and at one of the great cities, he entrusted the relics of the Martyrs of Thane to the Latin missionaries. He finally arrived at Khanbaliq, where the Yuan emperor lived in a palace with pillars made of gold and covered with animal fur. Odoric presented himself at the court of the emperor and stayed at Khanbaliq for three years, from c.1324 to 1327, making inquiries about the land and its people. The empire, he found, was far greater than he had ever imagined, divided into twelve provinces and very well-populated.

The Latin Church was flourishing in China, having found the people as receptive to missionaries as the Indians had been. Giovanni of Montecorvino was still alive: the founder of the Latin Church in India and China was by then eighty years old and had completed translating the Bible into Mandarin and Uighur. Other missionaries had joined him and built churches across the land and the old Franciscan was as respected by the emperor's court as by the Vatican. A year after Odoric left Khanbaliq and travelled north, Giovanni would pass away and be given a state funeral in the imperial capital, attended by the notables of the land, including the Latins and his old adversaries from the Nestorian Church. Of all the remarkable men of the Latin Church who travelled in the East, Giovanni's career would be the most legendary and successful.

Journeying through Central Asia and quite possibly visiting Tibet on the way, Odoric reached Europe towards the end of 1329 after thirteen years in the East. In Hormuz, on his way to India, Odoric had met and befriended a friar named James from Ireland, who stayed with him through the journey and the return trip. In 1330, Odoric dictated his account at a Franciscan house in Padua and finally deposited the head of the Thane martyr Thomas with the Franciscans at the latter's birthplace in Tolentino. He then travelled to Avignon to meet the pope, but became unwell. He resolved to visit his home in Pordenone, but died en route.

By then his fame had reached Pordenone and the people insisted that he be given a grand funeral on account of his travels to India and China. They also gave a present to Friar James to appreciate his travels with Odoric. As accounts of his travels were copied and read, many miracles began to be ascribed to Odoric at his tomb and he was beatified in 1755.

Odoric found the Latin Church had taken root in the East and was thriving. He also confirmed to Europeans that the Hindus and Chinese, with their diverse beliefs, were welcoming to holy men of all faiths. Perhaps it was possible for the East and the West to meet.

Eight years after Odoric died on the road to Avignon, a forty-year-old Franciscan travelled to the papal seat to meet the incumbent, Benedict XII. The Franciscan was Giovanni de Marignolli, born to a patrician family in Florence. In terms of learning, he was of the Giovanni Montecorvino mould and had taught theology at the University of Bologna.

Pope Benedict XII was at heart a scholar and in public policy a peacemaker. He preferred to spend his time writing on theological matters. Lately, the Franciscan Order had been engaged in a dispute with the Church hierarchy, pointing out that Jesus and his first followers had not been known for their ostentation and wealth. Among the most severe critics of the Church's notables was the English Franciscan philosopher and logician William of Ockham, now known for the Occam's razor principle. In the year that Marignolli travelled to Avignon, Ockham brought out his *Tractatus Contra Benedictum* against the incumbent pope. Benedict XII in turn tried to mend fences with the Franciscans, gently sparred with Ockham through his own written responses and tried to introduce reforms such as reducing instances of favouritism towards the relatives of high-ranking clergymen. Benedict also hoped for a reunion between Rome and Constantinople and was interested in the Latin missions to the East.

In 1338, the pope received a letter from Yuan Emperor Toghun Temur in Khanbaliq. Written a year earlier, it informed his Holiness that the Latin Church, although thriving, had been without a designated archbishop since the demise of Giovanni Montecorvino nearly a decade previously and that the pope should send a replacement. Among the four envoys to Khanbaliq chosen by Benedict XII was Marignolli. A group of fifty clerics in total started out from Naples and, passing through the Byzantine Empire, reached Caffa on the Black Sea.

The route they were to take was different from what had been used by the previous missionaries to China. Instead of going through the Strait of Hormuz to India, they set out overland, because they were to minister to other parts of the Mongol Empire as well, besides Yuan China.

It was a different view of the world. They spent the bitter winter of the Russian steppes at Sarai, the capital of the Golden Horde north of the Caspian Sea. Travelling east again in the spring of 1340, the papal envoys reached Chagadai Khanate territory and stayed at the city of Armalec in what is now the northern part of Xinjiang Uighur region of China. By the summer of 1342, after three and a half years of travel, Marignolli and his companions, although reduced in numbers by the difficulties of the journey, arrived at Khanbaliq.[4]

Montecorvino's legacy was still intact, and as the Yuan emperor had informed the pope, had been growing stronger. Latin missions were secure under Yuan protection. At Khanbaliq, the Franciscans had a cathedral of their own next to the emperor's palace, while the Latin archbishop had a residence suitable to his position and there were several churches around the great city. Latin clergymen still received generous stipends and other perquisites from the imperial court.[5]

Marignolli stayed at Khanbaliq for four years and grew very fond of the Chinese, not to mention the Yuan courtiers, and was pleased with their politeness and hospitality. Towards the end of 1347, Marignolli and the other papal legates started their journey back to Europe by a different route. Travelling by land for three weeks to the Strait of Taiwan, the Franciscan reached Zayton. The city had three large Franciscan churches by then, and the order had also started getting involved in business. From here he boarded a ship passing through the Strait of Malacca to India's Malabar Coast.

Marignolli made landfall at Kollam in the spring of 1348 and visited the Latin church of St George in the city, built by Jordanus, who had passed away by then. Marignolli lived in the church complex for a year and a half and found that in Malabar too, Latin Christianity was thriving and the congregation had grown in the years after Jordanus. He helped decorate the church with paintings in the then current Italian style, and also funded the construction of a marble pillar in the building, containing the emblem of Benedict XII as well as Marignolli's own seal as papal envoy, and a bilingual inscription in Latin and a local language, presumably Malayalam.

From Kollam the Franciscan sailed around Sri Lanka to Mylapore on pilgrimage to the tomb of the apostle Thomas and met the Syrian Christian community which lived around the sacred site. Marignolli discovered that the Syrians of the Malabar and Coromandel coasts were very prosperous in his time and controlled a substantial part of the spice trade on both coasts, as well as steel smelting sites. At Kollam, Marignolli had been warmly hosted by the community and had been given a lot of gifts when he left the city.

The Franciscan also met an old man who had been born a Brahmin and had sailed across both the Arabian Sea and the Bay of Bengal—apparently, caste restrictions on sea voyages were different in that period, or perhaps more relaxed. The man had then converted to Latin Christianity and was living out the rest of his days on land. Marignolli thoroughly questioned the old sailor about all the numerous fantastic islands and realms across the seas he had heard of in legend, but the man told him he had never seen any of them.

Around this time, it appears a gang of poisoners administered a strong toxin to Marignolli to steal his belongings. He survived, but was considerably weakened for nearly a year. By then he had somehow managed to visit Mylapore and complete his pilgrimage. From the Coromandel Coast he sailed to Java, where a local woman healer gave him herbal medicines and advised him to eat sparingly, and he was cured. He found Javanese society to be much different from his native land. The women were politically and financially more powerful—he was hosted and entertained by a queen—and confirmed that nobody reliable had ever seen a monster of any kind, although there were some animals which had humanoid features, possibly referring to orangutans.

On his way back to India, Marignolli also visited Sri Lanka, and of all the many wonderful places he passed through on his circuitous journey, the Florentine clergyman apparently loved the island the most.

The visit did not begin well. Almost immediately on landing at a small port, he was arrested by a local administrator, a Muslim eunuch named Khoya Jaan, who took away treasure worth the substantial amount of 60,000 marks from Marignolli under the pretext of a loan. This treasure in the form of gold, silver, silk and precious stones had included gifts from the Yuan emperor, the Latin and Syrian Christian merchants of India and the Queen of Java, and had been meant for the pope. After four months, Marignolli was released, but did not get most of the gifts back.

At the centre of the island, said Marignolli, the land rose to a mountain peak which was the closest to the Garden of Eden as any place in the world could be. The mountain, Adam's Peak, contained a footprint which Marignolli and his fellow Latins believed was of the first man. In Buddhist tradition, the footprint is of the Buddha, while for the Hindus, it is the mark of Shiva. Marignolli had very little interest in Buddhism and did not connect the Buddhists of Sri Lanka with those he had met in China. He reported that a very large statue of a seated man pointing to the distance was that of one of the biblical patriarchs, or possibly Adam himself.

Inadvertently, however, we find an interesting parallel between the monastic Christian ideal and Buddhist orders. On Adam's Peak, Marignolli found a group of men who were clearly not Christian but lived, he was happy to note, a life of temperance, chastity and simplicity. Among the Buddhist monks he had found echoes of the kind of life his fellow Franciscans back in Europe, such as William of Ockham, had been demanding of princes of the Church.

From Sri Lanka he returned to Kollam and then sailed up the Konkan Coast before turning west to Hormuz. From the great Persian Gulf port, he journeyed by land to a small town in the neighbourhood of what had once been the city of Nineveh in ancient times and then reached Edessa.

At that Syrian Christian heartland, Marignolli found the first signs of the calamity that was to fall on the Christians of the Middle East. The Ilkhanate was passing through a crisis and the rule of law had fractured. Marignolli spent four tense days there before journeying west again to Damascus. By the end of 1353, after a journey lasting fourteen years, he had reached Avignon with letters from the Yuan emperor and whatever gifts he had been able to salvage from Khoya Jaan in Sri Lanka.

Marignolli was optimistic in narrating the situation of the Latin Church in the East, as indeed he should have been. But even as he was returning to Europe, the clouds had begun gathering in the East.

Cataclysm

By the fourth decade of the fourteenth century, it appeared that Western Christianity, and by extension Europe, had established a secure presence in South and East Asia. An unprecedented degree of awareness and engagement with the Indians and Chinese had contributed to European understanding of the true size and complexity of the known world. Among the kings of Europe and the leaders of the Latin Church, it was thought that this process of engagement would become stronger and more secure as time passed.

But already the delicate balances of power which had created and contributed to this era were changing. Less than five years after Odoric left Khanbaliq and Giovanni received a state funeral, the Yuan dynasty began to be wracked by a series of convulsions within the empire. Famines and civilian unrest tested the frame of the structure created by Great Khan Qubilai and his descendants.

Indigenous Han sentiment against the Mongols found an outlet through the White Lotus Society, a millenarian Buddhist movement that, among other beliefs, expected an imminent arrival of the Buddha Maitreya and the occurrence of other events in Chinese Buddhist eschatology. This combination of nativism and religious dogma was worrying to the Mongols, who banned the group, which then went underground and proliferated. A Buddhist monk named Peng Yingyu led at least two rebellions in the 1330s, in the second of which he was killed by Yuan forces.

The White Lotus Society continued to gather more followers, who eventually adopted the signature red headgear which gave the name to what would come to be called the Red Turban Rebellion, the most successful indigenous revolt against Mongol rule in any part of the world.[1] By 1355, it was led by a charismatic and intelligent young man named Zhu Yuanzhang.

Zhu was born to a poor farmer's family in what is now Anhui Province in eastern China. When he was in his teens, drought and famine caused the death of almost his entire family. Burying them himself, Zhu became an apprentice monk and also travelled the countryside, seeing the devastation the natural disasters had caused.

When he was twenty-four, Zhu's monastery was destroyed by Yuan forces during yet another revolt in 1352, and Zhu joined the rebels. By then he was considerably well educated, and his natural intelligence combined with a keen tactical mind helped him become the leader of the rebels. In 1356, his forces captured Nanjing, which became his capital, from where the army of Yuan Emperor Toghun Temur was unable to dislodge them. Twelve years later, the Yuan emperor fled Khanbaliq to Inner Mongolia, and Zhu was victorious. Toghun Temur's descendants would retreat farther to Mongolia proper, and rule as the Northern Yuan, but Qubilai's dynasty had been ejected from China, and the Han Chinese had a native ruler once more.

Zhu Yuanzhang, or Hongwu, became the first emperor of the Ming dynasty, and instituted large-scale changes in Chinese polity. Yuan traces were removed from the military and bureaucracy, and Confucianism (albeit with detectable modifications) returned to its position of pre-eminence in the administrative structure and imperial philosophy of China.[2] But Emperor Hongwu and his successors also cracked down on those who had been seen by Han nativists as collaborators with the hated Yuan. Among them were the leaders of the Nestorian Church and the Latins. The Nestorian Church in particular, without the kind of diplomatic or missionary status which Latin preachers had in popular Han imagination, was severely hit by the advent of the Ming dynasty and gradually declined in China.

Dynastic collapse was not a new event for European kings or the Latin Church. Perhaps, at some point in the future, Ming emperors would accept another Giovanni Montecorvino. China was yet not a lost cause, although the ouster of the Yuan was a significant setback.

But the Latin Church's engagement with the East was utterly dependent on the fate of the Ilkhanate, under whose patronage Dominican and Franciscan houses had flourished at Sultanieh. And the next catastrophe occurred in Persia.

In c.1332, a new disease erupted in China. Amid the famine and unrest already sweeping the Yuan Empire, people started dying of a mysterious infection. It spread rapidly and civilian administrators proved utterly incapable of either understanding or dealing with it. Within a few years it had reached Central

Asia. Sweeping through the four divisions of the Mongol Empire, it arrived at the Crimean port of Caffa in 1347. A short while later, from Caffa and through other routes in the Mediterranean, it had reached Genoa and the Italian cities. In three more years, the whole of Europe was in the grip of the Black Death.

The plague devastated Europe, including its overcrowded cities. There was little escape in the countryside either. More than 50 per cent of the populations of England and Germany, and similar numbers in France and Italy, perished. Kings and bureaucrats proved unequal to the task of saving the people, and so did the Church. Dominican and Franciscan monks were among the hardest hit, because the mendicant orders stayed on in the ravaged cities and villages to tend to the sick and the dying, and themselves perished.[3]

The Black Death was among the most fearsome pandemics that have stalked the earth in recorded history, killing anywhere between 70 million and 200 million people. The Plague of Justinian in the sixth century which had stalked the Byzantine and Sassanid empires had been terrible, as Church annals revealed to those who cared to look into them 800 years later. But the world was much more closely connected in the fourteenth century than it had ever been before and no land, however mighty, prosperous or god-fearing, was spared. It would remain the deadliest pandemic ever, till Spanish influenza swept the globe in the aftermath of World War I.

In China, famine, other diseases and the Black Death killed nearly 20 million people. How much of this was directly because of the Black Death may perhaps never be known, but the pandemic certainly first occurred there. Arab chroniclers, themselves desperately trying to survive the plague when it hit the Middle East, would record that India was devastated, like Central Asia and Europe.

Curiously, there is very little evidence of the Black Death in India in that period. Plagues did turn up in the country at different periods: it was too well connected with global commerce in the Middle Ages and had far too many busy international ports to avoid the entry of deadly diseases. In the seventeenth century, during the reign of Mughal Emperor Shahjahan, a pneumonic plague pandemic swept the Deccan after arriving at Gujarat and the Malabar Coast. But, judging from the absence of any mention in Delhi Sultanate records, the Black Death, for reasons yet to be understood, did not quite reach India in the fourteenth century. It is possible that chroniclers at other places, on getting news of the devastation in Europe and China, assumed India too had been affected.

Long before the Black Death crippled the secular and ecclesiastical structure of Europe, it had arrived in Persia, where city after prosperous city, port after port, reeled under the deaths or flight of thousands of residents. In 1335, Abu Said, the sixth Ilkhan of Persia, descendant of Chinggis, contracted the plague and died at thirty-one years of age, and so did several of his sons. The eventual successor, Arpa Keun, ruled for barely a year before he was killed in a revolt by the governor of Baghdad. Persia descended into anarchy and civil war as the different noble houses of the Ilkhanate fought for supremacy.[4]

The dynasty that had been the most stable patron of Western Christianity in Asia was gone. The position of the missionaries of Sultanieh became increasingly precarious amid the bloodshed across Persia.

The Nestorian Church was no less affected. The small communities of Eastern Christians that lived along the Silk

Road from Khanbaliq through Central Asia to Tabriz, Hormuz and Sultanieh withered and died as the plague went through them. In the cities of Mesopotamia and Syria, such as venerable old Edessa, among the piles of the dead were the cream of the Nestorian Church.

Death had always been a constant in the Middle Ages. As Pestilence and Plague rode through Eurasia, the Fourth Horseman, said the wise, would surely not be far behind.

Timur was born in Kesh, a city some 80 km from the great Silk Road trading centre of Samarkand in what is now Uzbekistan. He was from a Mongol tribe, but not of the line of Chinggis. By all accounts a brilliant general and leader, he would embark on a campaign of conquest that sought to emulate Chinggis himself.

Despite all the great deeds he would accomplish, and the devastation he sowed in Eurasia, Timur truly desired two things which he knew he could never hope to gain. He wanted to be a khan, perhaps even a Great Khan, for that is what Chinggis, Mongke and Qubilai had been. But he was not a descendant of any of the four sons of Chinggis, so he could never be called 'khan'. Instead, he had to be content with the title of 'emir' or general, in which capacity he served the increasingly marginalized Chagadai khans at the beginning of his career. Eventually, he would reduce them to figureheads and rule as he pleased, but he could never quite be a second Chinggis. He tried to get close to the mantle of the Chinggisids by marrying a princess from the well-populated dynasty, thus becoming a Chinggisid son-in-law. Such were the rules of the world, and even he could not break them.

But Timur was also a Muslim, and he desired the greatest prize the House of Islam possessed: to be Caliph of the

Faithful. The general was to be denied that as well, for he was not a descendant of the Qureish tribe to which the Prophet had belonged and from which all caliphs were supposed to be chosen. To compensate for this, Timur began styling his campaigns as true jihad, as wars of conquest for the greater glory of the Faith, as victories that would rival and outdo the long-ago achievements of the Umayyads. He would persist with this fiction even as he slaughtered his way through the Muslims of Asia.[5]

By the early 1380s, Timur controlled Central Asia and all the former Chagadayid dominions. He then invaded the eastern part of the Ilkhanate, long ago lost to any of the feuding factions of Persia. His methods were as brutal as any of the Chinggisids: the city of Herat, now in western Afghanistan, was utterly destroyed. By 1384, Timur had reached Sultanieh and two years later, he had taken Tabriz.

Meanwhile, the warlords of the Golden Horde in what is now Russia, with whom he had a reasonably amicable relationship at the beginning, turned on him and Timur invaded the north, advancing so far that his soldiers objected, saying the days and nights were of completely different lengths than in the rest of the world and they could not keep track of the times for namaz. By 1391, he had defeated the Golden Horde and was master of most of Russia. By the middle of the 1390s, Timur ruled over Chagadai, Golden Horde and Ilkhanate lands and his dream of reuniting the domains of Chinggis was well on its way.

Timur saw symbolism in many of his acts, and was conscious of how history would record him. He went to extraordinary lengths for this. His chroniclers steadfastly claimed that he had been born in 1335–6, when evidence now indicates he was born in the previous decade. But 1335–6 was significant:

by claiming birth in the year that the last great Ilkhan, Abu Said—a Muslim like him but also a descendant of Chinggis—passed away, Timur could, or so he thought, claim he was in truth an inheritor of the Chinggisid legacy.

In 1397, Timur did what even Chinggis had not come around to doing—he led a full-scale invasion of India. Nasir-ud-Din Mahmud Shah Tughluq had been ruling the Delhi Sultanate for four years by then. The sultanate was a shadow of what it had been under Ghiyath al-Din or Muhammad bin Tughluq, and whatever remained was wracked by civil war between Turkic factions. A far cry from the time of Alauddin Khilji and the Battle of Amroha.

Timur's army swept through the breakaway principalities of Punjab, capturing Multan and Lahore. The emir then arrived at the gates of Delhi. Nasir-ud-Din Tughluq, as with any Indian king worth his name, had elephants—those animals which had seventy years earlier so impressed Jordanus. Surely there was no army that could resist war elephants. But Timur was the Fourth Horseman, so he heaped bales of straw on camels, set them on fire and sent the animals charging into the ranks of the Tughluqid elephants, which stampeded and fled the field. So did the Sultan of Delhi with his retinue.

Timur entered Delhi, and his men took the spoils of the greatest city in South Asia. But a section of Delhi's citizens, outraged at the loot, revolted and killed Timurid soldiers. Perhaps they had not been told of what had befallen the people of Herat and the Persian cities. Over three days, Timur's men slaughtered the people of Delhi and left piles of heads around the stricken city, before ransacking it again and returning west across the Indus. Delhi would not fully recover till the beginning of the sixteenth century. Nasir-ud-Din somehow managed to retain his throne for fifteen more years, after which the Tughluqs were ousted from power.[6]

The indefatigable Timur, who was quite advanced in years by then, had other places to go and conquer. Two years after the sack of Delhi, he was in Armenia and Georgia, depopulating both Christian lands and claiming the title of 'ghazi' or holy warrior. He then invaded Mamluk dominions in Syria, sacked Damascus and Aleppo and, in a nod to Mongke and Hulagu, sacked Baghdad and slaughtered its residents.

In 1402, Timur turned his attention to Bayezid, sultan of the Ottoman Empire, and invaded Anatolia, defeating Bayezid at the Battle of Ankara. The Ottoman ruler was captured and died a prisoner. The Byzantines in Constantinople got a very slight breathing space from the Ottoman advance towards them.

European rulers, still recovering from the plague, were in two minds about what to make of Timur. On the one hand, he had defeated the Ottomans, who had been shaping into a very potent threat to Constantinople and the West. On the other hand, the old emir was known for leaving cities considerably denuded of human life when he captured them, and had defeated some of the mightiest kingdoms of that period. Even Hulagu and the Mongols had not been able to give such a bloody nose to the Mamluks of Egypt. Despite his slaughter of Christians in the Middle East and Armenia, the Europeans sent tentative diplomatic feelers to him.

Timur, as he surveyed his empire, was conscious of just one more campaign which was necessary to make him the equal of Chinggis. The greatest prize of them all was still outside his grasp. In his twilight years, the emir set out to take the Mongol heartland and China. The Ming Empire had not been polite to him. In 1394, Emperor Hongwu, the novice monk who had toppled the Yuan dynasty had, in broad terms, told Timur to accept Ming overlordship. Timur knew how to respond to that. But in 1405, as he set out to invade China, he died at Otrar, the old city which Chinggis had sacked 200 years earlier, and whose governor Inalchuq had been fed molten gold.

Timur's genocidal legacy and the vast numbers of people his armies slaughtered from India to Anatolia hides the many small communities which became extinct in the wake of his campaigns. The Nestorian Christians of the Silk Road, already devastated by the plague, were summarily put to the sword on the orders of the great ghazi. Nestorian churches and prominent Christian centres in Persia and Mesopotamia were brought down, the prelates executed along with the other residents of the hapless cities. Within a few decades, as a combined result of the Black Death, the fall of the Yuan dynasty and, particularly, the campaigns of Timur, the Nestorian Church had gone from being the most widespread branch of Christianity to surviving only in a few pockets of northern Mesopotamia.

Across the Arabian Sea, however, the Nestorian Church endured in the Malabar Coast. The Eastern Christians of India had roots that were too deep to be affected by the cataclysm in the Middle East and Central Asia. While it was true that in Syria, the heart of Eastern Christianity, the community never recovered its former position, Indian Christians far from the shadow of Timur were to continue as in the centuries before.

The Latin Christians of Persia suffered as well. The bishopric of Samarkand, which had been established in 1329, barely got a few years to expand its reach before the plague arrived, followed by Timur, who was determined to uproot

Christianity, Western or Eastern, from his capital first before ravaging the world.

The Latin archbishopric of Sultanieh, within a few decades, lost its missions in Central Asia and China. Very soon, as a wave of rulers sought to remake Persia, the old Mongol policy of a free religious market was discarded. As in China, Western Christianity was no longer welcome in Persia. And once Sultanieh ceased to be the centre from where missionaries could venture East by land and sea, Europe's direct engagement with India and China, too, ebbed.

The Vatican continued to appoint archbishops for Sultanieh, but after Timur, it seemed to be a futile gesture. Certainly there were no more bishops for Kollam or Samarkand, or archbishops for Khanbaliq, and the missions there were left to fend for themselves. Of these only the Indian mission, which was not facing direct persecution or a nativist uprising unlike that in China or Central Asia, could have survived without guidance from the West, at least for a little while longer. In time, the Latin Christians would be subsumed in the larger Syrian Christian community of the Malabar Coast.

By 1450, with the resurgent Ottomans at the gates of Constantinople, Europe's last direct links to Asia were on the verge of being lost. That year, Pope Nicholas V formally declared that the archbishopric of Sultanieh was no longer a residential see but a titular one. Archbishops would continue to be appointed, but only in name, and the appointees never ventured to Persia. Yet again, the West had retreated. In 1926, the titular archbishopric too was suppressed.

The Colonial
Period

Swearing by a Bent Cross

On the morning of 3 February 1509, a cannon on the deck of the *Flor do Mar*, a 400-ton carrack, fired a single shot at the mouth of Diu harbour, signalling the start of one of the most significant battles in naval history. On the deck of the carrack stood Dom Francisco de Almeida, viceroy of Portuguese possessions in India. Under his command were nine carracks and nine other ships with 800 Portuguese men and around 400 Nairs from the Malabar port of Kochi. Ranged against them were 450 Mamluk soldiers and sailors from Egypt in ten carracks, six galleys and ten other smaller ships. Just behind this fleet were 150 small and agile war boats, on which were 5000 rowers and soldiers of the Gujarat Sultanate.

The subcontinent was passing through yet another post-imperial upheaval, with the attendant chaos and flux that occurred in such periods. The Sultanate of Delhi was ruled by the Afghan Lodhi dynasty. The sultanate was not what it had been under Alauddin Khilji or Muhammad bin Tughluq, and was limited to the Indo-Gangetic plain and Sindh. The reigning sultan, Sikandar Lodhi, was content with strengthening the kingdom's finances and writing poetry. The Hindu Rajputs of Rajasthan were independent and free to feud among themselves over territories too insignificant in the global scheme of things, while south and east of Sindh, the Sultanate of Gujarat ruled over the ports of western India. Nearly 1600 km north of Diu, in Kabul, a twenty-six-year-old descendant of Timur named Zahir-ud-Din, more famously known as Babur, was trying to retain control of the city he had conquered five years earlier. The Mughal Empire was some distance in the future.

By 1509, Portuguese ships had seriously disrupted commerce between India, Persia and Egypt. Portuguese carracks were better armed with stronger cannon, and their soldiers and crew had muskets, placing other navies at a definite disadvantage. And the Portuguese actively sought to engage with merchant ships not under their control, or with any armed adversaries in the Arabian Sea. The Mamluks were getting alarmed at the loss of revenue.

So were the Venetians, who depended directly on trade with the Mamluks and the Ottoman Empire. The Venetians suggested a naval expedition against the upstart Portuguese, a request which was also made by the Zamorin of Calicut (Kozhikode) on the Malabar Coast, whose ships had been repeatedly attacked by the Portuguese. In an echo of William of Adam's idea, the Venetians helped assemble ships in the Red Sea for the Mamluks. The fleet's commander was the Kurd Amir Hussain, and they sailed out on the Red Sea in November 1505—over 1100 Turks, Venetians and Mamluks. While the ships had guns similar to the Portuguese fleets', the soldiers had only bows and arrows, which would be a crucial tactical disadvantage. Two years later, the multinational expedition reached Diu, where they were welcomed by Malik Ayyaz, governor of the Sultan of Gujarat, who was also interested in resuming trade with the Mamluks and Ottomans and getting rid of the Christian Portuguese. In the Malabar, the ruler of Kozhikode also approved of this expedition.

In March 1508, the Mamluks fought the Portuguese at Chaul (now in Raigad district in the state of Maharashtra) and won. Among the Portuguese dead was Louranco de Almeida, son of the Portuguese viceroy, who then vowed revenge. Disregarding the arrival of a new viceroy from Lisbon, Dom Francisco sailed north in December of that year, and after a game of hide-and-seek for months, met the Mamluk-Gujarat Sultanate-Venetian alliance at Diu. Also present was a contingent sent by the Zamorin, while Nair soldiers from Kochi, opposed to the Zamorin, were with the Portuguese fleet.

The Portuguese cannons and small arms prevailed against the lighter Mamluk cannons and Turkish bowmen. By the evening, almost the entire Mamluk force had been captured or killed, while Amir Hussain fled to the mainland and eventually reached Egypt. The Portuguese were left masters of the Arabian Sea, although the Mamluks would mount some attempts to regain supremacy afterwards.

The Battle of Diu marked the beginning of European control over the Arabian Sea and the Indian Ocean, which would last till the end of the colonial period in the twentieth century. The Mamluks and Ottomans were no longer the controllers of East-West trade, while the Venetians found themselves outflanked by the Portuguese and faced an uncertain economic future.[1]

A European fleet with Hindu allies from the Malabar Coast; a decisive victory of the West over a combined task force of Egyptians, Turks and even an Indian sultanate; complete mastery of the Arabian Sea and disruption of Indian maritime commerce with Aden. It was exactly what William of Adam had suggested nearly 200 years previously in the *Tractatus*, and what Marino Sanudo had said was essential if Europe were to prevail in a crusade over Egypt. There was even an Italian city state that allied with the Muslims. William would have said the Italians could still not be trusted, while Sanudo, who had decried European merchants' willingness to trade with Egypt at the cost of Jerusalem, would have perhaps been embarrassed that his own city had fought on the Mamluk side. And yet neither crusade strategist would have approved of either the Portuguese or the circumstances leading to that naval victory. They would not have felt at home among these new Europeans.

Once again, the world had changed faster than anybody could have predicted, and the Church of Rome had changed with it. Three years after the archbishopric of Sultanieh was declared temporarily defunct, the Ottoman Turks took Constantinople in 1453, ending the Byzantine Empire and the last vestiges of what had once been the Empire of Rome. In 1439, Byzantine Emperor John VIII Palaiologos negotiated a formal reunion between the Latin and Greek churches. Even at that late hour, it was opposed by the Greek clergy and people, while the response of the Latin Christian kings of Europe was lukewarm. The union was ultimately repudiated. The Ottomans took Constantinople, and Emperor Constantine XI Palaiologos, brother and successor of John, died defending it.[2]

The Middle Ages in Europe, which had begun with the demise of the Western Roman Empire in 476, ended with the fall of Constantinople. Europe now directly faced the rising Ottoman Empire. The West was as far from Jerusalem as it had been since Salah ad-Din had retaken it. Now, the armies of Islam had taken the initiative once more.

Ottoman control extended into the Mediterranean as well. All vestiges of European presence in the Middle East had gone, and the eternal trade routes from China and India now went through either the Mamluks, who still held Egypt, or the Ottomans.

By the 1450s, the Kingdom of Portugal had been raiding northern Africa and had occupied some parts of it. King Afonso V wanted these campaigns to be ratified as Crusades proper by the pope, and wanted legitimization of conquests and actions in Muslim lands, including the taking of slaves. In 1452, with the Ottomans at the gates of Constantinople, Pope Nicholas V called the Christian kings to come to the aid of the Byzantines. Afonso responded, and said Portugal would carry on the fight against the Ottomans. In exchange, Nicholas was to declare Portuguese activities as part of a just war.

Christendom appeared to be in peril, and the Portuguese seemed to be willing to defend the faith, so the pope agreed. The result was the bull known as *Dum Diversas* (Until Different). This document proclaimed that the monarchs of Spain and Portugal had complete authority to wage war on the 'enemies of Christ'—a term which the bull said included Muslims and pagans—and that the two kingdoms were free to invade, raid and occupy any territory or city held by these enemies anywhere in the world. Also, any Muslim or pagan captured in these campaigns could be legally considered a slave for all time.[3]

Dum Diversas was to fundamentally alter the way in which Spaniards and Portuguese, who were leading the Age of Exploration, interacted with the non-European people they met across the world. From that period, the explorations would carry the menace implicit in the bull. In 1454, Nicholas issued a second bull, the *Romanus Pontifex*, which expanded on the *Dum Diversas*. The Portuguese were charged with exploring the seas and finding a route to India, 'whose people are said to worship Christ', and to convince the Indians to join an alliance with Europe against the Muslims.[4] Nicholas and his advisers seem to have completely misread Church history on the situation in India, and assumed that Indians were mostly Christian. All the lands that the Portuguese would conquer on these campaigns, according to *Romanus Pontifex*, would be theirs alone and no other European Christian monarch could contest Portuguese rule in those parts.

The Portuguese explorations in Africa and later in the Indian Ocean would be accompanied by large-scale violence, the enslavement of non-Christians and their persecution and conversion, and relentless war against Muslims. The Portuguese colonies that were established in the New World and Asia afterwards would be run on the policies that emerged from this period, in an arrangement known as the 'padroado' (patronage). Under this arrangement, the Portuguese royal establishment would directly administer the Church and its components in the numerous Portuguese colonies around the world. The Portuguese Empire, therefore, would be both a temporal and religious structure, which not only practised slavery as a matter of state policy but also was committed to the war against non-Christian people. These aspects of Portuguese colonialism were a direct legacy of *Dum Diversas*, *Romanus Pontifex*, and those difficult decades in the middle of the fifteenth century.

The imperial structure that emerged from this saw the Church of Rome as a client, a subservient partner, of the

Portuguese Crown. This was unprecedented in the history of Western Christianity. When Emperor Constantine walked into the Council of Nicaea and participated as a non-voting observer of the deliberations, he was acting on the lines of a long-standing Roman imperial tradition. Roman emperors, beginning with Caesar Augustus, had attended hearings of the senate as a symbolic—and fictional—reassurance that the republic had not fallen after all. Constantine's presence at the council which shaped the official Christian creed was a reassurance that the Roman imperial structure was merely overseeing the Christian faith but would not intervene in doctrinal or theological matters. It was a very Roman attempt at balancing the requirements of religious and political structures. In the years after Constantine, when Nicene Christianity became the state religion, Roman emperors had promoted the faith at the expense of other religions, borrowing a leaf or two from the Persian imperial model, but the Church had not been considered a client in any imperial expansion projects. In the Middle Ages, the Church of Rome had periodically sought alliances with monarchs who showed imperial promise, like Charlemagne. But kings and popes had tried to work as allies in imperial ventures or crusading campaigns, on the few occasions when such campaigns did take off. Occasionally, a pope or two might have found themselves hostage to the ambitions of European kings, but these were individual incidents and never institutionalized, and their impact had remained localized.

The padroado system was significantly different from these precedents. By agreeing to allow representatives of the Church to function in Portuguese colonies under the supervision of the crown, the pope had made the Church of Rome a subservient participant in the excesses of the Portuguese Empire in Africa, Asia and the New World. This was a position with which scholars such as William of Adam would not have agreed.

The Church's legitimization of the enslavement of non-Christians, which would become an important aspect of the Spanish and Portuguese empires, was also a policy with which Christians who had lived and worked in India in the fourteenth century would not have agreed. Observing the slave trade in the Persian city of Tabriz, William had called enslavement of Christians and non-Christians alike 'the most un-Christian of acts'. By the beginning of the sixteenth century, the Roman Church was a willing participant in an imperial structure which extensively practised slavery. The very definition of Christian virtues had changed.

On the Iberian Peninsula, at the time of the fall of Constantinople, the 700-year-old Reconquista, the Christian fightback against Muslims, was drawing to a close. Generations of bitter battles against Arab and Berber armies, and complex alliances between Christian and Christian, or Christian and Muslim warlords, princelings and kings had led to the Christian Spaniards and Portuguese recovering most of the peninsula. By 1252, only the Emirate of Granada, on the southern fringe of the peninsula, remained in Muslim hands. In 1492, Queen Isabella of Castile and King Ferdinand of Aragon annexed Granada after a decade-long campaign. The Reconquista was over.

But while monarchs and dynasties can and often do replace one another, and flags can be brought down and others raised, the general populace are a different matter. The Iberian Peninsula, at the end of the Reconquista, contained a large number of Muslim and Jewish converts to Christianity. The philosophy of the Roman Church, too, had changed by the end of the fifteenth century. It now officially questioned the reliability of new converts in Iberia. Could they, perhaps, be secretly practising their former faiths? It became necessary not only to ensure the sanctity of the Christian world, but also to test the faith of newcomers. It was no longer enough to believe that arguments such as those in the *Summa Contra Gentiles* of the thirteenth-century theologian Thomas Aquinas would be enough to strengthen Christianity in the hearts of converts, or indeed among other Christians. Faith needed to be tested on the rack and by the fire.

It was a potent idea. In 1478, Ferdinand and Isabella started what would come to be called the Spanish Inquisition, under which Christians and new converts were interrogated and tortured and sometimes executed if their faith was found inadequate. In 1492 and 1502, the remaining Jews and Muslims in Spain, including those who remained in Granada, were given the stark choice—convert or leave the kingdom. The Spanish Inquisition would come to an end only in 1834, by when more than 150,000 had been tried for heresy, and more than 5000 had been executed. Although other inquisitions and investigations of heresy had existed in Europe, the Spanish Inquisition was unarguably the most extensive, the most organized and the most brutal.[5]

The Age of Exploration achieved its greatest feats with this ideological milieu in the background and never too far away. With Iberia completely under Christian rule, and with forts in North Africa such as Ceuta and Melila, the Spanish and Portuguese now manned the western fringe of the Mediterranean. Their carracks and other ships gradually improved in design and carried better, stronger cannon than the Ottomans. But holding the western Mediterranean was no strategic advantage. The Ottomans held the east, and Mamluk Egypt held the Red Sea. The keys to global commerce and prosperity were very much in Muslim hands.

Some Europeans were willing to adjust to the changed strategic climate. The Venetians continued trading with the Mamluks and Ottomans. They understood that their city's prosperity hinged on Constantinople and Alexandria being the funnels through which commerce with the East was routed to Europe.

The Spaniards and Portuguese began exploring the western African coast, convinced that if the hitherto unnavigable waters around that continent were crossed, they could, eventually, find an alternate route to the East. In 1488, Bartolomeu Dias rounded the southern tip of Africa. Four years later, the Italian Christopher Columbus, funded by Ferdinand and Isabella, accidentally discovered the New World. Six years after Columbus, in 1498, Vasco da Gama arrived in the port of Kozhikode on the Malabar Coast. Europe now had direct maritime access to the East for the first time in history.

Vasco was a product of his times, and exemplified the kind of captain that Portugal produced during the Age of Discovery, seafarers associated with or inspired by Prince Henry the Navigator. Vasco's father Estevao had been a knight with a Portuguese prince, and later governor of a city. His mother was a noblewoman whose family was descended from an English adventurer of Gloucestershire in the fourteenth century.

The Portuguese expedition comprised four ships, including Vasco's flagship, the carrack *Sao Gabriel* and the *Sao Rafael*, under his brother Paulo. The ships' composition was typical of Portuguese voyages during the Age of Discovery and afterwards, during the early colonial period: command used to be in the hands of noblemen like Vasco, while the crew consisted almost entirely of pardoned convicts or similar hard men with a lot of sailing experience. The fleet which would find a sea route to India contained no member of the clergy or scholars, no Dominican or Franciscan, nobody familiar with the subcontinent, and none who had read the accounts of the founders of the Latin Church 200 years earlier. Like the papal advisers who had drafted the *Romanus Pontifex*, Vasco apparently had the idea that India was mostly Christian, and was quite prepared to deal with any Muslim forces that interfered with his voyage.[6] The notion that the subcontinent had a people called the Hindus, or the enormous complexities of the East, never occurred to him. But Vasco would have understood the old prophecy that Latin Christianity would one day triumph in the East. An idea which would have been ludicrous to Jordanus, the pope and the kings of Europe in the fourteenth century was now a goal that could be striven for. In essence, Vasco was bringing the militaristic philosophy of the last days of the Reconquista to a sea voyage meant as a commercial venture.

The result illustrates the tragedy that occurs when soldiers play at being businessmen. Vasco was received with traditional hospitality by the Zamorin (Samuthiri), the ruler of Kozhikode, but the Portuguese cargo—which included a box of European sugar and six hats—was hardly exciting for the Indians. The Muslim traders in the city, wary of the Europeans and their ominous ships bristling with cannon, told the Zamorin that they thought Vasco was just a pirate and not an ambassador from the King of Portugal. The Zamorin, meanwhile, refused to let Vasco post a guard for his cargo while the Portuguese fleet returned home, and insisted that they pay the customs duty.

Vasco's response was to take some of the Zamorin's soldiers and a few fishermen hostage and sail off. The return journey to Portugal was ill-advised and during the wrong season. Storms delayed the fleet's passage across the Indian Ocean, and a ship was lost. Along the way, Paulo da Gama died of fever.

From these ominous beginnings, Portuguese voyages to India continued to be marked with violence and disruption. The second expedition, in which Vasco was not present, ended in a fight on the streets of Kozhikode between the Portuguese and Muslims from Aden, and seventy of the former were killed. In 1502, the fourth expedition arrived with fifteen heavily armed ships and a crew of 800 led by Vasco. The fleet captured a ship carrying pilgrims to Mecca and slaughtered them. Laying off Kozhikode, Vasco trained his cannons on the city and directed the Zamorin to throw out all the Muslims first. When the king refused, Vasco's fleet bombarded Kozhikode relentlessly for two days.

In the years that followed, the Portuguese established their presence more strongly in the Indian Ocean, establishing enclaves in Goa and the Malabar Coast. And then the Battle of Diu happened. The precedent set by Vasco and the early expeditions was followed as policy by the Portuguese. With the arrival of Jesuits, there was a greater degree of understanding about India and its people, but the aggressive militaristic behaviour remained a constant, and so did the missionaries' approach to proselytism and heresy.

In Europe, the Church was facing a new crisis. Eight years after the Portuguese victory at Diu, Martin Luther published his *Ninety-Five Theses*, leading to the Protestant Reformation. The Catholic Church now faced schisms across the heart of Europe. These were not new converts in contested lands, but people reacting to the perceived corruption and autocracy of the Vatican. As the Catholic hierarchy moved to control the damage, heresy became the greatest fear among them. Heretics and schismatics, those who were not firm in the faith of the true Church, were considered the real enemies of Christianity.

In May 1542, a thirty-five-year-old Jesuit named Francis Xavier arrived in Goa from Lisbon. A Basque from the Kingdom of Navarre, Xavier, like Vasco, was very much a product of his time and class. His father, a doctorate in law from the University of Bologna, had been the royal finance minister of Navarre. Xavier's brothers had fought against the Castilian army when Ferdinand invaded Navarre. Under reduced circumstances after the Navarrese defeat, Xavier studied at the University of Paris, where he was a bit of a star athlete. He then taught philosophy, specializing in Aristotelian thought, at the university.

In 1534, Xavier was one of the original seven university students, along with Ignatius of Loyola, who took vows and founded the Jesuit Order. Eight years later he was in India, having been appointed a papal diplomat to the East, effectively given the commission that had once been granted to Giovanni Montecorvino, Giovanni Marignolli and Jordanus Catalani.

Xavier's discovery of India, however, was completely different from those men. Montecorvino and Jordanus had found an India full of wonderful sights and customs, and a people who welcomed Christianity; rulers and host societies who did not resist conversions. Jordanus during his mission had seen how converts to Latin Christianity were accepted by others without hesitation, and how readily Indian Hindus, Christians and Parsis were willing to explain their rites and scriptures, and show him their sacred places.

Xavier came from a different Church and saw a different India. Accommodation and understanding were no longer possible between faiths in the age of colonialism and the padroado. With very little success among the upper castes, his missionary work was confounded by his observation that some communities of Indians, who had recently been converted, had slipped back into their traditional pagan beliefs.[7] Even the Portuguese community, particularly the working class and pardoned convicts who were in such large numbers, had started marrying non-Christians. A situation that would have been unimaginable in the Iberian Peninsula after the Reconquista.

Therefore, in India, too, faith needed to be tested. In May 1546, Xavier wrote to the king of Portugal, summarizing his views on the Catholic mission in India, and recommended that the Inquisition be started in Goa.[8] He had left India a year earlier, and after travelling and preaching through Indonesia, Taiwan and Japan, passed away in China in 1552.

In 1560, the Goa Inquisition was launched, under which Hindus were severely persecuted in Portuguese territory, while Muslims were taxed. And the small Jewish communities of coastal areas which happened to fall under Portuguese domination suffered the same treatment as their co-religionists had in Spain and Portugal. Newly converted Catholics fared no better, facing interrogation, torture and execution on charges of heresy or reverting to their former religions. And then there was the 'xenddi' tax on Hindus, modelled on the 'jizya'. Like the Spanish and Portuguese versions of it, the Goa Inquisition continued till 1820, and the exact number of people tried, imprisoned or executed under it will never be known.[9]

The Portuguese and Catholic Church's India policy triggered reprisals from Hindus and Muslims. The accord that had existed at the arrival of Western Christianity in India, the notion that new religions could take peaceable roots in a land which had so many, lay in ruins.

The policies of the Catholic Church also progressively dismantled the ecumenism that Pope John XXII had expressed while appointing Jordanus as the Bishop of Kollam in 1329. The Syrian Christians of India were at first willing to hold ecumenical discussions with the Portuguese Catholic clergy. This, too, was as old a tradition as the Zamorin's welcome to Vasco in 1498. The Syrians had hosted and accompanied Latin missionaries in the fourteenth century, and had been present when Jordanus established his ministry at Kollam. The Catholic missions from Portugal received a similar warm welcome. At the beginning.

In 1534, the Portuguese established the Diocese of Goa. By 1558, there was a second at Kozhikode, with the Portuguese recognizing that the Malabar Coast contained the largest concentration of Syrian Christians. Progressively, Portuguese Catholic clergy tried to bring the Syrians under their direct authority. In 1599, at a council in Udayamperoor, Kerala, it was announced that the Syrian Church in India was united with the Catholic Church. This led to an immediate schism, with the East Catholic Syro-Malabar Church being formed as a Western Christian denomination. Several scriptures and rites practised by the Syrian Christians of India were prohibited, and a large number of Eastern Christian books burnt.[10]

The Syrians who remained in the original Eastern Church now began suffering persecution from the Portuguese, and resentment grew. In 1653, a Syrian Christian clergyman named Ahatallah arrived in India and said he had been appointed Patriarch of the Church of the East for India and China. A prestigious appointment, even though the Eastern Church had long withered away in China. The Portuguese immediately sequestered him from the Syrians of Kozhikode, and refused to allow them to meet Ahatallah, claiming he was an impostor. Ahatallah later disappeared, and although there are some indications that he was taken to Europe and died of old age in Paris, doubts lingered in India.

Syrians had been in the subcontinent practically from the earliest days of Christianity. They had survived and created strong, stable communities in Malabar and, once upon a time, farther north. They had endured, while the Church of the East, which had spread from Edessa to Khanbaliq, died out from the rest of the world. The Portuguese treatment of Ahatallah would be the last straw in this struggle between Western and Eastern Christianity.

On 3 January 1653, the Syrians of Kozhikode, said to number more than 2,00,000, gathered at a church at Matancherry in the city and swore not to accept the authority of the Catholic Church. Syrian Christian tradition has it that the people tied themselves with ropes to a large cross, and so great was the press of the crowd that the arms of the cross were bent. This, the most singular instance of defiance of the Catholics by the Syrians, would come to be known as 'Koonan Kurishu Satyam' (Oath of the Bent Cross). Of the Syrians of Kozhikode, only 400 stayed loyal to the Catholic Church, according to local lore.[11]

The forced union between Eastern and Western Christianity in India had ended after fifty-four uneasy years. The oath led to further schisms, with some Syrian denominations in communion with the Catholic Church, others staying with the Church of the East and yet others joining Oriental Orthodoxy.

The legacy of religious intolerance and militarism which was brought by the Portuguese to India ultimately derived from the Reconquista, the Reformation and the Iberian inquisitions. The return of Western Christianity to the subcontinent, which was heralded by Vasco, was of a far different nature than what the founders of the Latin Church had expected or hoped for 200 years prior to the Age of Exploration. It was a new Europe and a different Church. Admirals of armadas conducted trade negotiations, while clergymen found heresy where they chose to see it. Few of the many remarkable Europeans who had travelled to, written about or lived and died in India in the Middle Ages would have recognized these descendants of theirs. Nor would they have approved of what European presence in the subcontinent was shaping into. This was no Crusade, and it certainly wasn't an account of marvels.

New Jerusalem

As the Catholic Church and the Portuguese attempted to expand their presence in the subcontinent through increasingly disruptive methods, the Vatican was dealing with a crisis in Europe itself. The Protestant Reformation had spread across the continent under leaders such as Martin Luther, Calvin and Zwingli. The schism became a political conflict between Catholic and Protestant countries, resulting in the Eighty Years' War which lasted till 1648. One of the reasons for Dutch unhappiness with Spanish rule over them, which triggered the conflict, was the imposition of Catholicism and the Inquisition on an increasingly Protestant population.

Protestant ideas spread rapidly in Northern Europe, including Scandinavia, which had been Christianized much later than Western Europe. The ideas of Martin Luther's followers became popular in countries like Denmark. In 1536, Lutheranism became the state religion, and the country formally broke with the Vatican. As the Eighty Years' War devastated large swaths of Europe, the Lutherans started persecuting

Catholics. It was only 150 years later that the Catholic Church was allowed to return, but Lutheranism was still the state religion of Denmark and continues to be so.

As the Age of Exploration became the Age of Colonies, the Danes too decided to expand maritime trade across the world. In the annals of the colonial experience in India, however, the Danish venture would unarguably be the most inept.

The Danish East India Company, modelled on and named after the Dutch and English versions, was established at Copenhagen in 1616 during the reign of King Christian IV. The king and his advisers thought this was the right time to begin trade with Indian kingdoms. The Portuguese had, in a major reversal of fortune, lost the Battle of Swally near Surat to the English four years earlier. The English were opposed to the Catholics like the Danes, and any reversal to Catholic imperialists, no matter how far away, was welcome to the Danes. But they also knew that the English or the Dutch were not quite ready to step into Portuguese shoes and be masters of the Indian Ocean. The Danes wanted to exploit this advantage.

Shortly after the company was established, a Dutch ship captain arrived in Copenhagen in his capacity as a diplomat from the court of the king of Sri Lanka, who wanted help against the Portuguese and had originally thought of going to the Dutch East India Company. In a portent of the way the Danes would conduct themselves in India, they sent a single ship to Sri Lanka, where the king seems to have persuaded the captain, a Dutchman named Roelant Grappe, to declare war against the Portuguese all by himself in 1618.

As could be expected, the Danes did not fare well against their Catholic foes in an engagement off the Coromandel Coast in what is the state of Tamil Nadu today. Grappe barely escaped with some men and took shelter with the Naik of Tanjore (Thanjavur). Meanwhile, the Danes had sent a fleet under an admiral, Ove Gedde, to India. The Danish understanding of Portuguese strength seems to have been very optimistic, because the fleet actually consisted of two fighting ships and three merchantmen, while the admiral was a zealous but inexperienced twenty-four-year-old.

Gedde was a quick learner and made a treaty with the Sri Lankan king, and then sailed to Thanjavur, where he found that Grappe had been given a site at a place called Tharangambadi by the Naik. Thus the first and most important Danish colony in India was established at the place they called Tranquebar. A fort was built and named Dansborg, and the Danes began establishing what they hoped would be their own colonial empire in the East.

It was a difficult task from the beginning. Portuguese influence had spread up the Coromandel by then, and a little more than 30 km to the south of Tranquebar was the Portuguese colony of Nagapattinam, and Jesuit missionaries had been working among coastal communities for a while by the time the Danes arrived.

For a decade or two till 1636, with Tranquebar as the nerve centre, Danish colonies and factories extended to Surat in Gujarat, Masulipattam and Pondicherry in the Coromandel and even in Bengal, where they had a factory in what is now the village of Pipli in North 24 Parganas district. Reports from Tranquebar to Copenhagen, however, were unduly optimistic. The king was informed of factories in the Gangetic plain, such as the city of Patna, whereas these were trade depots of relatively minor size. They also set up factories and depots in Java and Sumatra.

By the middle of the seventeenth century, the Dutch and the English were contesting for mastery of the seas. Between 1652 and 1674, England and the Netherlands fought three wars at home bases and in the Atlantic. Inevitably, Anglo-Dutch rivalry spilled over into South and South East Asia. By then the Danish East India Company was in deep trouble. Following financial problems in Denmark and the effects of the Eighty Years' War, trade had dried up. The Company found it difficult to attract likely people to endure the hardships of the long sea voyage and settle in the East.[1] For over three decades till 1669, no ship arrived in Tranquebar from the home country. The Danes in India had to manage with local trade along the coast, and even this was not an easy task.

In 1640, a Danish ship ran aground at Pipli and had to be scuttled. The Danish crew were taken prisoner by the local Mughal authorities. The Danish response to this was to capture a ship full of Muslims. This sparked a riot, and two years later, a mob vandalized the Danish factory at Pipli. The Dutch, who were clubbed with the Danes by the Mughal administration and locals who could not differentiate between one European nation and another, did not take kindly to this disruption in peaceful commerce. With no trade from Europe, and finding themselves unpopular among both Indians and other European companies, the Danes chose a course of action which sounds incredible in hindsight. They declared war on Shahjahan's Mughal Empire and began attacking Mughal ships in the Bay of Bengal, even sailing inland up the Hooghly river.[2]

By 1645, the Danes of Tranquebar had become pirates in every sense of the term, and had captured nearly forty ships of all flags. They had also become infamous among Indians for forcing the conversion of captured crewmen to Lutheranism and then selling them off at ports along the bay. This practice earned the Danes money and also helped them claim, in their records, that they were promoting Lutheranism among the Indians.[3]

Among the people who were thoroughly irritated by the Danes' misadventures were the Dutch, who found their ships seized and their merchants harassed by Mughals looking for Danish pirates. The Dutch began attacking the Danes, capturing Scandinavian crewmen and bringing them to Mughal officials. The Mughals responded to the pirates with increasingly harsh measures, and sometime in 1647, the governor of Balasore in Odisha poisoned nearly forty Danish prisoners. In all the annals of European presence in Mughal India, only the Danes, the least powerful of the European nations in the subcontinent, would be at war with the Mughal Empire during the height of its power.

But the Danish East India Company could hardly be expected to stutter along as a piratical venture, reviled by Indians and Europeans alike. In 1650, the company was dissolved. Twenty-one years later, the Danish economy had begun recovering, and merchants in Copenhagen began dreaming of profits from the East again, so the second Danish East India Company was formed. But the authorities at Tranquebar still hadn't got their Mughal policy in order. The new governor general, Sivert Adeler, sent two armed ships to Bengal to sign a treaty with the Mughals. Both sides demanded a large sum of money as war reparations, and matters looked grim. Finally, a treaty was concluded, to the considerable relief of the Dutch and English. By the end of that century, it appeared that Danish commerce in India, chiefly in textiles, sugar and saltpetre, could actually have a future. But by 1702, the Dutch and English had started bringing in massive amounts of sugar to Europe from the West Indies, and the Danes were left behind once again. Tranquebar soon went back to its loss-making ways.[4]

The dismal fortunes of Danish merchants in India were also reflected in the fate of Lutheranism there in that period. Tranquebar had pastors from the home country, but for most of the seventeenth century, they apparently showed no inclination to preach to Indians in the Coromandel Coast, partly because the Portuguese Jesuits of Nagapattinam were backed by a sizeable armada from Goa. Danes might have taken to piracy for profit, and might have ventured into an ill-advised war with the Mughals, but fighting the Portuguese for the sake of the right kind of Christianity was not something the merchants of Tranquebar were comfortable with. The Lutheran pastors of Tranquebar did not venture out for missionary work in Thanjavur, and appear to have been content with ministering to the Danes alone. This was how matters continued for the rest of the century.

In 1681, a Lutheran clergyman named Jacob Worm arrived at Tranquebar. The circumstances under which the thirty-eight-year-old turned up in India were, in one word, hasty. Worm had been a preacher at Viborg in Denmark, and apparently a very learned man. But he had a tendency to be puritanical in his views on secular administrators, and acquired a reputation for railing against corrupt government officials, writing anonymous poems and satirical works which were widely circulated. These works, whose quality was not really of the highest standards, appealed to working-class Danish sentiments but not to the powerful. Worm also seems to have had perennial problems with fellow clergymen who he thought had been unjustly promoted over him despite being of lesser merit, qualifications and talent. He even wrote satirical works on the Danish king and his numerous illegitimate children, and about corruption among royal officials. In 1680, Worm seems to have pressed his luck a little too far, refusing to join in a toast to the king on the latter's birthday, and was jailed, with an execution imminent. After a Copenhagen notable interceded on his behalf, Worm's execution was stayed, but he was sentenced to exile in India. While the Portuguese had started their empire with pardoned convicts, the Danes were sending a pardoned clergyman to their congregation in Tranquebar.

Afterwards, Worm's life in Tranquebar became hagiographic for the Lutheran Church in Copenhagen. It was said that he preached successfully among the Indians and won many converts in Thanjavur, and translated the Bible into Tamil, in keeping with Protestant scholars' efforts to spread the Good News in local languages. After his death in 1691, it was said that his body, like that of Francis Xavier, was incorruptible, and his countrymen started calling him the Danish Apostle of India. An honourable appellation, but later Danish Lutherans found no trace of his translated Bible, and no sign of the large number of Indians he had converted. Worm's exploits can be seen as a desire by the Danish Lutherans to step into the shoes of Francis Xavier, whom the Portuguese were very proud of because he had preached and converted large numbers of Indians and had built several churches along the coast. Ultimately, Worm's exaggerated career was a conscious attempt at projecting Lutheranism as the legitimate successor to the earliest apostolic traditions in Christian history. Thomas had come to India and been martyred not 270 km from Tranquebar. Worm was not to be given martyrdom, but astonishing success and supernatural intervention in the subcontinent was still the measure by which

the worth of a Christian denomination was to be judged. Worm
is said to have been buried in the cemetery near Dansborg, but
years of search, including some efforts by this writer, have not
led to the discovery of his grave.

In August 1699, Frederick IV became king of the
Norwegian-Danish union. Frederick was deeply interested in
Lutheran proselytism, and discovered that there had not been
a real missionary from his country to India from the beginning.
He resolved to remedy this. It is indicative of the manner
of functioning of Danish colonies in India that, just like the
founding of Tranquebar by a Dutchman, the propagation of
Danish Lutheranism was entrusted to two German missionaries,
Heinrich Plutschau and Bartholomaus Ziegenbalg, who arrived
at Tranquebar in 1706 on board the *Sophia Hedewig*.

Ziegenbalg, a native of Pulsnitz, a small town some 24 km
from Dresden in the German state of Saxony, was twenty-three
years old when he arrived at Tranquebar. He was picked by his
teacher and recommended to the Danish king as an ideal choice
to preach in India—he was learned in theology and committed
to missionary work. There was already a church at Dansborg,
the Zion Church, established in 1701, which today is among
the oldest surviving Protestant churches in the subcontinent.
Surely all the two missionaries had to do was begin their work.

The Danish merchants of Tranquebar and the authorities of
the fort, however, reacted to the missionaries' arrival with utter
hostility. Proselytism was a fine idea, but not when it was very
likely to cause disturbances among the Indians or Portuguese.
On that first day, Ziegenbalg and Plutschau were left to bake
in the sun while the authorities refused to step out of the fort
and meet them, despite the royal orders they carried. It was
a situation that would have been unthinkable in a Portuguese

The inept Danish colonial venture in India, and Ziegenbalg's remarkable career, were both centred at Dansborg Fort in Tranquebar colony, where senior Catholic clergymen were part of the administrative structure.

Left to their own devices, with no cooperation from secular officials, the Lutheran preachers embarked on their mission. Ziegenbalg might have been the archetypical prospective missionary in the eyes of the Danish king, but he was also a perceptive man, despite being new in India. The Tamils, he saw, used to write using their own script—which he realized was distinct from other parts of the country—with an iron stylus on palm leaves. Tranquebar veterans told him the natives in that part of India were hardly sophisticated thinkers like the Europeans thought they were. Ziegenbalg not only realized this was not true, but also inferred the cause—Europeans did not know Tamil, and much had been lost in translation between the two people. If he was to understand the Tamils, and if they were to understand him, translation was the key. It was a leap in logic which had been made in the past by other missionaries, now forgotten in Protestant Europe. Giovanni Montecorvino, in his decades among the Chinese in the fourteenth century, had always considered his translations of the Bible and other texts into Mandarin and Uighur as his greatest achievements. Now, in the eighteenth century, quite unaware of Giovanni, Ziegenbalg independently decided to embark on understanding the Tamils.

It was not an easy task. While Plutschau concentrated on missions farther south along the Coromandel Coast, Ziegenbalg began reaching out to Tamil scholars, learning the script and reading their works. He would afterwards admit he had arrived in India completely unprepared, believing the Tamils were an unlettered people with haphazard systems and structures, and that his mission was to bring order to them. This had, after all, been the fondly held opinion of the Danish Lutherans in Copenhagen and of the king himself. Ziegenbalg's long studies of Tamil showed him the richness and vitality of the language, and of the culture and systems of the people, so that in a few years, he would look back on his older self with some chagrin.

Ziegenbalg remained a committed Lutheran, but acknowledged the Tamils and the other Indian people had managed the feat of believing in what he had been told were 330 million gods, and believing in all of them simultaneously. And then there was the caste system, which the missionary understood in greater detail than even Jordanus Catalani had. The Tamils, Ziegenbalg found, had a total of ninety-six sub-castes within the major castes, with rigid social rules and hierarchies.

Ziegenbalg attempted to preach not only to these Indian castes, but also to a new category, perhaps even, in the inevitable Indian way, a new caste which had emerged in the colonial period. These people were broadly called 'black Portuguese' by the Danes of the Coromandel Coast, and were born of marriages between European Portuguese Catholics and Indians. Native Portuguese speakers, these people spoke almost no Tamil, and dressed as Europeans. Despite Jesuit opposition, the two Lutherans reached out to this Catholic congregation along the coast. And then there were the Sunni Muslims, which again were of two kinds in Tamil lands. Foreign-born or descended Muslims were called 'Turukan' and spoke mainly Hindi and very little Tamil, while native Muslims spoke Tamil and used Arabic only at religious seminaries. Ziegenbalg was living in a complex society indeed.

In three years, Ziegenbalg had mastered Tamil, taking such extreme steps to speed up his learning as not reading a word of either German or Latin during this period, and had begun writing in the native language. He also began writing comparative lists of Tamil works, with commentaries on them, and sending them home. He also found time to write critical pieces on the works of Portuguese missionaries in the region, including some in Tamil. Among his major achievements in those years was a comparative study of 119 books of Hindu scripture, translated from Tamil, and a study of eleven books on Islam by noted clerics. He would send out people to scour what are Tamil Nadu and Kerala for valuable works he could read. Ziegenbalg did not have much money at any point, and the officials of Tranquebar still did not get along with him, so they could not be expected to fund his research, which made absolutely no sense to them. So the Lutheran had to find his own means to get books in Tamil. He discovered that widows of Brahmins were quite willing to sell the family library to him at reasonable rates, and this formed a key source of such texts over the years.

Inevitably, Ziegenbalg ended up compiling the first Tamil dictionary, which in just four years contained 40,000 words. In the first column was the Tamil word, in the second its phonetic transliteration in the Roman script, and in the third was the translation in German. Then the Lutheran compiled a dictionary of poetry, under the guidance of Tamil poets, putting together 17,000 words which were particularly to be found in Tamil verse.

Ziegenbalg's contribution to the Tamil language and European understanding of Tamil was seminal. In 1712, the Lutheran mission also received a printing press. It wasn't the first press in the subcontinent. In 1556, the Jesuits had brought one from Portugal. It was originally meant for printing the Bible in Ethiopia, but the press for various reasons could not be taken out of Goa to Eastern Africa, so the missionaries in India made use of it. These works of Catholic scholars, including writings of Francis Xavier, were printed for distribution in Portuguese territory, including Nagapattinam. The Danish Lutheran press was mainly used for printing missionary material.

Over time, Ziegenbalg's work as a missionary became subsumed under his research into Tamil, Sanskrit and Arabic works. By the time he passed away in 1719, at just thirty-seven years of age, he had created an opus that would be rivalled only by the British scholars who came after him in the nineteenth century. One of the original Indologists, he took the Protestant commitment to understanding local languages and bridged the divide between missionary work and true scholarship. In this, as in his research and writings, he would stand at the beginning of a long line of scholarly Protestant missionaries who advanced the idea and understanding of India in Europe.

This, ultimately, would be the greatest achievement and most enduring legacy of the Danes' colonial experiment in India. Out of piracy and ineptitude, ineffectual commercial ambitions and stillborn imperial aspirations, something immeasurably valuable had emerged and grown in Tranquebar.

The second version of the Danish East India Company had a somewhat better fate than the first, but it never quite matched the power and wealth of the British, French or the Dutch in Asia. In 1772, its monopoly over commerce between Denmark and India was taken away. Seven years later, all of the company's possessions in India were taken over for direct administration by the crown. By then the British East India Company was in control of Bengal and large parts of the Deccan, and the colonial race had been all but decided in the subcontinent, with only the French still in the reckoning.

At the beginning of the nineteenth century, with Europe in the throes of the Napoleonic Wars, British fleets conducted campaigns against Danish possessions in India, particularly Tranquebar. There was no future to serious Danish aspirations in India, if there had ever been any. In 1845, the Danes transferred control of Tranquebar to Britain and returned home. The fort and the settlement, not being significant for British strategic or commercial interests, declined in importance over the remainder of the colonial period.[5]

The Danish Lutheran mission in India continued, with other inheritors of Ziegenbalg's legacy. The German pastor who came to India and found a different focus for his life's work could have told Copenhagen's unrealistic empire builders and the Lutheran Church a fundamental truth he had chanced upon not long after arriving in India: imperial ambitions are seldom easy to realize, and proselytism from a position of assumed superiority is just as deceptively attractive. Only informed engagement with the complexities of the subcontinent could create a legacy which might outlast empires.

For the British, the new masters of the subcontinent, to arrive at this insight would take a long time and many missteps.

Imperium

When the British East India Company won the Battle of Plassey in Bengal in 1757 and found itself master of a substantial and prosperous part of the crumbling Mughal Empire, it had achieved what no other European colonial power had managed in 250 years—political control beyond the Indian coast. Europeans of the Middle Ages would never have dreamt of it, and even the British were unprepared for the enormity of the situation.

In Europe, the Enlightenment was creating a school of thought which would eventually lead to the American and French Revolutions and to secularism. Writers were exploring the idea that the world could be viewed through prisms apart from the strictly religious. Western Europe was beginning to re-examine itself.

But this nascent self-awareness did not immediately extend to European presence in the East. The Enlightenment, in fact, bore unexpected fruit in British India. The late eighteenth and early nineteenth centuries were the time of scholars like the polyglot William Jones, discoverer of Sanskrit for the West, proponent of the theory of the Indo-European linguistic family tree and founder of the Asiatic Society of Bengal (now the Asiatic Society). It was the time of the Orientalist James Prinsep, who deciphered the Kharosthi and Brahmi scripts of Ancient India and rediscovered the edicts of Emperor Ashoka, introducing the Mauryan monarch to an India which had quite forgotten all about him. History, it seemed, had come full circle. The children of the Enlightenment, born of ideas tracing their lineage to the Ancient Greeks, had reached back into history and found evidence of India's long and intimate contact with Hellenism, of Mauryan diplomats in the courts of Greek Eurasia and Greeks in India.

It was a time of Orientalists, of amateur but brilliant linguists, archaeologists and historians marvelling at the treasures the subcontinent kept revealing. With the whole of India open for exploration, there seemed to be no end to the amount of research that could be done.[1]

But the scholars would not have the day so easily, for there was another group which was trying to explain how the British had triumphed in India, and was trying to influence how British rule would be shaped in the subcontinent. Charles Grant, an ex-soldier who had become wealthy in the silk business in Bengal and would later become member of Parliament and chairman of the East India Company in London, was a born-again evangelist. Member of the Clapham Sect, a group of Christians who were against slavery, Grant was completely convinced, living in England and looking back on his time in India, that his country had achieved so much in the subcontinent despite the political and social upheavals in Europe because of Christianity, that is, Christianity of the right kind. This group would be the Evangelists. The British East India Company's policy discouraging missionary activity in India because it interfered with commerce (a view shared by the Danes and the Dutch) was a matter of acute discomfort for people like Grant. If India, or large parts of it, had been delivered to Britain, surely this was for a purpose greater than mere commerce.[2] They saw divine intervention in events in the subcontinent over the eighteenth century.

The Company had clawed its way to supremacy in India, beginning in the early seventeenth century. Company merchants had arrived on the Indian coast to find the Dutch had already begun manoeuvring against the long-established Portuguese, who in turn had given up hoping for an Indian empire to rival their prized possession in South America, Brazil. The Portuguese concentrated on keeping their naval supremacy intact, but the English and Dutch soon caught up with them. The English struck the first major blow, defeating the Portuguese near Surat in the Battle of Swally in 1612. For six decades, the Anglo-Dutch rivalry raged in the Indian Ocean and the Bay of Bengal till the English prevailed.

But there were still the French, who had set up factories from Malabar to Bengal. In 1707, the last great Mughal emperor, Aurangzeb, died on campaign in the Deccan, and his overextended empire, which was already in economic crisis, passed into the hands of descendants less capable than him and began crumbling. Provincial governors carved out their own kingdoms, from Oudh (Awadh) in the Gangetic plain to the nawabs of Bengal and the Nizam of Hyderabad in the Deccan. The Marathas, who had fought Aurangzeb for years, began rapid expansion and at one time, were even poised to replace the Mughals as a new imperial power in north and west India.

With the passing of the Mughals, the age of Gunpowder Empires, those three behemoths of the Muslim world from South Asia to Europe, had ended. The oldest of these empires, the Ottomans, had at one time been poised to claim a large part of Europe itself, but by the turn of the eighteenth century had fallen into stagnation and eventual decline. The third Gunpowder Empire, the Safavids of Persia, would last only a brief while longer, but Persia would defy European colonialism for a long while yet.

Crusading had long ceased to be of importance for a Europe torn by Protestant schisms. Egypt had not been an enemy for more than 250 years, ever since the Ottomans had ousted the Mamluks and captured that fertile land in 1517. The war between Christendom and Islam was apparently over, but in an unexpected way: the Muslim world was in decline and European Christians no longer thought much of Jerusalem. As a new group of scholars began studying the Middle Ages and Antiquity in the late eighteenth century, the Crusades became an academic subject, a matter of as little immediate significance for Europeans as the economic policies of the Ancient Roman emperors.

At a time of post-imperial vacuum in India, the rivalry between the British and French found fertile ground for transplantation. The Seven Years' War between the two old foes might not have rivalled the duration of their 100-year conflict in the fourteenth and fifteenth centuries, but it divided Europe in two, with every major power taking either the British or the French side. From Europe to North America, from the Atlantic to Africa and the Philippines, the two adversaries grappled for victory in direct or proxy conflicts.

The British and French had already fought two wars in the Deccan prior to the Seven Years' War. It ended in a stalemate in the First Carnatic War. The British proxy Muhammad Ali became Nawab of Carnatic, a feudatory of the Hyderabad Nizam, at the end of the Second Carnatic War in 1754, and the French were defeated.

Plassey, therefore, was a turning point for the Anglo-French wars. On 23 June 1757, Robert Clive's East India Company forces defeated Nawab Siraj-ud-Daulah and his French allies. Over the next few decades, the British expanded their control over the Gangetic plain while cornering the French in the Deccan.

There were reverses for the British elsewhere in the world, such as when the American colonies won their independence in 1783. But it was not going well at all for the French, and in 1789, the French Revolution swept away the monarchy and the Catholic Church in that country. From the ashes of the revolution emerged Napoleon and a secular France, and the British faced the wiliest foe they had ever seen in the Continent.

In 1792, the British besieged Seringapatam, capital of Tipu Sultan in Mysore, now in the state of Karnataka. Tipu lost the siege and signed a treaty, reducing his power and dominions considerably. Although Tipu would remain in power for seven more years, 1792 was the defining moment for British supremacy in the Deccan. For the French, who had expectations from Tipu, it was the end of their ambitions in India.

In the same year that Tipu lost the Siege of Seringapatam, Charles Grant, back in London from India two years earlier, wrote an essay titled 'Observations on the State of Society among the Asiatic Subjects of Great Britain', arguing that greater missionary activity in India would benefit the natives in every way. Britain's position as a rising power in India was more secure than ever, and surely this was the time to remember that his countrymen had prevailed in that land because of Christ and Anglican values, where the slave-trading Portuguese and the Roman Catholic Church had failed. Twelve years later, as chairman of the Company, Grant would begin sponsoring chaplains to travel to India to both minister to British expatriates and proselytize if they could. It was not exactly the great evangelical revolution he wanted, but the best he could do. In 1799, Grant was instrumental in establishing the Society for Missions to Africa and the East.[3] It is now known as the Church Mission Society, an umbrella organization of Protestant and Anglican denominations, and has continued to be present in Asia, Australia and Africa.

Grant's fellow members in the Clapham Sect included Zachary Macaulay, former assistant manager at a sugar plantation in the West Indies, abolitionist and an evangelical Christian who believed that Britain was truly a civilizing force in the East, and that it was the duty of the East India Company to promote missionary activity in India. This idea would be central to the philosophy of his more famous son, the historian and politician Thomas. In February 1835, Thomas Macaulay would present his Minute on Indian Education to Governor General William Bentinck, calling for reform in the education system in British India so that they would have knowledge of 'useful' subjects in English, and not Persian or classical Indian languages. He did not know Sanskrit or Persian and had no desire to learn them, but he said he had looked into them and formed an idea of their worth, which in his eyes was not much. 'A single shelf of a good European library was worth the whole native literature of India and Arabia,' he infamously declared. Thomas Macaulay's reforms would change the history of the subcontinent and create an Anglicized class of Indians originally intended to shoulder administrative responsibilities of the empire.

But Thomas Macaulay's philosophy, predicated on European supremacy over the East, was less concerned with Christian evangelism and more with the cultural and intellectual values of the West. His father's ideas, on the other hand, had evangelism as their core. In 1813, after bitter arguments between the Orientalists and Evangelists, the latter won. The British Parliament passed the Charter Act, renewing the East India Company's rule over India, subservient to the Crown. The Charter Act officially permitted Christian missionaries, for the first time, to work in the subcontinent with complete freedom.

The model that emerged was an expression of religion as extension of empire. It was not a new model and went back to the earliest days of Western Christianity. Emperors such as Theodosius and Justinian, with their idea of Christianity as the official faith of the Roman Empire, would have understood people such as Charles Grant and Zachary Macaulay. An empire had an obligation to propagate its faith.

This model was different from other European systems which India had seen till then. For the Portuguese, there was an official obligation to promote the Catholic faith in their dominions, even though their reach never extended beyond pockets of the Indian coast. The Danes, struggling to be commercially viable, were always uncomfortable with missionary activities by their countrymen. The British model approached the problem from the other side. Finding themselves in possession of a growing empire, the Evangelists promoted Christianity as the cause of, and bulwark of, this success.

Missionary work without the protection of imperial power had always been a fraught venture. Paul the Apostle had walked into the heart of a hostile pagan Rome and had been martyred. Jordanus Catalani had single-handedly shouldered missionary responsibilities with no expectation of political support, and had been gratified by the welcome he received in Indian society. Even Giovanni Montecorvino had laboured against the polite disdain of the Nestorians in China without making Western Christianity a political tool for European expansionism. But when missionaries began to be seen as agents of empire, there were bound to be repercussions among host societies.

The Charter Act of 1813 opened the floodgates for a massive and concerted amount of missionary work in British India. Cities like Bombay and Calcutta, creations of the British and nerve centres of the empire, saw sustained activities by missionaries, who reached out to all the diverse communities of Indian society. Twenty years later, the Government of India Act would reduce the East India Company to an administrative body, taking away its right to commercial activities. But the missionary outreach created by the Charter Act remained.

In 1839, two Parsis were baptized in Bombay, an event which caused considerable consternation among India's Zoroastrians, who had established themselves in the subcontinent after fleeing centuries of persecution in their native Iran. A small community even when Jordanus had met them in the fourteenth century, the Parsis of Bombay were alarmed at the conversions to Christianity. Four years later, a young Marathi Brahmin man named Narayan Sheshadri, who had studied at a college in Pune run by Scottish missionaries, decided to be baptized, becoming the first Brahmin to convert in Bombay. Then his

CARPENTERS AND KINGS 268

younger brother Shripat, just sixteen years old, also chose to convert. Two Parsis had caused alarm. Now, said orthodox and even western-educated Hindus, the missionaries were coming for Brahmins. There was uproar. Shripat was just sixteen years old, and Hindu upper-caste opponents of the missionaries, and those of the Bombay British sympathetic to them, went to court. They found support among the Parsis and Muslims, who also felt the weight of the empire and the increasing presence of missionaries. It was an unprecedented event in the history of the British presence in India. The Hindus won, with the court refusing to permit Shripat's baptism on account of his age.[4]

This created a fresh conundrum. Shripat had eaten with his Christian elder brother, so what was to become of his caste? The matter was debated across the land, even among the learned in Varanasi. Finally, with a lot of elaborate rituals, Shripat was reinducted into the caste fold under the eye of educated middle-class Hindus of Bombay. But orthodox Hindus still maintained that this was very unusual because there was no scriptural sanction for reconversion if caste was lost in this manner. Hinduism never had a provision for conversion, so a person who had been removed from the caste structure could not be accommodated again. But others felt that Hinduism had to respond to such missionary activities, and if caste rules had to be relaxed to bring somebody back, so be it.

The Shripat Sheshadri case has been largely forgotten by modern Indians, but should not be. The Hindu Right of today has created a system called 'ghar wapasi' (return home) under which the aim is to reconvert Muslims and Christians to Hinduism. But in Shripat's time, it was the ideological forebears of the Right, the orthodox Hindus, who had opposed this re-conversion, and the Hindu liberals who had carried it out.

Shripat's case had a tragic ending which illustrates the problems of bridging religious and doctrinal divides while ignoring the lives and emotions of individuals caught in between. Orthodox Hindus refused to accept that he had regained his caste, and boycotted him. His family, facing intense social censure, in the end severed relations with him. Not allowed to convert to Christianity, and not allowed to 'return home', the only family member who stayed by Shripat's side was Narayan Sheshadri, who had become a pastor. Caught between forces beyond his comprehension, Shripat lived a lonely life and died at twenty-nine years of age in 1856.

The Shripat Sheshadri case would demonstrate the difficulties the missionaries had stirred up among the Indians by being seen to function with impunity because of the empire. Combined with reform movements that had begun among Indians, and colonial policies such as new colleges which promoted modern education for men and women, the activities of missionaries led to a sense of distrust among orthodox Indians.

And then the Revolt of 1857 erupted. A complex event resulting from several causes, the conflict was not just about disaffected Indian soldiers and ousted kings taking on the British Indian army. The numerous other smaller conflicts based on caste and gender too were a part of the violence during that period, and new research is probing these events. But religion too was an important part of the conflict. The coming of Europeans and their military campaigns across the land had deeply affected entrenched Hindu and Muslim hierarchies. British administrators, not to mention military officers, had an understanding of caste by then but failed to realize how deeply internalized it was. After all, this was a land where even

Muslim society had birth-based hierarchies which were carried over from the Hindu societies from which their ancestors had converted. As the Portuguese eventually realized, and as the perceptive Ziegenbalg had seen 150 years earlier, even those born of mixed marriages, the 'black Portuguese' and Anglo-Indians, were on their way to becoming a caste proper, with clothing and other markings as social signifiers.

The British should have anticipated the events of 1857. Long before the soldiers of Meerut Cantonment turned on their officers and marched to Delhi, a few hundred Indian sepoys of the Madras Army had mutinied in the Fort of Vellore, 140 km inland from Madras (now Chennai) in July 1806. The Vellore Mutiny was the first mass rebellion by Indian soldiers against the East India Company, and the reason was caste and religion. The dress regulations of the Madras Army had recently been changed, and Hindus had been forbidden from putting tilaks or other caste marks on their foreheads, while Muslims had been ordered to shave their beards. There had been no rumours of bullet cartridges greased with beef or pork fat, as would be the case in 1857.

The last straw for the Hindu and Muslim soldiers at Vellore had been the new regimental headgear, a round hat which was associated by the people of the Deccan with Anglo-Indians or those who had newly converted to Christianity. And if this were not enough, the cockade on the hat was made of leather.

Caste, religion, a hat and the slur of being ridiculed by their fellow Hindu and Muslim civilians as Christians. Hundreds of sepoys at Vellore mutinied and killed their officers. As in 1857, they planned to rouse the populace and install deposed royalty—in their case, the sons of Tipu Sultan who had been housed near the fort for a while. Only a desperate dash by British forces from Arcot 25 km away and hard fighting at close quarters prevented the mutiny from spreading.[5]

The elements which led to the Vellore Mutiny were present during 1857 as well, and so was the hatred of Christians, not to mention white people. The sepoys who marched into Delhi and declared the amiable Mughal Bahadur Shah Zafar as Emperor of India also rounded up and killed Christians in the city. Prominent among the victims was the Anglican missionary Midgley John Jennings and his family.

Anglo-Indians, who participated on both sides or were non-combatants, were targeted by both sides. Joseph Skinner was a prominent Delhi resident, grandson of a Rajput woman and son of the legendary cavalryman, Col. James Skinner, who founded the 1st and 2nd Skinner's Horse regiments and built St James Church, which still stands at Delhi's Kashmiri Gate area. The 1st Skinners is also still around, as the 1st Horse armoured regiment of the Indian Army. Joseph Skinner and his family were killed by mutineers in Delhi during the first days of the 1857 rebellion.

The soldiers of Maj. William Hodson, now chiefly known for the murder of three sons of Bahadur Shah Zafar after Delhi was recaptured in 1858, also killed the entire Christian Anglo-Indian contingent of bandsmen of the 28th Bengal Native Infantry, who had fought on the side of the rebels. And then there was Felix Rotton, an Anglo-Indian ex-soldier who had served with the Nawab of Oudh, and stayed with the rebels after Lucknow was overrun, until he was captured by British forces. Loyalist Anglo-Indians were counted as Christian enemies by the rebels, while rebels from the community were held as worse traitors than Hindus and Muslims. In a complex conflict which defied categorization, religion mixed with ethnicity and created a toxic concoction of carnage.[6]

The Hindu and Muslim attitude towards Christians, particularly missionaries, during the rebellion was a direct fallout of the ideas of people such as Zachary Macaulay and Charles Grant. The idea that Christianity had been responsible for the empire had led to repercussions against Christians in India. In the decades after the rebellion, as Indian nationalist consciousness emerged and borrowed from European thought, Christians, and in particular new converts, had to struggle to deal with this recent legacy of distrust in a land where their faith had been present for nearly 2000 years.

The lessons of 1857 were learnt at a bitter cost, and after the British Crown took over administration of India and dissolved the Company, the activities of missionaries were administered with greater caution than earlier. While a new Indian middle class emerged, Europe too changed over the nineteenth century. Even the Portuguese eventually acknowledged the change. The Inquisition had ended in Spanish and Portuguese territories around the world, and the Catholic Church prepared to face the Industrial Age.

Missionaries still continued to proselytize in India, but not as adjuncts of the empire. The Catholic orders focused on the centuries-old legacy of learning that the Dominicans and Franciscans had once sought to bring to the East. Schools and colleges were built by Protestant and Catholic clergymen, where the children of the new Indian middle class and resident Europeans were taught modern subjects—and a bit of the classics too.

As Christian missionaries negotiated the complex social structures of the subcontinent, some of them had ventured out into those parts which had only recently been added to the idea of India. In 1826, the British signed the Treaty of Yandabo with the Burmese after the Third Anglo-Burmese War, and found themselves in control of the erstwhile Kingdom of Assam, east of Bengal. The new province comprised the Brahmaputra river valley surrounded by hills extending into Tibet and Burma. While the population of the valley comprised caste Hindus and indigenous tribes which had kept their independence from the Mughal Empire, the hills had not been Hinduized. Barring a few Portuguese mercenaries and two Jesuits in the early seventeenth century, Christians had not ventured over the difficult terrain into north-east India.

In 1836, two American Baptist missionaries, Nathan Brown and Oliver Cutter, arrived at the eastern end of the Brahmaputra valley just south of the Himalayan foothills. The tropical climate and dense vegetation of the region was not a hindrance for them because they had just recently been in Burma. Brown, a New Hampshire native, had brought a printing press with him like Ziegenbalg, and followed the German Lutheran's template to the letter. By 1848, he had learnt Axomiya, the local Indo-European language, and had translated the New Testament and notable Baptist writings. But he had also been reading on the history of the erstwhile Ahom Kingdom, preserved in detailed documents called 'buronjis', and had been translating and printing them as well as works on mathematics in Axomiya.[7]

Like Ziegenbalg, Brown's legacy as a missionary would be subsumed by his research into the language, culture and history of his hosts. Unlike the British Evangelists of the early nineteenth century like Zachary Macaulay, Brown had very few illusions about the supremacy of the West. However, like them, he was a committed abolitionist and when the debate over emancipation of slaves grew more strident in his home country, Brown returned to the United States and stayed there through the Civil War, delivering a series of sermons in the North in support of abolition. In 1872, he sailed to Japan and immediately began working on Japanese translations of Scripture. He passed away in that country sixteen years later.

Brown was the archetype of the charismatic Protestant missionaries who would find their way into the hills around the Brahmaputra valley, including the Khasi, Jaintia and Garo Hills (now the state of Meghalaya) between Assam and Bengal, the Lushai Hills (now Mizoram) and Naga Hills (now Nagaland) on the border with Burma. The tribal political and social structures in these places, far from the Indian heartland, did not have the complex caste and religious structures of Indian Hindus and Muslims which had reacted to missionary zeal and imperial missteps. The tribes were restive and rebelled against British authority on several occasions. The most remote part of the north-eastern Naga Hills proved so forbidding a terrain, full of such relentlessly hostile a people, that it was designated an Unadministered Tribal Area and the people were left to their own devices. But elsewhere in the hills, Baptist, Anglican and Presbyterian ministries slowly spread.

The coming of Christianity to these newly co-opted parts of India also brought some significant social churn. The Kingdom of Manipur, which lay between the Naga Hills and Lushai Hills, became one of the Princely States of the Indian Union by the turn of the twentieth century. The Meiteis, the dominant group in Manipur, had gone through a process of Hinduization with influences from neighbouring Bengal while holding on to their indigenous belief systems. Shortly after World War I, Haipou Jadonang, a young farmer from the Rongmei Naga tribe in Manipur, started a revivalist movement, calling on his fellow Nagas to resist Christian proselytism. The Heraka movement that he started was significant because of the polytheism it propounded, while maintaining the presence of a supreme god. In many ways, it borrowed monotheistic ideas from Christianity and Islam, the latter of which had been spreading in the easternmost part of Bengal next door. The Heraka movement was suppressed by British administrators who saw its potential of being a nationalist unifying force for Manipuri Nagas. Far from Indian orthodoxies, on the periphery of the subcontinent, such reactions and syncretism with monotheisms continued till much after India got independence.

This, too, is a part of the story of how Western Christianity arrived at an idea of India and an understanding of a vast and complex land.

Conclusion

In a neighbourhood called San Thome, in a part of Chennai known as Mylapore, stands the San Thome Cathedral Basilica. It is one of the most important Christian churches in the world, because it was built over the tomb of Thomas the Apostle. There are only two other cathedrals which were ever built over tombs of the Twelve Apostles. There is St Peter's Basilica in the Vatican and there is the Cathedral of Santiago de Compostela in north-western Spain, which has the tomb of James the son of Zebedee.

The San Thome Cathedral, built in the neo-Gothic style, is an impressive structure in white, with a spire that rises 64 m high. Syrian Christians had been praying for centuries at the site where the apostle was believed to have been martyred. In the tenth century, they built a church over the tomb and a settlement came up. It was this church which was visited by Jordanus Catalani, Giovanni Marignolli and Odoric of Pordenone in the fourteenth century. By the time of Portuguese arrival on the Coromandel Coast in the early sixteenth century, perhaps as a

San Thome Cathedral Basilica is one of the most sacred Christian
pilgrimage sites in the world

result of conflict in the region, the original church was in ruins and the Syrians did not have the resources to rebuild it.

The Portuguese seem to have taken their position as the vanguard of Western Christianity too literally. Local tradition maintains they moved the tomb to what they considered a more appropriate spot nearby and by 1525, had built a new, suitably Catholic, church. In 1606, it was given the status of a cathedral. In 1893, the British administration undertook to rebuild it, while still maintaining its status as a Catholic shrine, and in 1956, it was declared a Minor Basilica.

San Thome Basilica represents, in a single structure, the complex history of Christianity—both Western and Eastern—in India. A structure and history founded on the martyrdom of an apostle and nurtured by Eastern Christians under the guidance of ecclesiastical figures from northern Mesopotamia practically since the beginning of Christianity. A place visited in the Middle Ages by Western Christian missionaries, who discovered the deep roots of Syrian Christians in India and hoped for both ecumenism and a lasting Latin Church in the subcontinent. A structure taken over and rebuilt by Portuguese Catholics who believed they were truly doing the Lord's work, no matter how violent or disruptive the means they adopted. And the final structure, which stands today—an edifice constructed by the British who took care neither to radically change the site nor the Roman Catholic identity of the place, but insisted they had to do some construction of their own while they were there, with the final structure reflecting a very British architectural sensibility.

The Latin Church might have fragmented into Catholic, Anglican and Protestant denominations by the time it returned with the Age of Exploration, but ecumenism has progressively occurred between Western and Eastern Christians in India. The Syro-Malabar Catholic Church is a denomination originally Syrian but now in full communion with the Catholic Church, and at 3 million members, is the fourth-largest Christian denomination in the country. The Syro-Malankara Catholic Church, which has a similar arrangement, has a little more than 300,000 members, with both denominations predominantly to be found in Kerala. Then there is the Malankara Orthodox Syrian Church, with 2.5 million members; the Malankara Mar Thoma Syrian Church and Jacobite Syrian Christian Church, which have remained in Eastern Christianity as part of what is known as Oriental Orthodoxy, which includes the Coptic, Armenian and Ethiopian churches worldwide, essentially the oldest continuously surviving Christian denominations. The Chaldean Syrian Church, derived from Nestorian Christianity, is also very much alive, with an estimated 50,000 members.

The Roman Catholic Church in India has more than 12 million members, making it the largest Christian denomination in the country. In Kerala, Catholics form more than 61 per cent of the state's 6.2 million Christians, who themselves make up 18 per cent of the total population of the state.

In December 1961, fourteen years after India got independence and was partitioned, the Indian Army invaded Portuguese territories, including Goa, which is today an Indian state. Christians, overwhelmingly Roman Catholic, number 365,000 and form a quarter of the population in Goa. There are significant numbers of Goan Catholics settled in Portugal and other countries after decolonization. Diu, once a strategic prize proposed as a naval base for a crusade by William of Adam, and contested by the Portuguese and the Egyptians in the early colonial period, now forms part of the federally administered

Union Territory of Daman and Diu, where Christians number a little more than 1 per cent. As with other parts of the world, the Portuguese language has survived in that country's former colonies, although it is limited to liturgical functions and is a first language among only a few residents.

The populations of three Indian states have a Christian majority and all of them are in north-east India. Mizoram has 1.10 million people, of whom 87 per cent are Christian, mainly Presbyterians. More than 96 per cent of the 2 million people of Nagaland are Christian, three-fourths of them Baptists. There are 2.55 million Christians in Meghalaya, making 85 per cent of the population, with Presbyterianism the largest denomination.

Christianity is India's third-largest religion with nearly 30 million members. In relative terms, in the second most populous country in the world, this makes a little more than 2.3 per cent of the residents. But Christians also form a significant productive part of the population, and their human development indices are perceptively high. Nearly 85 per cent of India's Christians are literate, which is considerably higher than the national average of 74 per cent, while the percentage of Indian Christians with high academic degrees is also much larger than the national average.

Catholic orders run some of the most prestigious schools and colleges in the country, while scholars and researchers from the mendicant orders have made invaluable contributions in research and higher education.

But there have been problems as well. The Hindu Right, which is on the rise in the country at present, is led by an ideology that believes Islam and Christianity are not indigenous religions and, therefore, Muslims and Christians are not as Indian in their hearts as Hindus, Jains or Sikhs. Muslims are often considered fifth columnists for Pakistani jihadists.[1] It is not easy to assign a quarrelsome neighbour next door who would be a similar patron for Indian Christians, so that task has been given to the Vatican, a position which ignores doctrinal differences among Christian denominations.[2]

The rise of the Right has led to targeted attacks against Indian Christians, particularly in central and eastern India, where people of non-Hinduized tribes often convert to Christianity. Incidents of attacks on missionaries and vandalism of churches are reported from these areas.[3] In 1999, the Australian missionary Graham Staines and his sons, aged ten and six, were burnt alive by a mob in Odisha.[4] The man who led the mob is alleged to have links with the Hindu Right.

The rise of majoritarian, fascist politics has other, more insidious effects on the internal mechanisms of minority societies. In 2018, a Roman Catholic nun alleged that a bishop had raped her multiple times between 2014 and 2016. There have been other allegations of sexual misconduct by Christian clergymen in the country. In some cases the victims, who include nuns and lay believers, have not spoken out because of the power their assailants have within the Church hierarchy. However, several nuns have also admitted that, considering the prevailing political climate in India, they are unwilling to publicly accuse their assailants because of the concern that it would tarnish the image of the Church and of Christians, and lead to criticism about the faith by Hindu hardliners.[5] In an environment where genuine problems within the community cannot be addressed because of fear of majoritarian criticism, much-needed reforms in the Church power structure and method of functioning cannot be expected to occur.

The story of how Christianity arrived and found a home in India has lessons for Indians as well as the West. The Hindu

Right's idea of India is based on the fondly nurtured fiction that there was a single identifiable entity called India at some point in the past, and this entity was Hindu in faith and created solely by 'indigenous' people.

No civilization has been built by the people of a land in isolation. The strongest, most enduring cultures have been those which have internalized ideas from elsewhere, being enriched in the process. India has always been connected to the East and the West, and there were always people and ideas arriving in the subcontinent to contribute in small and large measures. Christianity, which has been here for 2000 years, is as Indian a religion as any other. And if only religions originating from the subcontinent are legitimately Indian, the Hindu Right will need to explain how Buddhism disappeared from India long before Islam arrived.

Nativism of the kind promoted by the Hindu Right was never a part of Indian society. In the fourteenth century, Han Chinese rebels waged war on the Yuans because the latter were Mongols. The rebels persecuted Nestorian Christianity because it was a foreign faith. Contemporary accounts from India indicate no such feelings of xenophobia against Syrian or Latin Christians, and no persecution of missionaries or converts by Hindus. The delegitimization of Christians and Muslims as Indians by the Hindu Right today is a result of the twentieth-century nationalist movement in the country which has been co-opted by the Right into a xenophobic narrative which has no historical basis.

The story of Western Christianity in India also shows how the interplay between faith and political structures depends on the fundamental doctrines of the religion. Christianity was never meant to be a political or imperial religion. The earliest

Christians were part of an underground movement driven by piety and humility, living a precarious existence under two empires—Roman and Persian—which persecuted them ruthlessly. Churches like Rome and Constantinople grew and evolved in an imperial climate and Christianity benefited from being considered a state religion. The medieval Latin and Catholic churches passed through phases where they tried to purge decadent elements and return to the spirit of Early Christianity, and phases when they sought to act as imperial entities or representatives of such entities themselves, such as during the Inquisitions or through the Portuguese padroado system. It has been a chequered history, but it is also undeniable that Western Christianity, both in India and in the West, has been at its best when it was represented by reasonable, kind and gentle people. When the carpenters were in charge, not the kings.

This story is about such people across faiths. It is about Jordanus, Giovanni Montecorvino, William of Tyre and Usamah ibn Munqidh, or Ziegenbalg and Nathan Brown. It was these people who made the effort to understand one another, and the world around them, who were in the truest sense ambassadors of their faith. Western Christianity was at its best when it was truly Christian.

It is a cautionary tale for the Indian Right and for those who believe that the only solution to an alliance of religion and the state is more religion, not less. Christianity was never meant to be a political structure, which is why reformist movements like the Franciscans and Dominicans, or the Protestants, began as a reaction to the political nature of the Catholic Church. It is another matter that some of the Protestant movements were co-opted by monarchies of those European countries. But because the core of Christianity is a non-political set of humanitarian ideas, it has been possible for these reforms to moderate, to some extent, the imperial tendencies of the late medieval and early modern Church. If Western Christian prelates could eventually understand that religion should not be an organ of the state, but should instead be confined to personal or theological matters, there is no reason why the Indian state should, at this point in the history of our species, opt for discarding secularism.

But if it does, and this process of Hinduization of state institutions continues, what will be affected is the idea of India. This has never been a land for a single people, or culture or religion. No community has ever been exiled from the subcontinent at any point. No people have been delegitimized or have had their history here denied. If the Hindu Right succeeds in doing this, it might arrive at its own perverted idea of India. But it would not be what India truly is, and has always been.

Bibliography

Primary Sources

Afsar-e Shirazi, A. (ed.), *Motun-e arabi va farsi dar bare-ye Mani va manaviyyat*, Tehran, 1956.

Boyle, J.A. (tr.), *Tarikh-i Jahan-gusha by Atamalik Juwayni*, Boston, Harvard University Press, 1958.

Church, A.J., Brodribb, W. (tr.), *The Annals of Tacitus*, Book XV, London, Macmillan, 1884.

Constable, G. (tr.), *Tractatus Quomodo Sarraceni Sunt Expugnandi by William of Adam*, London, Dumbarton Oaks, 2011.

Contini, R., 'Hypotheses sur l'arameen manicheen', *Annali di Ca' Foscari 34*, Venice, University of Venice, 1995.

Cruse, C.F., Boyle, I. (tr.), *The Ecclesiastical History of Eusebius Pamphilus, Bishop of Cesarea in Palestine, and an Historical View of the Council of Nice*, New York, Thomas N. Stanford, 1856.

Dodge, B. (tr.), *The Fihrist of al-Nadim*, New York and London, Columbia University Press, 1970.

Dewing, H.B. (tr.), *Procopius, History of the Wars*, Cambridge, Harvard University Press, 1914.

Freese, J.H. (tr.), *The Library of Photius I*, New York, The Macmillan Co., 1930.

Funk, W.P., 'The Reconstruction of the Manichaean Kephalaia', Mirecki, P., BeDuhn, J. (eds), *Emerging from Darkness: Studies in the Recovery of Manichaean Sources*, Leiden, Brill, 1997.

Gibb, H.A.R., Beckingham, C.F. (trs), *The Travels of Ibn Battuta: A.D. 1325–1354 IV*, London, Routledge, 2017.

Giverson, S., *Cahiers d'orientalisme 14*, Geneva, Patrick Cramer, 1986.

Godley, A.D., (tr.) *The Histories of Herodotus, Section 1*, Cambridge MA, Harvard University Press, 1920.

Golubovich, G. (ed.), *Liber Recuperationis Terrae Sanctae by Fidenzio of Padua*, Biblioteca Bio-Bibliografica della Terra Santa e dell'Oriente Franciscano II, Quarachhi, 1906.

Gospel of John, Chapter 20, New Testament, *The Holy Bible*, King James Version.

Guillaume, A, (tr.), *The Life of Muhammad: A Translation of Ishaq's Sirat Rasul Allah*, Oxford, Oxford University Press, 1955.

Hamilton, H.C., Falconer, W. (trs), *The Geography of Strabo*, London, George Bell and Sons, 1903.

Hitti, P.K. (tr.), *Kitab al-Itibar by Usamah ibn Munqidh*, New York, Columbia University Press, 1929.

Jackson, P., *The Mission of William of Rubruck*, London, The Hakluyt Society, 1990.

Jacobs, J. (ed.), *Barlaam and Josaphat: English Lives of Buddha*, London, David Nutt, 1896.

James, M.R., 'The Acts of Thomas', *The Apocryphal New Testament*, Oxford, Clarendon Press, 1924.

Koenen, L., Romer, C., *Der Kolner Mani-Kodex*, Opladen, Westdeutshcer Verlag, 1988.

Lang, D.M. (tr.), *The Balavariam (Barlaam and Josaphat): A Tale from the Christian East*, London, George Allen and Unwin, 1966.

Lock, P. (tr.), *Liber Secretorum Fidelium Crucis by Marino Sanudo Torsello*, London, Ashgate Publishing, 2011.

McCrindle, J.W. (ed.), *The Christian Topography of Cosmas, an Egyptian Monk*, New York, Cambridge University Press, 1897.

MS No. 351, Pelliot Tibetain Collection, Bibliotheque Nationale, Paris

MS of epistle I of Jordanus Catalani in pp. 549–550, Quetif, J. and Echard, J., *Scriptores Ordinis Praedicatorum*, Paris, 1721; epistle II in pp. 359–61, Wadding, L., *Annales Minorum VI*, 1654.

MS of *Mirabilia Descripta* of Jordanus Catalani, published in facsimile form in *Recueil de Voyages et de Memoires*, Paris, Society of Geography, 1839. For a translation see Yule, H. (tr.), *Mirabilia Descripta: The Wonders of the East by Friar Jordanus*, London, The Hakluyt Society, 1863.

MS of the account of Odoric in pp. 123–6, Wadding, L., *Annales Minorum A.D. 1331 VII*, 1654. For translations of the text see Yule, H., *Cathay and the Way Thither I*, London, The Hakluyt Society, 1866; Beazley, C.R., *Dawn of Modern Geography III*, Oxford, Clarendon Press, 1906.

MS of papal bull on Jordanus Catalani in Raynaldus, O., *Annales Ecclesiastici, 1330, folios LV, LVII*, Rome, Barri-Ducis, Guerin, 1864.

MS of *Pontifex Romanus* in Davenport, F.G., *European Treaties Bearing on the History of the United States and its Dependencies to 1648*, Washington, Carnegie Institute, 2004.

Onon, U. (tr.), *The Secret History of the Mongols*, London, Routledge Curzon, 2001.

Price, R., Gaddis, M., *The Acts of the Council of Chalcedon*, Liverpool, Liverpool University Press, 2005.

Rhys Davids, T.W., Fausboll, V. (tr.), *Buddhist Birth Stories, Or, The Jataka Tales*, London, Trubner and Co., 1880.

Schaff, P. (ed.), McGiffert, A.C. (tr.), *Eusebius Pamphilius: Church History, Life of Constantine, Oration in Praise of Constantine by Eusebius*, Grand Rapids, Christian Classics Ethereal Library, 1890.

Schaff, P., Wace, H. (eds), *A Select Library of the Nicene and Post-Nicene Fathers of the Christian Church*, Vol. III, Series II, New York, Christian Literature Co., 1908.

Schoff, W.H. (tr.), *The Periplus of the Erythraean Sea*, London, Longmans, Green and Co., 1912.

Sundermann, W., *Berliner Turfantexte* 4, Berlin, Brepols, 1973.

Wadding, L., *Annales Minorum VI*, 1654, for facsimiles of epistles I and II of Giovanni Montecorvino. For English translation see Yule, H., *Cathay and the Way Thither III*, Hakluyt Society, London, 1863.

Walford, E. (tr.), *The Ecclesiastical History of Evagrius: A History of the Church from AD 431 to AD 594*, Merchantville, Evolution Publishing, 2008.

West, M.L., *The Hymns of Zoroaster: A New Translation of the Most Ancient Sacred Texts of Iran*, London, I.B. Tauris, 2010.

Wood, P. (tr.), *The Chronicle of Seert: Christian Historical Imagination in Late Antique Iraq*, Oxford, Oxford University Press, 2013.

Wright, T. (tr.), *Gesta Romanorum*, London, J.C. Hotten, 1871.

Yule, H., *Cathay and the Way Thither II: Odoric of Pordenone*, London, The Hakluyt Society, 1863.

Secondary Sources

Alberigo, G., Sherry, M., *A Brief History of Vatican II*, Ossining, Orbis Books, 2006.

Allsen, T., *Mongol Imperialism: The Policies of the Grand Qan Mongke in China, Russia and the Islamic Lands, 1251–59*, Berkeley, University of California Press, 1987.

Allsen, T., 'The Rise of the Mongolian Empire and Mongolian Rule in North China', in Twitchett, D.C., Franke, H., Fairbank, J.K. (eds), *The Cambridge History of China VI: Ancient Regimes and Border States, 710–1368*, Cambridge, Cambridge University Press, 1994.

Almond, P.A., 'The Buddha of Christendom: A Review of the Legend of Barlaam and Josaphat', *Religious Studies 23*, Cambridge, Cambridge University Press, 1987.

Ames, G.J., *Vasco Da Gama: Renaissance Crusader*, London, Longman, 2004.

Asbridge, T., *The First Crusade: A New History*, Oxford, Oxford University Press, 2004.

Atiya, A.S., *The Crusade in the Later Middle Ages*, London, Methuen, 1938.

Beazley, C.R., *Dawn of Modern Geography I–III*, Oxford, Clarendon Press, 1906.

Blois, F. de, *Burzoy's Voyage to India and the Origin of the Book of Kalilah wa Dimnah*, London, Royal Asiatic Society, 1990.

Boardman, J., Edwards, I.E.S., Hammond, N.G.L., Sollberger, E., *The Cambridge Ancient History*, Vol. III, Part II, Cambridge, Cambridge University Press, 1992.

Brodrick, J., *Saint Francis Xavier (1506–1552)*, London, Burns, Oates and Washbourne, 1952.

Chadwick, H., *East and West: The Making of a Rift in the Church: From Apostolic Times until the Council of Florence*, Oxford, Oxford University Press, 2003.

Clasquin-Johnson, M., 'The Centuries-Old Dialogue between Buddhism and Christianity', *Acta Theologica 2*, Bloemfontein, 2009.

Embree, A.T., *Charles Grant and British Rule in India*, London, George Allen and Unwin, 1962.

Evans, G.R., *The First Christian Theologians: An Introduction to Theology in the Early Church*, Hoboken, Blackwell Publishing, 2004.

Feldbaek, O., *The Organisation and Structure of the Danish East India, West India and Guinea Companies in the 17th and 18th Centuries*, Leiden, Leiden University Press, 1981.

Fenger, J.F., Francke, E. (tr.), *History of the Tranquebar Mission*, Tranquebar, Evangelical Lutheran Mission Press, 1863.

Forbes Manz, B., 'Temur and the Problem of a Conqueror's Legacy', London, *Journal of the Royal Asiatic Society, Third Series, 8: 1*, 1998.

France, J., 'The Election and Title of Godfrey de Bouillon', *Canadian Journal of History XVIII*, Toronto, University of Toronto Press, 1983.

Frykenberg, R.E., *Christianity in India: From Beginnings to the Present*, Oxford, Oxford University Press, 2010.

Geddes, M., *The History of the Church of Malabar*, London, Smith and Walford, 1694.

Ghosh, A., 'Evangelism in Assam: Schools and Print Culture (1830s–1890s)', *Proceedings of the Indian History Congress 75*, New Delhi, 2014.

Gottfried, R.S., *The Black Death: Natural and Human Disaster in Medieval Europe*, London, Simon and Schuster, 2010.

Grabar, O., Nuseibeh, S., *The Dome of the Rock*, Boston, Harvard University Press, 2006.

Grainger, J.D., *The Syrian Wars*, Boston, Brill, 2010.

Greatrex, G., *Rome and Persia at War, 502–532*, Cambridge, Francis Cairns, 1998.

Gronseth, K., *A Little Piece of Denmark in India*, Oslo, University of Oslo, 2007.

Haldon, J., *The Byzantine Wars*, Stroud, The History Press, 2008.

Harris, J., *The End of Byzantium*, New Haven, Yale University Press, 2012.

Herlihy, D., *The Black Death and the Transformation of the West*, Cambridge (MA), Harvard University Press, 1997.

Hillenbrand, C., *Turkish Myth and Muslim Symbol: The Battle of Manzikert*, Edinburgh, Edinburgh University Press, 2007.

Hilton, B., *The Age of Atonement: The Influence of Evangelicalism on Social and Economic Thought, 1785–1865*, London, Clarendon, 1993.

Holmqvist, W. (ed.), *Excavations at Helgo, Part I, Report for 1954–56*, Stockholm, Kungl. Vitterhets Historie och Antikvitets Akademien, 1961.

Hough, J., *The History of Christianity in India IV*, London, Seeley and Burnside, 1839.

Housley, N., *The Avignon Papacy and the Crusades, 1305–1378*, Oxford, Clarendon Press, 1986.

Housley, N., *The Later Crusades, 1274–1580: From Lyons to Alcazar*, Oxford, Oxford University Press, 1992.

Hoyland, R.G., *Seeing Islam as Others Saw It*, Princeton, The Darwin Press, 1997.

Husain, A., 'Mission to Crusade: Friar William of Rubruck's Journey to the Mongols' in Glenn, J. (ed.), *The Middle Ages in Text and Texture: Reflections on Medieval Sources*, Toronto, University of Toronto, 2011.

Jackson, P., *The Delhi Sultanate: A Political and Military History*, Cambridge, Cambridge University Press, 2003.

Jackson, P., *The Mongols and the West: 1221–1410*, Oxford, Routledge, 2005.

John, S., *Godfrey of Bouillon: Duke of Lower Lotharingia, Ruler of Latin Jerusalem c. 1060–1100*, London, Routledge, 2017.

Keay, J., *India Discovered: The Recovery of a Lost Civilization*, London, HarperCollins, 2001.

Kelly, J.F., *The Ecumenical Councils of the Catholic Church: A History*, Collegeville, Liturgical Press, 2009.

Kennedy, H., *The Great Arab Conquests: How the Spread of Islam Changed the World We Live In*, Philadelphia, Da Capo Press, 2007.

Khanbaghi, A., *The Fire, The Star and the Cross: Minority Religions in Medieval and Early Modern Iran*, London, I.B. Tauris, 2006.

Kosmin, P.J., *The Land of the Elephant Kings: Space, Territory and Ideology in the Seleucid Empire*, Cambridge MA, Harvard University Press, 2014.

Lawrence, C.H., *Medieval Monasticism: Forms of Religious Life in Western Europe in the Middle Ages*, London, Routledge, 2015.

Lea, H.C., *A History of the Inquisition of Spain*, New York, I.B. Tauris, 2011.

Le Roulx, J.D., *La France en Orient au XIVe Siècle: Expeditions du Maréchal Boucicaut I*, Paris, E. Thorin, 1886.

Llewellyn-Jones, R., *The Great Uprising in India, 1857–58: Untold Stories, Indian and British*, London, Boydell Press, 2007.

Macquarrie, J., *Mary for All Christians*, London, A&C Black, 2001.

Majumdar, R.C., 'Social Life: Hindu and Muslim Relations' in *The History and Culture of the Indian People VI: The Delhi Sultanate*, Bombay, Bharatiya Vidya Bhavan, 2006.

Mason, P., *A Matter of Honour: An Account of the Indian Army, Its Officers and Men*, London, Jonathan Cape, 1974.

Mathisen, R.W., 'Barbarian Bishops and the Churches "in Barbaricus Gentibus" during Late Antiquity', *Speculum 72: 3*, University of Chicago Press, July 1997.

Mentgen, G., 'Crusades', in Levy, R.S., Bell, D.P., Donahue, W.C., Madigan, K., Morse, J., Shevitz, A.H., Stillman, N.A. (eds), *Antisemitism: A Historical Encyclopedia of Prejudice and Persecution*, Santa Barbara, ABC-CLIO, 2005.

G.G. Merlo; Robert J Karris; Jean François Godet-Calogeras; (trs), *In the Name of St Francis: A History of the Friars Minor and Franciscanism until the Early Sixteenth Century*, Allegany, Franciscan Institute Publications, 2009.

Meyendorff, J., *Imperial Unity and Christian Divisions: The Church 450–680 A.D.*, Crestwood, St. Vladimir's Seminary Press, 1989.

Millar, F., *The Roman Near East, 31 B.C.–A.D. 337*, Cambridge MA, Harvard University Press, 1982.

Monteiro, S., *Portuguese Sea Battles I—The First World Sea Power 1139–1521*, Lisbon, Monteiro, 2010.

Morgan, D., *The Mongols*, Boston, Blackwell, 1990.

Moriyasu, T., *A Study of the History of Uighur Manichaeism*, Osaka, University of Osaka, 1991.

Mote, F.W., *The Cambridge History of China VII: The Ming Dynasty, 1368–1644 Part I*, Cambridge, Cambridge University Press, 1988.

Muldoon, J., *Popes, Lawyers and Infidels*, Philadelphia, University of Pennsylvania Press, 1979.

Muldoon, J., 'The Avignon Papacy and the Frontiers of Christendom', Rome, *Archivum Historiae Pontificiae* 17, 1979.

Naum, M., Nordin, J.M. (eds), *Scandinavian Colonialism and the Rise of Modernity*, New York, Springer, 2013.

Palsetia, J.S., 'Parsi and Hindu Traditional and Nontraditional Responses to Christian Conversion in Bombay, 1839–45', *Journal of the American Academy of Religion 74:3*, Claremont, Oxford University Press, 2006.

Panzer, J.S., *The Popes and Slavery*, New York, Alba House, 1996.

Pourshariati, P., *Decline and Fall of the Sasanian Empire: The Sasanian-Parthian Confederacy and the Arab Conquest of Iran*, London, I.B. Tauris, 2008.

Priolkar, A.K., *The Goa Inquisition: The Terrible Tribunal for the East*, Panaji, Rajhauns Vitaran, 2010.

Rao, R.P., *Portuguese Rule in Goa: 1510–1961*, Bombay, Asia Publishing House, 1963.

Rapson, E.J., *Ancient India: From the Earliest Times to the First Century A.D.*, Cambridge, Cambridge University Press, 1914.

Ray, A., 'Mughal-Danish Relations in Bengal in the 17th and 18th Centuries', Bangalore, *Proceedings of the Indian History Congress, 58th Session*, 1997.

Reeves, J.C., 'The Elchasaite Sanhedrin of the Cologne Mani Codex in Light of Second Temple Jewish Sectarian Sources', *Journal of Jewish Studies* 42, Oxford, University of Oxford Centre for Hebrew and Jewish Studies, 1991.

Robinson, C.F., *Abd al-Malik*, London, Oneworld Publications, 2005.

Robinson, C.F., *Empires and Elites After the Muslim Conquest: The Transformation of Northern Mesopotamia*, Cambridge, Cambridge University Press, 2000.

Rowe, W., *Crimson Rain: Seven Centuries of Violence in a Chinese County*, Stanford, Stanford University Press, 2007.

Runciman, S., *A History of the Crusades*, Cambridge, Cambridge University Press, 1987.

Salomon, R., *Indian Epigraphy: A Guide to the Study of Inscriptions in Sanskrit, Prakrit and the Other Indo-Aryan Languages*, Oxford, Oxford University Press, 1998.

Saunders, J.J., *The History of the Mongol Conquests*, Philadelphia, University of Pennsylvania Press, 2001.

Schwinges, R.C., 'William of Tyre, the Muslim Enemy and the Problem of Tolerance', in Gervers, M., Powell, J.M. (eds), *Tolerance and Intolerance: Social Conflict in the Age of the Crusades*, Syracuse, Syracuse University Press, 2001.

Senocak, N., *The Poor and the Perfect: The Rise of Learning in the Franciscan Order, 1209–1310*, Ithaca, Cornell University Press, 2012.

Spuler, B., Drummond, H. and S. (trs), *History of the Mongols*, London, Routledge & Kegan Paul, 1972.

Subramanyam, S., *The Career and Legend of Vasco da Gama*, Cambridge, Cambridge University Press, 1998.

Tardieu, Michel, DeBevoise, M.B. (tr.), *Manichaeism*, Chicago, University of Illinois Press, 2008.

Tyerman, C., *God's War: A New History of the Crusades*, Boston, Harvard University Press, 2006.

Uray, G., 'Tibet's Connections with Nestorianism and Manichaeism in the 8th–10th Centuries', in Steinkellner, E., Tauscher, H. (eds), *Contributions on Tibetan Language, History and Culture*, Wien, Arbeitskreis fur tibetische und Buddhistische Studien, University of Wien, 1983.

Ware, K., *The Orthodox Way*, Yonkers, St Vladimir's Seminary Press, 1995.

Weatherford, J., *The Secret History of the Mongol Queens: How the Daughters of Genghis Khan Rescued His Empire's Crown*, New York, Broadway Books, 2011.

Zutshi, P.N.R., 'The Avignon Papacy' in Jones, M. (ed.), *The New Cambridge Medieval History c. 1300–c. 1415*, Cambridge, Cambridge University Press, 2000.

Notes

Antiquity

The Second Carpenter

1. James, M.R., 'The Acts of Thomas', *The Apocryphal New Testament* (Oxford: Clarendon Press, 1924, with revision by Muller, A., 2006), p. 865. The text translated here is from a Greek manuscript, with reference to Syriac versions of the *Acts*.
2. *Gospel of John*, Chapter 20, New Testament, *The Holy Bible*, King James version.
3. James, M.R., 'The Acts of Thomas', *The Apocryphal New Testament* (Oxford: Clarendon Press, 1924, with revision by Muller, A., 2006), p. 865.
4. Ibid.
5. The word used in the Greek manuscript is 'tekton', which is also used in the canonical Gospels to refer to the profession of both Jesus and his human father Joseph. The word is contextually understood to mean an artisan specializing in woodcraft, stonework or house construction. The common

translation in European languages has traditionally been 'carpenter'.

6. For an understanding of the process by which Western Christianity arrived at an official position on New Testament apocrypha and related doctrines such as Docetism, see Kelly, J.F., *The Ecumenical Councils of the Catholic Church: A History* (Collegeville: Liturgical Press, 2009).

7. Godley, A.D., (tr.) *The Histories of Herodotus*, Section 1 (Cambridge MA: Harvard University Press, 1920).

8. For an understanding of Hellenism in the Seleucid Empire, see Kosmin, P.J., *The Land of the Elephant Kings: Space, Territory and Ideology in the Seleucid Empire* (Cambridge MA: Harvard University Press, 2014). For an analysis of Seleucid retreat in Persia and their conflict with Egypt, see Grainger, J.D., *The Syrian Wars*, (Boston: Brill, 2010).

Schism

1. Mathisen, R.W., 'Barbarian Bishops and the Churches "in Barbaricus Gentibus" during Late Antiquity', *Speculum* 72: 3, University of Chicago Press, July 1997.

2. Salomon, R., *Indian Epigraphy: A Guide to the Study of Inscriptions in Sanskrit, Prakrit and the Other Indo-Aryan Languages* (Oxford: Oxford University Press, 1998). For an understanding of the context of the Heliodorus inscription, see Rapson, E.J., *Ancient India: From the Earliest Times to the First Century A.D.* (Cambridge: Cambridge University Press, 1914).

3. Schaff, P. (ed.), McGiffert, A.C. (tr.), *Eusebius Pamphilius: Church History, Life of Constantine, Oration in Praise of Constantine by Eusebius* (Grand Rapids: Christian Classics Ethereal Library, 1890).

4. Schaff, P., Wace, H. (ed.), *A Select Library of the Nicene and Post-Nicene Fathers of the Christian Church*, Vol. III, Series II (New York: Christian Literature Co., 1908).

5. *Eusebius Pamphilius*, p. 346 (footnotes). For an analysis of the location of the Sindi people in the Black Sea region, see Boardman, J., Edwards, I.E.S., Hammond, N.G.L., Sollberger, E., *The Cambridge Ancient History*, Vol. III, Part II (Cambridge: Cambridge University Press, 1992).

6. Isager, S., Friis-Jensen, K., Olsen, B.M., Skydsgaard, J.E. (eds), *Classica Et Mediaevalia: Revue Danoise de Philologie et D'Histoire XLVI*, (Copenhagen: Museum Tusculanum Press, University of Copenhagen, 1995).

7. Church, A.J., Brodribb, W. (tr.), *The Annals of Tacitus*, Book XV (London, Macmillan, 1884).

8. Cruse, C.F., Boyle, I. (tr.), *The Ecclesiastical History of Eusebius Pamphilus, Bishop of Cesarea in Palestine, and An Historical View of the Council of Nice* (New York: Thomas N. Stanford, 1856).

9. Schaff, P., Wace, H. (ed.), *A Select Library of the Nicene and Post-Nicene Fathers of the Christian Church*, Vol. II, Series II.

10. Walford, E. (tr.), *The Ecclesiastical History of Evagrius: A History of the Church from AD 431 to AD 594* (Merchantville: Evolution Publishing, 2008). For an account of the Council of Chalcedon, see Price, R., Gaddis, M., *The Acts of the Council of Chalcedon* (Liverpool: Liverpool University Press, 2005). For an understanding of the schism between Eastern and Western Christianity after Chalcedon, see Meyendorff, J., *Imperial Unity and Christian Divisions: The Church 450–680 A.D.* (Crestwood: St Vladimir's Seminary Press, 1989).

The Many Errors of Mani

1. Tardieu, Michel, DeBevoise, M.B. (tr.), *Manichaeism* (Chicago: University of Illinois Press, 2008).

2. Reeves, J.C., 'The Elchasaite Sanhedrin of the Cologne Mani Codex in Light of Second Temple Jewish Sectarian Sources',

Journal of Jewish Studies 42 (Oxford: University of Oxford Centre for Hebrew and Jewish Studies, 1991).

3. West, M.L., *The Hymns of Zoroaster: A New Translation of the Most Ancient Sacred Texts of Iran* (London: I.B. Tauris, 2010).

4. Afsar-e Shirazi, A. (ed.), *Motun-e arabi va farsi dar bare-ye Mani va manaviyyat* (Tehran, 1956).

5. Evans, G.R., *The First Christian Theologians: An Introduction to Theology in the Early Church* (Hoboken: Blackwell Publishing, 2004).

6. For Aramaic sources on the life and teachings of Mani, see Contini, R., 'Hypotheses sur l'arameen manicheen', *Annali di Ca' Foscari 34* (Venice: University of Venice, 1995). For Greek and Latin sources, see Koenen, L., Romer, C., *Der Kolner Mani-Kodex* (Opladen: Westdeutshcer Verlag, 1988). Sources for Manichaeism in Mesopotamia can be found in facsimile form by Giverson, S., *Cahiers d'orientalisme* 14 (Geneva: Patrick Cramer, 1986) and in Funk, W.P., 'The Reconstruction of the Manichaean Kephalaia', Mirecki, P., BeDuhn, J. (eds), *Emerging from Darkness: Studies in the Recovery of Manichaean Sources* (Leiden: Brill, 1997). For Persian and Turkic sources, see Sundermann, W., *Berliner Turfantexte* 4 (Berlin: Brepols, 1973).

7. Moriyasu, T., *A Study of the History of Uighur Manichaeism* (Osaka: University of Osaka, 1991).

Fruits of the Wisdom Tree

1. Jacobs, J. (ed.), *Barlaam and Josaphat: English Lives of Buddha* (London: David Nutt, 1896).

2. Clasquin-Johnson, M., 'The Centuries-Old Dialogue between Buddhism and Christianity', *Acta Theologica* 2 (Bloemfontein, 2009).

3. Wright, T., *Gesta Romanorum* (London: J.C. Hotten, 1871).

4. Almond, P.A., 'The Buddha of Christendom: A Review of the Legend of Barlaam and Josaphat', *Religious Studies 23* (Cambridge: Cambridge University Press, 1987).

5. Rhys Davids, T.W., Fausboll, V. (tr.), *Buddhist Birth Stories, Or, The Jataka Tales* (London: Trubner and Co., 1880).

6. For the Old Georgian version of the legend, see Lang, D.M. (tr.), *The Balavariam (Barlaam and Josaphat): A Tale from the Christian East* (London: George Allen and Unwin, 1966).

7. Dodge, B. (tr.), *The Fihrist of al-Nadim* (New York and London: Columbia University Press, 1970).

8. De Blois, *Burzoy's Voyage to India and the Origin of the Book of Kalilah wa Dimnah* (London: Royal Asiatic Society, 1990).

9. Hamilton, H.C., Falconer, W. (tr.), *The Geography of Strabo* (London: George Bell and Sons, 1903).

10. Holmqvist, W. (ed.), *Excavations at Helgo, Part I, Report for 1954–56* (Stockholm: Kungl. Vitterhets Historie och Antikvitets Akademien, 1961).

An Amateur at Sea

1. Dewing, H.B. (tr.), *Procopius, History of the Wars* (Cambridge: Harvard University Press, 1914). For an understanding of the Roman-Persian Wars till the fourth century, see Millar, F., *The Roman Near East, 31 B.C.–A.D. 337* (Cambridge: Harvard University Press, 1982); for an overview of the conflict between the Byzantines and the Sassanids in the early sixth century, see Greatrex, G., *Rome and Persia at War, 502–532* (Cambridge: Francis Cairns, 1998).

2. Schoff, W.H. (tr.), *The Periplus of the Erythraean Sea* (London: Longmans, Green and Co., 1912).

3. McCrindle, J.W. (ed.), *The Christian Topography of Cosmas, an Egyptian Monk* (New York: Cambridge University Press, 1897).

4. Stahl, W.H. (tr.), *Macrobius: Commentary on the Dream of Scipio* (New York: Columbia University Press, 1952).
5. Dewing, *Procopius, History of the Wars*, 1914. For an Arabic account of the expedition, see Guillaume, A. (tr.), *The Life of Muhammad: A Translation of Ishaq's Sirat Rasul Allah* (Oxford: Oxford University Press, 1955).
6. Freese, J.H. (tr.), *The Library of Photius I* (New York: The Macmillan Co., 1930).

The Middle Ages

The Forge of the World

1. Haldon, J., *The Byzantine Wars* (Stroud: The History Press, 2008).
2. Kennedy, H., *The Great Arab Conquests: How the Spread of Islam Changed the World We Live In* (Philadelphia: Da Capo Press, 2007).
3. Hoyland, R.G., *Seeing Islam as Others Saw It* (Princeton: The Darwin Press, 1997).
4. Pourshariati, P., *Decline and Fall of the Sasanian Empire: The Sasanian-Parthian Confederacy and the Arab Conquest of Iran* (London: I.B. Tauris, 2008).
5. Robinson, C.F., *Empires and Elites after the Muslim Conquest: The Transformation of Northern Mesopotamia* (Cambridge: Cambridge University Press, 2000).
6. Wood, P. (tr.), *The Chronicle of Seert: Christian Historical Imagination in Late Antique Iraq* (Oxford: Oxford University Press, 2013).
7. Robinson, C.F., *Abd al-Malik* (London: Oneworld Publications, 2005). For a study of the inscriptions in the Dome of the Rock and their significance for the early history of Islam, see Grabar, O., Nuseibeh, S., *The Dome of the Rock* (Boston: Harvard University Press, 2006).

8. MS No. 351, Pelliot Tibetain Collection, Bibliotheque Nationale, Paris. For a translation and analysis of the passage, see Uray, G., 'Tibet's Connections with Nestorianism and Manichaeism in the 8th–10th Centuries', Steinkellner, E., Tauscher, H. (eds), *Contributions on Tibetan Language, History and Culture* (Wien: Arbeitskreis fur tibetische und Buddhistische Studien, University of Wien, 1983).

9. Jackson, P., *The Delhi Sultanate: A Political and Military History* (Cambridge: Cambridge University Press, 2003).

'Deus Hoc Vult'

1. Macquarrie, J., *Mary for All Christians* (London: A&C Black, 2001).

2. Ware, K., *The Orthodox Way* (Yonkers: St Vladimir's Seminary Press, 1995).

3. Chadwick, H., *East and West: The Making of a Rift in the Church: From Apostolic Times until the Council of Florence* (Oxford: Oxford University Press, 2003).

4. Alberigo, G., Sherry, M., *A Brief History of Vatican II* (Ossining: Orbis Books, 2006).

5. Runciman, S., *A History of the Crusades* (Cambridge: Cambridge University Press: 1987). For an understanding of the significance of the Battle of Manzikert for Turkish history and cultural identity, see Hillenbrand, C., *Turkish Myth and Muslim Symbol: The Battle of Manzikert* (Edinburgh: Edinburgh University Press, 2007).

6. Asbridge, T., *The First Crusade: A New History* (Oxford: Oxford University Press, 2004).

7. Tyerman, C., *God's War: A New History of the Crusades* (Boston: Harvard University Press, 2006). For an understanding of the role of pogroms in the crusading period and the larger history of anti-semitism in Europe, see Mentgen, G., 'Crusades', in Levy, R.S., Bell, D.P., Donahue, W.C., Madigan, K., Morse, J.,

Shevitz, A.H., Stillman, N.A. (eds), *Antisemitism: A Historical Encyclopedia of Prejudice and Persecution* (Santa Barbara: ABC-CLIO, 2005).

8. John, S., *Godfrey of Bouillon: Duke of Lower Lotharingia, Ruler of Latin Jerusalem c. 1060–1100* (London: Routledge, 2017).

9. Runciman, *A History of the Crusades* (Cambridge, 1987).

10. France, J., 'The Election and Title of Godfrey de Bouillon', *Canadian Journal of History XVIII* (Toronto: University of Toronto Press, 1983).

11. Schwinges, R.C., 'William of Tyre, the Muslim Enemy and the Problem of Tolerance', in Gervers, M., Powell, J.M. (eds), *Tolerance and Intolerance: Social Conflict in the Age of the Crusades* (Syracuse: Syracuse University Press, 2001).

12. Hitti, P.K. (tr.), *Kitab al-Itibar by Usamah ibn Munqidh* (New York: Columbia University Press, 1929).

13. Merlo, G.G., Karis, R.J. and Bonanno, R. (trs), *In the Name of St Francis: A History of the Friars Minor and Franciscanism until the Early Sixteenth Century* (Allegany: Franciscan Institute Publications, 2009).

14. Lawrence, C.H., *Medieval Monasticism: Forms of Religious Life in Western Europe in the Middle Ages* (London: Routledge, 2015).

15. For an understanding of the establishment of scholarly traditions in the early years of the Franciscan order, see Senocak, N., *The Poor and the Perfect: The Rise of Learning in the Franciscan Order, 1209–1310* (Ithaca: Cornell University Press, 2012).

The Hammer of Dajjal

1. Onon, U. (tr.), *The Secret History of the Mongols* (London: Routledge Curzon, 2001).

2. Boyle, J.A. (tr.), *Tarikh-i Jahan-gusha by Atamalik Juwayni* (Boston: Harvard University Press, 1958).

3. Spuler, B., Drummond, H. and S. (trs), *History of the Mongols* (London: Routledge & Kegan Paul, 1972).

4. Khanbaghi, A., *The Fire, The Star and the Cross: Minority Religions in Medieval and Early Modern Iran* (London: I.B. Tauris, 2006).

5. Jackson, P., *The Mongols and the West: 1221–1410* (Oxford: Routledge, 2005).

6. Morgan, D., *The Mongols* (Boston: Blackwell, 1990).

7. Saunders, J.J., *The History of the Mongol Conquests* (Philadelphia: University of Pennsylvania Press, 2001).

8. Runciman, S., *A History of the Crusades* (Cambridge: Cambridge University Press, 1987).

Our Khan in Persia

1. Weatherford, J., *The Secret History of the Mongol Queens: How the Daughters of Genghis Khan Rescued His Empire's Crown* (New York: Broadway Books, 2011).

2. Jackson, P., *The Mongols and the West: 1221–1410* (Oxford: Routledge, 2005).

3. Jackson, P., *The Mission of William of Rubruck* (London: The Hakluyt Society, 1990). For an understanding of the crusading context behind the friar's mission, see Husain, A., 'Mission to Crusade: Friar William of Rubruck's Journey to the Mongols' in Glenn, J. (ed.), *The Middle Ages in Text and Texture: Reflections on Medieval Sources* (Toronto: University of Toronto).

4. Morgan, D., *The Mongols* (Oxford: Oxford University Press, 1986). For a detailed analysis of Mongol activities leading to the Syrian campaign, see Allsen, T., *Mongol Imperialism: The Policies of the Grand Qan Mongke in China, Russia and the Islamic Lands, 1251–59* (Berkeley: University of California Press, 1987).

5. Zutshi, P.N.R., 'The Avignon Papacy' in Jones, M. (ed.), *The New Cambridge Medieval History c. 1300–c. 1415* (Cambridge: Cambridge University Press, 2000). For an understanding

of the Avignon Papacy and crusading activities during this period, see Housley, N., *The Avignon Papacy and the Crusades, 1305–1378* (Oxford: Clarendon Press, 1986).

6. Muldoon, J., *Popes, Lawyers and Infidels* (Philadelphia: University of Pennsylvania Press, 1979).

7. Muldoon, J., 'The Avignon Papacy and the Frontiers of Christendom', Rome, *Archivum Historiae Pontificiae* 17, 1979.

The Pioneers

1. Beazley, C.R., *Dawn of Modern Geography III* (Oxford: Clarendon Press, 1906).

2. Facsimile of epistle I (1305) in pp. 69–72 and epistle II (1306) in pp. 91–2, Wadding, L., *Annales Minorum VI*, 1654; for English translation see Yule, H., *Cathay and the Way Thither III* (London: Hakluyt Society, 1863).

The Source of All Evil

1. Runciman, S., *A History of the Crusades* (Cambridge: Cambridge University Press, 1987).

2. Golubovich, G. (ed.), *Liber Recuperationis Terrae Sanctae by Fidenzio of Padua*, Biblioteca Bio-Bibliografica della Terra Santa e dell'Oriente Franciscano II, Quarachhi, 1906.

3. Le Roulx, J.D., *La France en Orient au XIVe Siècle: Expeditions du Maréchal Boucicaut I* (Paris: E. Thorin, 1886).

4. Atiya, A.S., *The Crusade in the Later Middle Ages* (London: Methuen, 1938).

5. Housley, N., *The Later Crusades, 1274–1580: From Lyons to Alcazar* (Oxford: Oxford University Press, 1992).

6. Lock, P. (tr.), *Liber Secretorum Fidelium Crucis by Marino Sanudo Torsello* (London: Ashgate Publishing, 2011).

7. Constable, G. (tr.), *Tractatus Quomodo Sarraceni Sunt Expugnandi by William of Adam* (London: Dumbarton Oaks, 2011).

8. Ibid., p. 83.
9. Runciman, S., *A History of the Crusades II: The Kingdom of Jerusalem and the Frankish East, 1100–1187* (Cambridge: Cambridge University Press, 1989).

Signs and Marvels

1. Jackson, P., *The Delhi Sultanate: A Political and Military History* (Cambridge: Cambridge University Press, 2003).
2. Majumdar, R.C., 'Social Life: Hindu and Muslim Relations' in *the History and Culture of the Indian People VI: The Delhi Sultanate* (Bombay: Bharatiya Vidya Bhavan, 2006).
3. *Mirabilia Descripta of Jordanus Catalani*, MS published in facsimile form in *Recueil de Voyages et de Memoires* (Paris: Society of Geography, 1839). For a translation see Yule, H. (tr.), *Mirabilia Descripta: The Wonders of the East by Friar Jordanus* (London: The Hakluyt Society, 1863).
4. Yule, H., *Cathay and the Way Thither II: Odoric of Pordenone* (London: The Hakluyt Society, 1863), pp. 119–25.
5. MS of epistle I of Jordanus Catalani in pp. 549–50, Quetif, J. and Echard, J., *Scriptores Ordinis Praedicatorum*, Paris, 1721; epistle II in pp. 359–61, Wadding, L., *Annales Minorum VI*, 1654.
6. Gibb, H.A.R. and Beckingham, C.F. (tr.), *The Travels of Ibn Battuta: A.D. 1325–1354 IV* (London: Routledge, 2017).
7. MS of papal bull on Jordanus Catalani in Raynaldus, O., *Annales Ecclesiastici, 1330, folios LV, LVII* (Rome: Barri-Ducis, Guerin, 1864).

The Courts of the Morning

1. Jackson, P., *The Delhi Sultanate: A Political and Military History* (Cambridge: Cambridge University Press, 2003).
2. MS of the account of Odoric in pp. 123–6, Wadding, L., *Annales Minorum A.D. 1331 VII*, 1654. For translations of the text see Yule, H., *Cathay and the Way Thither I* (London:

The Hakluyt Society, 1866); Beazley, C.R., *Dawn of Modern Geography III* (Oxford: Clarendon Press, 1906).

3. Wadding, L., *Annales Minorum A.D. 1331 VII*, 1654, p. 124.

4. Beazley, C.R., *Dawn of Modern Geography III* (Oxford: Clarendon Press, 1906).

5. Yule, H., *Cathay and the Way Thither I* (London: The Hakluyt Society, 1861).

Cataclysm

1. Rowe, W., *Crimson Rain: Seven Centuries of Violence in a Chinese County* (Stanford: Stanford University Press, 2007). For an understanding of Yuan polity see Allsen, T., 'The Rise of the Mongolian Empire and Mongolian Rule in North China,' in Twitchett, D.C., Franke, H., Fairbank, J.K. (eds), *The Cambridge History of China VI: Ancient Regimes and Border States, 710–1368* (Cambridge: Cambridge University Press, 1994).

2. Mote, F.W., *The Cambridge History of China VII: The Ming Dynasty, 1368–1644 Part I* (Cambridge: Cambridge University Press, 1988).

3. Herlihy, D., *The Black Death and the Transformation of the West* (Cambridge (MA): Harvard University Press, 1997). See also Gottfried, R.S., *The Black Death: Natural and Human Disaster in Medieval Europe* (London: Simon and Schuster, 2010).

4. Morgan, D., *The Mongols* (Oxford: Oxford University Press, 1986).

5. Forbes Manz, B., 'Temur and the Problem of a Conqueror's Legacy', *Journal of the Royal Asiatic Society, Third Series, 8: 1*, 1998.

6. Jackson, P., *The Delhi Sultanate: A Political and Military History* (Cambridge: Cambridge University Press, 2003).

The Colonial Period

Swearing by a Bent Cross

1. Monteiro, A.S., *Portuguese Sea Battles I—The First World Sea Power 1139–1521* (Lisbon: Monteiro, 2010).
2. Harris, J., *The End of Byzantium* (New Haven: Yale University Press, 2012).
3. Housley, N., *Religious Warfare in Europe 1400–1536* (Oxford: Oxford University Press, 2002).
4. Facsimile of MS of *Pontifex Romanus* in Davenport, F.G., *European Treaties Bearing on the History of the United States and its Dependencies to 1648* (Washington: Carnegie Institute, 2004). For an understanding of the Roman Church's legitimization of slavery in the fifteenth century and afterwards, see Panzer, J.S., *The Popes and Slavery* (New York: Alba House, 1996).
5. Lea, H.C., *A History of the Inquisition of Spain* (New York: I.B. Tauris, 2011).
6. Ames, G.J., *Vasco Da Gama: Renaissance Crusader* (London: Longman, 2004). For an understanding of the philosophy and personality of Vasco da Gama, see Subramanyam, S., *The Career and Legend of Vasco da Gama* (Cambridge: Cambridge University Press, 1998).
7. Brodrick, J., *Saint Francis Xavier (1506–1552)* (London: Burns, Oates and Washbourne, 1952).
8. Rao, R.P., *Portuguese Rule in Goa: 1510–1961* (Bombay: Asia Publishing House, 1963).
9. Priolkar, A.K., *The Goa Inquisition: The Terrible Tribunal for the East* (Panaji: Rajhauns Vitaran, 2010).
10. Geddes, M., *The History of the Church of Malabar* (London: Smith and Walford, 1694). For an analysis of the Eastern Christian texts proscribed by the Synod, see Hough, J., *The History of Christianity in India IV* (London: Seeley and Burnside, 1839).

11. Frykenberg, R.E., *Christianity in India: From Beginnings to the Present* (Oxford: Oxford University Press, 2010).

New Jerusalem

1. Naum, M., Nordin, J.M. (eds), *Scandinavian Colonialism and the Rise of Modernity* (New York: Springer, 2013).
2. Ray, A., 'Mughal-Danish Relations in Bengal in the 17th and 18th Centuries', Bangalore, *Proceedings of the Indian History Congress*, 58th *Session*, 1997.
3. Fenger, J.F., Francke, E. (tr.), *History of the Tranquebar Mission* (Tranquebar: Evangelical Lutheran Mission Press, 1863).
4. Feldbaek, O., *The Organisation and Structure of the Danish East India, West India and Guinea Companies in the 17th and 18th Centuries* (Leiden: Leiden University Press, 1981).
5. Gronseth, K., *A Little Piece of Denmark in India* (Oslo: University of Oslo, 2007).

Imperium

1. Keay, J., *India Discovered: The Recovery of a Lost Civilization* (London: HarperCollins, 2001).
2. Hilton, B., *The Age of Atonement: The Influence of Evangelicalism on Social and Economic Thought, 1785–1865* (London: Clarendon, 1993).
3. Embree, A.T., *Charles Grant and British Rule in India* (London: George Allen and Unwin, 1962).
4. Palsetia, J.S., 'Parsi and Hindu Traditional and Nontraditional Responses to Christian Conversion in Bombay, 1839–45', *Journal of the American Academy of Religion 74:3* (Claremont: Oxford University Press, 2006).
5. Mason, P., *A Matter of Honour: An Account of the Indian Army, Its Officers and Men* (London: Jonathan Cape, 1974).

6. Llewellyn-Jones, R., *The Great Uprising in India, 1857–58: Untold Stories, Indian and British* (London: Boydell Press, 2007).
7. Ghosh, A., 'Evangelism in Assam: Schools and Print Culture (1830s–1890s)', *Proceedings of the Indian History Congress 75*, New Delhi, 2014.

Conclusion

1. Gettleman, J, Raj, S., 'His Defense of Hindus Was to Kill a Muslim and Post the Video', *New York Times*, 8 December 2017.
2. Gomes, R., 'India's Catholic Bishops Condemn Fake Letter Defaming Church', *Vatican News*, 10 May 2018.
3. 'Chhattisgarh Church Vandalism: Four More Arrested', *Indian Express*, 7 March 2016.
4. 'Two Acquitted in Graham Staines Murder Case', *Times of India*, 27 February 2014.
5. 'History of Nuns Abused by Priests in India: Fighting off Advances Means Pinballing through Centuries-Old Clerical Traditions', Firstpost, 4 January 2019.